THE Big BOOK OF CHRISTIAN MYSTICISM

"McColman's book on Christian mysticism is a masterpiece of scholarship and wisdom. This author obviously earned his understanding of mysticism through years of research as well as his own personal spiritual journey and there is no more powerful combination for inspired writing."

—**Caroline Myss**, author of *Entering the Castle* and *Anatomy of the Spirit*

"Mysticism is not *mystifying* at all, but simple, always available, and utterly clarifying. Carl McColman's much-needed book will allow you to experience this for yourself! Christians and all Seekers will find both meat and dessert in such a full meal."

—**Richard Rohr**, OFM, author of *The Naked Now:*
Learning to See as the Mystics See and *Everything Belongs*

"Charmingly and conversationally written, but also rich in nuance and thorough in its coverage and its attention to detail, *The Big Book* is, as its name suggests, a big—even an enormous—contribution to our current literature on the subject. Highly recommended."

—**Phyllis Tickle**, author of *The Great Emergence: How Christianity*
Is Changing and Why and *God-Talk in America*

"It's accessible, human, well-informed, balanced, broad . . . just what we needed."

—**Brian D. McLaren**, author of *A New Kind of Christianity*
and *A Generous Orthodoxy*

"Carl McColman's wise and clear writing takes us on a wide journey through both classical and contemporary mystic guides. Ultimately he invites us to catch a glimpse of the heart of Mystery through concrete suggestions for mystical practice and be transformed ourselves."

—**Christine Valters Paintner, PhD**, author of *Water, Wind, Earth, & Fire:*
The Christian Practice of Praying with the Elements

"If you are looking for both a primer on Christian mysticism as well as an in-depth treatment of this oft-misunderstood aspect of the spiritual life, here is your book."

—**Paul Wilkes**, author of *Beyond the Walls: Monastic Wisdom for Everyday Life*

"I highly recommend this book not only for general readers interested in mysticism and spirituality, but also for undergraduate or graduate students who need an introduction to what Carl himself calls "this ancient wisdom tradition.""

—**Ed Sellner**, author of *Wisdom of the Celtic Saints*
and *Finding the Monk Within: Great Monastic Values for Today*

"McColman's book is wise and wonderful, deceptively simple! Are you interested in having a relationship with something that's ultimately unknowable? Me too. It's not easy, but dig in, here!"

—**Jon M. Sweeney**, author of *Almost Catholic*
and *The St. Francis Prayer Book*

"A wise and supportive guidebook for those going deeper on the Christian mystical path."

—**The Rev. Cynthia Bourgeault, Ph.D.**,
author of *Centering Prayer and Inner Awakening* and *The Wisdom Jesus*

"With his "Big Book," McColman has pulled off a tour de force: a work on Christian mysticism that is broadly accessible, but deep; scholarly but not pedantic; reverent, but judicious; thorough, but a good read; an excellent introduction to the subject for the general reader, but with plenty of meat for the specialist."

—**The Rev. Robert D. Hughes, III. Ph.D.**,
author of *Beloved Dust: Tides of the Spirit in the Christian Life*

"In this delightfully accessible book, Carl McColman dispels the notion that Christian mysticism exists somewhere in the ether, and reveals its solid, earthy roots. If you want a rich, nourishing life of faith and virtues that flourish like wildflowers, read *Christian Mysticism*, and let the good news in it transform you."

—**Claudia Mair Burney**, author of *God Alone is Enough:*
A Spirited Pilgrimage with St. Teresa of Avila

"Carl McColman has both studied and practiced the Christian mystical tradition, stressing its earthiness and 'ordinariness.' Like Thomas Merton, Michael Ramsey, and others, he holds that mysticism is not an esoteric realm reserved for the very holy, but is what all Christian life is about. I strongly commend this book."

—**Kenneth Leech**, author of *Soul Friend* and *Prayer and Prophecy*

The Big Book *of* Christian Mysticism

THE ESSENTIAL GUIDE
TO CONTEMPLATIVE SPIRITUALITY

Carl McColman

HAMPTON ROADS
PUBLISHING COMPANY, INC.

Hampton Roads Publishing Company, Inc.
Charlottesville, VA 22906

Cover and text design by Tracy Johnson
Cover photograph: Church of San Pantaleo, Martis, Sardinia © 2009 bacilloz/shutterstock.com.
Production Editor: Michele Kimble
Copy Editor: Laurel Warren Trufant, Ph.D.
Proofreader: Audrey Doyle
Typeset in Perpetua, Trade Gothic, and Requiem.

ISBN-13: 978-1-57174-624-5

Printed in the United States of America

�֍

The mystery of the kingdom of God has been granted to you....
for there is nothing hidden except to be made visible;
nothing is secret except to come to light.

MARK 4:11, 22 (NAB)

The Christian of the future will be a mystic or he will not exist at all.

KARL RAHNER[1]

Preface

Christian mysticism is many things.

It is Christianity's best-kept secret. It is a revolutionary way to approach God and Christ and spirituality. It is an ancient wisdom tradition, not a story line cooked up for an adventure novel or a feature film. It is a venerable lineage of spiritual teachings that can be traced back to the New Testament, which promises to transform the lives of people who seriously and sincerely apply its wisdom to their own life circumstances.

Christian mysticism is not the same as ordinary religious belief or observance. It has room for profound doubt and insistent questioning. It does not ask you to check your mind at the door and submit your will to some sort of external authority—whether that be a church, a priest or minister, or a book. Rather, Christian mysticism argues that any respect you pay to external authority can emerge only from a profound inner experience or conviction that God is real and present, and that it is both possible and plausible for the average person to have a truly experiential relationship with God.

This is not to suggest that Christian mysticism is some sort of alternative to religious Christianity. Far from it! Religion, after all, is simply spirituality expressed in social and communal ways. Since Christianity is about loving God and loving our neighbors, Christian mysticism encourages an optimistic, positive outlook toward other people, despite our human failings. Think of mysticism as a tool that can help you find joy in relating to others—even in organized religious settings like your neighborhood church.

Some interpreters of Christian mysticism insist that it necessarily involves supernatural visions and voices, or profound charismatic experiences that are miraculous in nature and extraordinary in scope. Indeed, such things are possible in the world of mysticism, because mysticism is all about possibility. But in its oldest and purest form, Christian mysticism is anchored in values like humility, trust, simplicity, and peacefulness. Christian mysticism is, in fact, completely ordinary, utterly down-to-earth, and entirely naturalistic. You can be a mystic without ever seeing visions or receiving secret messages from God. In fact, some of the greatest Christian mystics, like John of the Cross, felt that supernatural phenomena tended to be a problem, because they could so easily arise from non-mystical causes, like the human ego's need to feel important or special.

Christian mysticism invites us to look at God, Christ, the church, our own souls, and our understanding of such things as sin or holiness in new ways. Mysticism doesn't contradict traditional religious teaching. In many ways, however, it represents an element of Christianity that transcends human logic or reason. It can therefore appear, on the surface, to be subversive of mundane piety.

Well, it *is* subversive, and it has the potential to undermine everything—especially all of our cherished beliefs, sacred cows, and dogmatic illusions. It undermines all of our settled ways of looking at things, not because it seeks to cause chaos, but rather because it helps us open our hearts and minds to something that cannot be captured in ideology, or dogma, or theology, or philosophy.

And that "something" is God.

THE PARADOX OF MYSTICAL EXPERIENCE

Here is a central truth about Christian mysticism: the more it reveals, the more it conceals. Mysticism is concerned with mystery—spiritual mystery. Thus, its essence cannot be captured in words and any book on the subject will, of necessity, be incomplete, paradoxical, and, at times, confusing or ambiguous. Indeed, that confusion is rooted in the trans-rational nature of mysticism itself. Mystical experience opens you up to the love of God, yet forces you to give up all your limited ideas and concepts about God, discarding them all as mere mental idols. The deeper you go, the more elusive God becomes.

When you begin to explore mysticism through prayer, meditation, and contemplation, you embark on a journey by which you slowly respond to that elusive mystery we call God. Yet mysticism exists only in the present moment; it's not about what is going to happen tomorrow, or next year, or in the next life. It is about learning to live in joy, about transforming consciousness, about becoming holy. The world of Christian mysticism offers spiritual practices and exercises that help you cultivate a spiritual dimension to your life, yet the moment you focus your attention on practice, no matter how worthy or pious or spiritual it may be, you lose touch with the mystical. One popular notion of Christian mysticism depicts monks cloistered in monasteries, or hermits sheltered in the desert, or sages isolated on mountaintops, or women living sheltered from the noise of the world. In these antiseptic settings, they partake of sweet communion with God. Yet the famous twentieth-century mystic Thomas Merton had one of his most life-altering experiences not in a monastery but standing on a busy street corner in Louisville, Kentucky. The great fourteenth-century mystic Julian of Norwich did, in fact, withdraw from society, spending much of her life in a tiny cell sheltered from "worldly" concerns, where people came to seek her spiritual advice. Yet her most powerful mystical experiences occurred not while she was alone but during an illness, as she lay suffering in a room surrounded by loved ones. Others have reported that their most amazing encounters with God have occurred while working hard to alleviate the suffering of the poor, the sick, or the dying. Mysticism isn't about keeping your hands clean. Rather it impels you to get them dirty.

Christian mysticism is all about experience—the experience of union with God, or of the presence of God. But it's also about a spiritual reality that undermines experience itself, deconstructing all your masks and self-defenses and leaving you spiritually naked and vulnerable before the silence of the Great Mystery. It is the spirituality of bringing heaven to earth, and of going through hell while here on earth in order to get to heaven. While many books on mysticism approach it from a global, universal perspective, here I focus specifically on mysticism in the Christian tradition as a distinct, unique, and beautiful form of mystical experience. The Christian mystical tradition has a long and rich history that reaches back to the New

Testament and the first 500 years of church history. Unlike other books that take a primarily historical approach to that tradition, focusing on the lives and words of the great mystics and contemplatives of the past, I focus more on the present.

What does mysticism mean *today*? How can we apply the mysteries of mysticism and contemplation and Christian meditation to our current circumstances and situations? Rather than tell you *about* mysticism, I invite you to *encounter* it as a reality that can transform you and your relationship with God. First we investigate the mystery and paradox of mysticism; then we explore how the wisdom of Christian mysticism can make a real difference in your own life.

While I encourage you to study the works of the great mystics as a way to foster a deeper understanding and appreciation of what is distinctively good and beautiful about their faith, my larger goal is to inspire Christians and non-Christians alike to live according to their wisdom.

ACKNOWLEDGMENTS

Christianity is all about community, and writing a book is truly a communal act. Many people have helped in the creation of this book, in small and large ways. As a sacramental Christian, I affirm that marriage and family life are intended to be a means of grace: an opportunity for us to "be" Christ to and for one another. I am truly blessed to have a family that encourages belief in such a noble calling. My wife, Fran, and daughter, Rhiannon, have been patient and loving over the many hours I have devoted to this book.

Thanks to Greg Brandenburgh for his insight, challenge, and support, and to Linda Roghaar for making the connections (and for playing amateur counselor when necessary). Thanks to Meg Anderson, Nancy Carnes, Claudette Cuddy, Cliff Post, Michael Morrell, Gini Eagen, Bob Hughes, Greg Kenny, Darrell Grizzle, Phil Foster, Kenneth Leech, Emmett Jarrett, Natalia Shulgina, John Skinner, Brittian Bullock, Peter Rollins, Richard Rohr, Brian McLaren, and Jon Sweeney for your feedback, insight, encouragement, and suggestions.

Thanks to the readers of my blog (*www.anamchara.com*), who have, in many cases, been the first people exposed to the ideas and perspectives that eventually shaped this book. Your comments, questions, and support inspired me to persevere and made the final project much more valuable. Its limitations, naturally, remain my responsibility.

I especially want to thank the Trappist monks of the Monastery of the Holy Spirit in Conyers, Georgia, where I am blessed to be both a member of the lay associates community and an employee of the monastery's business division (I work in the bookstore). I owe immense thanks, not only for their witness as a community of faith, but also for the many small gestures of kindness and hospitality they offered as I worked and prayed alongside them. Members of this community have related to me as mentors, spiritual directors, confessors, teachers, business colleagues, and—most rewarding of all—friends. In particular, I wish to mention Fr. Tom Francis, Fr. Anthony Delisi, Br. Elias Marechal, Fr. Matt Torpey, and Fr. James Behrens, each of whom patiently endured my endless questions and occasional whining as I sought to understand the splendor of Christian mystical spirituality and to capture its beauty in the written word.

Because of my professional relationship with the monastery, I feel I must emphasize that this book represents my personal views and thoughts on Christian mysticism. Any errors or distortions within it are entirely my own fault. Of course, what little wisdom may be present in these pages is very much the result of my having access to a living contemplative community. For this, I am profoundly grateful.

Thanks also to the members of the Lay Cistercians of Our Lady of the Holy Spirit, especially Paco Ambrosetti, Jacquie Johnston, Linda Mitchell, Jacki Rychlicki, and Rocky Thomas, and to my colleagues at the Abbey Store and Monastery Industries. I'm always afraid when I write my acknowledgments that I will leave out someone who has really made an important contribution to my life and/or the project at hand. To such an unknown contributor, I can only offer my gratitude and beg for your forgiveness. You know who you are.

Carl McColman
Feast of Saint Scholastica, 2010

PART I

The Christian Mystery

Jesus looked at them and said, "For human beings this is impossible, but for God all things are possible."

MATTHEW 19:26 (NAB)

In Greek religion, from which the word [mysticism] comes to us, the myste were those initiates of the "mysteries," who were believed to have received the vision of the god, and with it a new and higher life. When the Christian Church adopted this term it adopted, too, its original meaning. The Christian mystic therefore is one for whom God and Christ are not merely objects of belief, but living facts experimentally known first hand; and mysticism for him becomes, in so far as he responds to its demands, a life based on this conscious communion with God.

EVELYN UNDERHILL[2]

CHAPTER 1

Hidden in Plain Sight

For it is the God who said, "Let light shine out of darkness,"
who has shone in our hearts to give the light of the knowledge of
the glory of God in the face of Jesus Christ.

II CORINTHIANS 4:6

For the sages say that it is impossible for rational knowledge of God
to coexist with the direct experience of God, or for conceptual knowledge of God
to coexist with immediate perception of God.

MAXIMUS THE CONFESSOR[3]

Mysticism is a vague word that is used in a variety of ways to mean different things. This is not just because human beings are sloppy and like to use words in imprecise ways—although, granted, that's part of the problem. Rather, mysticism as a word or concept is impossible to define because it is, by nature, linked to spirituality, to mystery, to subjective experience—all notoriously squishy subjects. In this book, we attempt to unlock the mystery of mysticism, not only by appealing to the wisdom of the great mystics from more than 2,000 years of Christian history and the scholars who have written about them, but also by exploring the ways in which mysticism can enlighten our spiritual lives today.

The history of Christian mysticism includes a wide array of colorful and sometimes eccentric characters who have much to teach us, not only about Christianity and mysticism, but also about life in general. When we take the time to understand their lives in a way that honors their wisdom, we begin to find ways to apply that wisdom to our own lives. Ultimately, our goal must be not just to explore an interesting philosophical concept, but rather to understand mysticism as a powerful tool for transforming our minds, hearts, and souls.

What do the Christian mystics tell us? That the wisdom they offer us can literally unite us with God—or at the very least, give us such a powerful experience of God's presence that it can revolutionize our lives. The purpose of such transformed lives is not primarily to achieve a goal (like enlightenment or spiritual bliss), but rather to participate in the Holy Spirit's ongoing activity—embodying the flowing love of Christ, love that we in turn give back to God as well as to "our neighbors as ourselves." The mystical tradition manifests in a particular tension that persists throughout Christian history and is, thus, distinct from other expressions of Christian spirituality. You can be a Christian without being a mystic, and you can be a mystic without being a Christian. If you want to embrace Christian mysticism, however, you begin by embracing Christianity, both in its external, "religious" form, and also in its inner exploration of prayer, meditation, and contemplation.

THE PROBLEM WITH MYSTICISM

Over the years, I have found that many—perhaps most—of the books, websites, and blogs that treat the mystical dimension of Christianity tend to fall into two categories: the overly fanciful, and the overly boring.

Christian mysticism gets overly fanciful when you place too much emphasis on having "cool" spiritual experiences like cosmic consciousness or secret visions. While it is true that mysticism is experiential, Christian mysticism is also *grounded* in the love of God—a love which leads to healing, transformation, and growth in holiness. In other words, Christian mysticism is never an end to itself. The point behind mysticism is not to dazzle the mind with ecstatic wonders or heady feelings, but to foster real and lasting changes, for the purpose of becoming more like Christ, which is to say, more compassionate, more forgiving, more committed to serving others and making the world a better place. In other words, the experience is really just a small part of the overall package.

Likewise, students of Christian mysticism lose their way when they get too caught up in quests for secret knowledge, or hidden teachings that are supposedly the key to higher realities, that somehow have been lost (or suppressed) by church authorities. I'm willing to go with the idea that many of the key principles of Christian mysticism have been marginalized, ignored, or even rejected by many followers of Jesus, but there's no need to get all conspiratorial about this. The keys to Christian mysticism have been hidden in plain sight.

Unfortunately, there is a certain allure to the idea that some sort of secret body of knowledge has been squirreled away in the Vatican or in a monastery somewhere on the Sinai Peninsula for the past 1,500 years. History is full of colorful characters who have promoted themselves as the guardians of such long-lost information, offering to share their esoteric teachings with a select worthy few—for a hefty fee.

The real mystical tradition in Christianity is much broader and deeper than that. It is the story of people who receive powerful mystical experiences, undergo amazing and beautiful transformations of consciousness, and embody the teachings of Jesus—*without* getting lost in a fantasy world.

Another variation of this kind of fanciful mysticism is the idea that the only "real" mysticism comes from the East, from venerable wisdom traditions such as Vedanta or Zen. Therefore, "Christian" mysticism is really just Hinduism or Buddhism with a little bit of Jesus mixed in. But in fact, Christianity has its own, homegrown mystical tradition with its own practices, wisdom, and values. While it is true that, generally speaking, Christian mystics are more open to the wisdom of other religions than most Christians, this openness is rooted in loyalty to the central wisdom teachings of Christ, the Bible, and the Christian tradition.

Where can we turn to find the most authentic expressions of Christian mysticism? To that tradition, as embodied in the great mystics of history (see Appendix A). Christian mysticism is rooted in an easily identifiable body of wisdom teachings that can be traced back to the very origins of the faith. Great saints, monks, nuns, theologians, philosophers, and artists throughout the centuries have made contributions to the faith that include their experience as mystics. Francis of Assisi, Hildegard of Bingen, Thomas Aquinas, and Augustine are just a few of the many Christian spiritual geniuses who lived by and taught the wisdom of encountering the mysterious presence of God. Because they didn't draw attention to themselves or their experiences, their mysticism is, in a very real way, hidden in plain sight. It is not secret or occult, or part of an underground conspiracy. It is a very simple, humble, down-to-earth spirituality that has slipped unpretentiously across the stage of history. The problem is not that mystical teachings are hidden, but rather that so few people bother to learn the principles of Christian mysticism, much less apply them to their own lives.

If some writers err on the side of the overly fanciful, however, others err on the side of boredom. Many of the teachers and scholars who write about the genuine tradition of Christian mysticism without resorting to sensationalism or exaggeration are brilliant, intelligent experts who produce profound studies filled with fascinating insights—all too often, replete with complex ideas and arcane terminology, much of it Greek or Latin. Since mystical spirituality is intimately related to theology which in turn is related to philosophy, most of these studies are as challenging to read as the works of Plato, Aristotle, or Kant. Even when these academics work hard to make their studies accessible to those of us who don't have graduate degrees in logic, their books are often unavoidably dry and dull.

Many of the serious and scholarly books on mysticism tend to focus on its heritage—on the lives and the teachings of great mystics of the past—and have little or nothing to say concerning why mysticism matters today. In other words, they do a great job of telling you *about* mysticism, but don't really make mysticism come alive in an intimate, practical way. It seems to me that the central question we need to ask is how and why that ancient wisdom can be relevant today. How can we take the authentic Christian mysticism of history and apply it to our own spiritual lives?

The Search for Authentic Experience

I'm writing about Christian mysticism because I love Christ, and because I hunger for the presence of God in my life. I'm writing about it because I believe that the wisdom of great mystics—Julian of Norwich, John Ruusbroec, Richard of St. Victor, Teresa of Avila—can be applied to our lives today. I believe that, if enough of us try to conduct our lives according to their teachings, we can change our lives and the world.

The mystics point us to Christ, and to the powerful message of the gospel. So make no mistake: this is a book about how to live according to the teachings of the Christian faith. We look at topics like repentance, holiness, sacrifice, and prayer—difficult topics with which you may or may not be comfortable, depending on your background and beliefs. All I ask as you consider them is that you try to keep an open mind. I believe one of the powerful gifts of Christian mysticism is that it can take the truths of the gospel—ideas that sometimes come across as rigid or repressive in many contexts—and transform them into exciting, spiritually luminous principles by which we can ignite our lives into a profound experience of God's love and healing presence. If you are a devout Christian, I likewise ask you to approach this book with an open mind. Mysticism does not change the gospel. But it does shine an entirely new light on it that can help you see what has always been there in powerful and exciting new ways.

Christian mysticism is a concept unto itself—not just a "flavor" of some generic mystic philosophy. The cross-fertilization between Christianity and mysticism created something entirely new—a unique belief system that is different from all other kinds of mysticism.

Likewise, Christian mysticism is not the same thing as basic Christianity. The two are not incompatible, however. On the contrary, authentic Christian mysticism reflects and reinforces authentic Christianity. Any perceived conflict between them arises only when something has gone awry with one or the other. When Christianity is true to itself as a liberating faith in Jesus, and Christian mysticism is true to itself as a Christian encounter with the awesome mystery of God, they flow together beautifully and harmoniously. Nonetheless, while it is helpful to draw a distinction between Christianity-the-religion and Christian mysticism, the tradition has consistently emphasized that you cannot be a Christian mystic without engaging with the social and communal dimensions of the Christian faith. Indeed, the more authentic a Christian mystic is, the more engaged he or she will be with even the most mundane aspects of religious Christianity.

Likewise, there are real differences between generic mysticism, Christian mysticism, and all the other types of mysticism—Buddhist, Jewish, Hindu, etc. These differences are not absolute and we can, in fact, talk about mysticism in general ways. For example, we can make this statement: "Mysticism concerns spiritual experience." This is true for mysticism in general as well as for Christian mysticism. But we must also acknowledge the real differences that distinguish Christian mysticism from world mysticism. For example, many forms of non-Christian mysticism are anchored in the idea that human beings are (or can become) *identical* with God. Christianity denies this, and Christian mysticism concurs. Christian mysticism pursues *participation* with God, *communion* with God, and even *experiences of union* with God, but always distinguishes creator from creature. To deny that distinction is to move away from Christian mysticism, even if you talk about Jesus all the time.

I'm belaboring this point because I anticipate three kinds of people will pick up this book: non-Christians who are interested in mysticism, but perhaps not favorably disposed to Christianity; Christians who are interested in, but perhaps not favorably disposed to, mysticism; and people who are interested in Christian mysticism (regardless of their faith). I point this out because I need to be clear about my own perspective: I love Christianity; I love mysticism in general—including all the different "types" of mysticism; and I love Christian mysticism and understand it as a unique phenomenon. It is, however, my goal to write an honest book, which means being honest about both my Christian faith and my fascination with mysticism.

Part of the challenge in writing about this topic is that there are plenty of people who love mysticism, but are suspicious of Christianity. And there are others who are committed to Christianity, but are unsure about mysticism. I want to write a book that honors readers wherever they are on their own spiritual journeys. I can't guarantee that I'll win anyone over to my point of view, but I can hope to give everyone who reads this book a new insight or two, or something to think about. If you have a positive attitude (or, at least, an open mind) toward both Christianity and mysticism, you will find plenty of information here to consider as you proceed on your own spiritual journey. My goal is to inspire and encourage you to make Christian mysticism a part of your life.

I believe Christian mysticism can transform you. It's a form of alchemy that integrates Christianity's promise of new life in Christ with mysticism's promise of experiencing the presence of God. It allows something to emerge that is greater than the sum of its parts; it illuminates a path by which you can open yourself to what the Apostle Paul calls "letting the mind (consciousness) of Christ be in you" and what the Apostle Peter calls "partaking of the divine nature." Christian mysticism invites you to do more than just know about God, or Christ, or spiritual transformation. It invites you *into* God, and *into* Christ, and *into* the experience of transformation that can come about only through the love and grace of God. It's intimate; it's heartful and mindful; it's oriented toward making a real, powerful, profound, and lasting difference in your life and your relationships.

Of course, whether you accept the invitation is entirely up to you.

CHAPTER 2

Defining Mysticism

For my thoughts are not your thoughts,
nor are your ways my ways, says the LORD.

Isaiah 55:8

What, then, is time? I know well enough what it is, provided that
nobody asks me; but if I am asked what it is and try to explain, I am baffled.

Augustine[4]

Some people think mysticism means having powerful spiritual experiences, like seeing heavenly visions, or hearing supernatural voices, or feeling a sense of communion with God, or undergoing profound shifts in consciousness. Others see it as a spiritual dimension to (and beyond) religion, in which the cultural, ethical, and theological differences between religions are somehow resolved in a trans-verbal state of unity. Still others dismiss it as the fuzzy, illogical, and irrational element that makes religion and spirituality so distasteful to those who prefer to conduct their lives according to science rather than faith (which they see as superstition). These, and other, ways of understanding mysticism all make sense in their own context. But none of them manages to appreciate mysticism's treasures fully.

Probably the first important thing that needs to be said about mysticism is that you can never adequately put it into words. And, although there are many different kinds of mysticism, the inability to describe them adequately with words—in other words, the *ineffability* of mysticism— holds true for them all. Indeed, trying to understand mysticism is futile, and we must begin our discussion with the recognition that it cannot be precisely defined.

LOVE IN A BOTTLE

It's like trying to put love in a bottle. It just can't be done. To begin with, love is not something that can be pinned down to a specific point in space and time. It is a spiritual reality that can never be defined, or enclosed or "captured."

Much the same is true of mysticism. Its essence simply cannot be captured in human language—indeed, not even by the most sublime reaches of human thought. We can use language to suggest mysticism—to allude to it, to point to it, to create poetic metaphors or analogies about it that ring true—but these linguistic interpretations are ultimately like attempts to empty the ocean with a teaspoon. Like God or spirituality or heaven, mysticism takes us beyond what the most eloquent and poetic language can ever express. It pushes you to the limits of your imagination and then says, "take another step." And another, and another.

Dr. Seuss once wrote a book called *On Beyond Zebra!* that explored all the meta-letters that exist in his imaginary alphabet, beyond the twenty-six of the standard English alphabet. Mysticism is like Seuss's alphabet. It pushes beyond the normal boundaries of human thought, human logic, and human rationality and knowing. It goes beyond the limits of philosophy, theology, psychology, and science. But whereas Dr. Seuss was just playing make-believe, mysticism points to something that countless witnesses, in cultures all across the world and in every age from the dawn of recorded history, insist is utterly real—maybe even more real than the universe and consciousness we normally inhabit.

You don't have to be an expert in etymology to figure out that the word "mysticism" is related to the word "mystery." Thus, the most we can hope to do is to use our feeble language to try to catch tiny glimpses of that heaven-sent *something*—that mystery—the great visionaries and saints have described as an experiential relationship with God. Maybe your heart will register a thrill of recognition as you read their writings, giving you some sense of what mysticism is. But, like love in a bottle, as soon as you try to put it into your own words, mysticism unfolds itself into a variety of paradoxes and seemingly contradictory truths that leave you as confused and befuddled as ever.

Christian mysticism is all about having a "relationship with God." Indeed, this is its bedrock principle. In some non-Christian forms of mysticism like Zen Buddhism or Taoism, God is not part of the equation at all. In these traditions, it is possible to be a mystic and an atheist—or at least, an agnostic. However, even some of the most profound Christian mystics talk about how *unknowable* God is. How can you have a relationship with something or someone who is fundamentally unknowable? And yet, that is where mysticism takes you. When we talk about mysticism, we can use words that try to make sense of the mystery—"God," or "the Absolute," or "the Ultimate Mystery"—until the words themselves fail us. Then we are left with only silence, facing the mystery again, and perhaps scrambling to find new words, new concepts, and new ideas.

The way I talk about mysticism will make the most sense in a Christian context—even when I'm discussing mysticism in general. After all, this is a book about Christian mysticism. But even within a specifically Christian framework, mysticism has an unnerving tendency to contradict itself and deconstruct itself in bewildering and playful ways. That dynamic gets even more complicated when we begin to talk about "world" mysticism, which is not limited to any one religious or spiritual tradition. As a dynamic spiritual force that has been at work in the lives of Christians throughout the history of the faith—and one that continues to show up in surprising ways among the faithful even today—mysticism remains perplexing and uncontrollable; it plays out in people's lives in unexpected ways.

The mystics themselves have long recognized the ultimate "unknowability" of this indefinable thing we call mysticism. Indeed, I warn you that I will fail utterly to explain what mysticism is. I am philosophical about that because, as a Christian, I know that grace is always present, even in the midst of our failures. So why, you may ask, do I try? As the mountain climber said when asked why he climbed mountains: "Because it's there." I write about mysticism, not because I have it all figured out (I don't), or because I think my book will help you figure it all out (it won't), but because I hope my attempt may contain some small glimmers of insight or encouragement that you can use on your own journey into the Ultimate Mystery.

Exploring the Unknowable

When we talk about mysticism, what exactly are we talking about? I can offer several snappy definitions:

> *Mysticism is the art of union with God.*
>
> *Mysticism is the experiential core of spirituality, contrasted with religion, which is an organized assembly of rituals, beliefs, and codes of conduct that are derived from spirituality.*
>
> *Mysticism is the heart of spirituality where all religious differences are resolved and we find unity in the Sacred.*

Each of these statements is useful, as far as it goes. The first is rather more useful in terms of God-oriented mysticism (like Christian mysticism), while the other two broaden the topic to include other mystical paths as well.

The problem with these pat definitions is that they leave all the major paradoxes and seeming contradictions of mysticism unexplained. How can mysticism be about God when even Christians don't all agree on who or what God is or how knowable he is? Can we really say that mysticism is about "experience," when there are some mystics (like Jean-Pierre de Caussade) who insist that our feelings are unreliable when it comes to spiritual growth? And what's all this about resolving religious differences? Is that really what mysticism is about, or is that just wishful thinking on the part of those who try to gloss over real and intractable differences between religions? Each of these definitions contains a measure of truth, but also a measure of distortion or limitation.

Mysticism is directly related to mystery, and indeed few topics are more puzzling or enigmatic. Here are some other definitions; the first comes from the *American Heritage Dictionary*; the others from writers and thinkers who have wrestled with the mystery:

Mysticism: Immediate consciousness of the transcendent or ultimate reality or God.[5]

Mysticism, according to its historical and psychological definitions, is the direct intuition or experience of God; and a mystic is a person who has, to a greater or less degree, such a direct experience—one whose religion and life are centered, not merely on an accepted belief or practice, but on that which he regards as first-hand personal knowledge.
—Evelyn Underhill [6]

The word "Mysticism" itself comes down to us from the Greeks and is derived from a root meaning "to close." The mystic was one who had been initiated into the esoteric knowledge of Divine things, and upon whom was laid the necessity of keeping silence concerning his sacred knowledge. The term "mystical," then might be applied to any secret cult revealed only to the initiated. [7]

Christian mysticism is a way of life that involves the perfect fulfillment of loving God, neighbor, all God's creation, and oneself. ... It is an ordered movement toward ever higher levels of reality by which the self awakens to, is purified and illuminated by, and is eventually fully united with, the God of love.[8]

With the exception of the dictionary definition, all of the above refer specifically to Christian mysticism. To make things more interesting, here are a few ideas about mysticism that come from non-Christian sources, or sources that are not exclusively Christian:

Mysticism is concerned with the possibility of personally encountering a spiritual reality which is hidden from our normal awareness like the sun behind the clouds. It is not concerned with propounding a philosophy that may be believed or doubted. The mystics tell us that higher consciousness is available to everyone, and by setting out on our own journey of spiritual exploration we can experience it for ourselves.[9]

Mysticism is that point of view which claims as its basis an intimate knowledge of the one source and substratum of all existence, a knowledge which is obtained through a revelatory experience during a rare moment of clarity in contemplation. Those who claim to have actually experienced this direct revelation constitute an elite tradition which transcends the boundary lines of individual religions, cultures and languages, and which has existed, uninterrupted, since the beginning of time.[10]

Mysticism is a manifestation of something which is at the root of all religion and all the higher religions have their mystical expressions.[11]

Mystical experience is the direct, unmediated experience of what Bede Griffiths beautifully describes as "the presence of an almost unfathomable mystery". ... This mystery is beyond name and beyond form; no name or form, no dogma, philosophy, or set of rituals can ever express it fully. It always transcends anything that can be said of it and remains always unstained by any of our human attempts to limit or exploit it.[12]

Imagine all these experts sitting in the same room trying to hammer out a universal definition of mysticism. It might get pretty loud in there.

TImothy Freke and Peter Gandy insist that mysticism is about "higher consciousness" that is "available to everyone," while Swami Abhayananda calls it an "elite tradition," which suggests that it is something only for the chosen few. Margaret Smith sees mysticism in terms of an "esoteric knowledge of Divine things" that is so exalted that mystics (whom she describes as "initiates") must forever remain silent about their "sacred knowledge." By contrast, Andrew Harvey insists that mysticism "always transcends anything that can be said of it and remains always unstained by any of our human attempts to limit or exploit it." In other words, there are no secrets to keep, because, far from being esoteric, mysticism is ineffable, and therefore impossible to put into words even if you wanted to.

ORIENTING GENERALIZATIONS

While it may be tempting to look at all these contradictory approaches to mysticism and simply decide that it is an impossible topic to explore, it is possible to build bridges between these various perspectives. American philosopher Ken Wilber writes about the connections between religion and science, between Eastern and Western spirituality, and about other broad areas of human knowledge. In his book *A Brief History of Everything*, Wilber argues that the best way to approach large and complex topics is to begin by looking for patterns of similarity between the different elements of the material being investigated. We can apply this same methodology to the complex and mysterious topic of mysticism.

Wilber uses the term "orienting generalization" to describe a broad and basic way of speaking about a difficult topic that can point toward an understanding, if not a precise definition, of complex issues. Even when experts can't find complete agreement, he notes, their perspectives may have enough commonality that orienting generalizations can be drawn from their differing viewpoints.

So what are the orienting generalizations of mysticism? We can make at least these initial observations based on the various and admittedly contradictory earlier definitions:

- *Mysticism concerns a higher reality*. Different religions and philosophies call this by different names; the traditional Christian name for this reality is "God."

- *Mysticism involves an experience, or conscious awareness, of this higher reality*. Precisely because this reality is "higher," however, there is an unavoidable and inexhaustible element of mystery surrounding it as well. In other words, mysticism seems to be grounded in experience, but simultaneously is something other than mere experience. It involves consciousness, but also transcends it.

- *Mysticism is often connected with religion*. Here I am using religion to mean the various social and cultural ways in which people relate to each other's common desire for contact with the Higher Mystery. This connection between mysticism and religion, however, exists alongside real differences and tensions. Certainly it is possible to be religious without exploring mysticism; and some expressions of mysticism do not require a religious setting. Since community is such an important element within Christianity, Christian mysticism is more overtly religious than other forms of mysticism. In fact, while mysticism in general is *often* connected with religion, I think the case can be made that genuine Christian mysticism is *always* religious (communal) in nature.

- *Since religion concerns values, beliefs, ethics, and dogma, these things all have an impact on mysticism in its religious forms*. That being said, it's important to remember that, just as religion includes many ideas and values about God (some clearly paradoxical, if not apparently contradictory), so too mysticism entails a rather dizzying array of ideas, beliefs, and values, among which many paradoxes and tensions can be found.

- *Along with its emphasis on personal experience and consciousness, mysticism also has a behavioral component.* In other words, mysticism is a way of life. People who explore it often do some pretty unusual things, including trying to live in a holy or sanctified manner, or (at the very least) embracing a regular practice of prayer, meditation, or contemplation. Such spiritual exercises are believed to foster or support the desired experience of intimacy with, union with, or even simply the felt presence of God.

Much of Wilber's work is devoted to understanding consciousness, which means that he has devoted a lot of effort to examining the role of spirituality in human life. In his book *Integral Spirituality*, Wilber suggests that the word "spirituality" can be understood in four distinct ways. He notes that many people regard spirituality as a rather vague, if not meaningless, concept and suggests this is because the word has a variety of meanings. It's not a question of which meaning is the "right" one—they are all correct, depending on the context in which the word is used. His point is that, only when we start taking these distinctions seriously do we begin to recognize the beauty and value of spirituality. Moreover, it becomes easier to communicate about it in meaningful and effective ways.

Wilber gives four orienting generalizations about spirituality that I believe can be applied to mysticism as well. Although spirituality and mysticism are not synonymous—all mysticism is spiritual, but not all spirituality is mystical—I think his four generalizations can aid our understanding of mysticism.

1. Mysticism can refer to a particular type of experience—a "peak" experience of God/the Ultimate Mystery, which can also be called a "peek" experience in that it provides a glimpse of previously unimagined possibilities. The Bible has numerous examples of such experiences, which, in traditional religious language, are called "epiphanies." The most dramatic is the conversion of Saint Paul, which followed an encounter with the risen Christ on the road to Damascus (Acts 9:3-9). Many, if not all, of the great Christian mystics experienced epiphanies of their own.

2. Mysticism also refers to a particular level of consciousness. This altered or heightened state—which has been known by many names, including enlightenment, holiness, sanctification, and the unitive life—is not an isolated event, but rather represents a fundamental shift in awareness to a higher/holier state. As Saint Paul put it: "Let the same mind be in you that was in Christ Jesus" (Philippians 2:5). Unlike an epiphany, which is transitory in nature, mysticism as heightened consciousness suggests a more or less permanent or longer-lasting change in awareness or knowledge of the Ultimate Mystery/God. While a mystical experience may involve having a glimpse of God's presence, mystical consciousness may mean an ongoing sense of being united with God.

3. Mysticism may also refer to a particular type of ability—what Wilber calls a "developmental line." Just as some people are naturally gifted at music or sports or mechanics, so mysticism is a particular aptitude for which a person may exhibit a greater or lesser degree of innate skill. This suggests that a "mystically gifted" person has an innate ability, not only to experience the presence of the Ultimate Mystery, but also to manifest extraordinary spiritual abilities—to heal, to prophesy, to teach or influence others through a deep spiritual charisma, to live a holy or sanctified life. Of course, such mystical ability, like all other aptitudes, exists on a continuum. Just as you can enjoy music or art or sports even if you are not a Mozart or a Michelangelo or a Michael Phelps, you don't have to be a mystical genius to have some capacity for the mystical.

4. Mysticism refers to a particular attitude that has more to do with values than with experience, consciousness, or ability. In this sense, being a mystical person may mean nothing more than being serious about your belief that God is real and at work in your life, or having a clear conviction of the world as operating

in harmony with God's plan, or consistently being more forgiving than judgmental about others' failings. Whereas the previous generalizations all seem to indicate that mysticism is something largely outside of your control (either you're born with a mystical ability or you aren't), a mystical attitude rests more on the choices and intentions you make. If you immerse yourself in mystical literature, if you are deeply engaged in the life of faith, if you choose to pray and meditate on a daily basis, you are cultivating an attitude of mysticism even if you never have an extraordinary experience, or sense a heightened consciousness, or display any supernatural ability. This may not be as dramatic a view of mysticism, but it has the virtue of being within the reach of the average person. Many Christian mystics, in fact, understood the spiritual life, not as something awesome and extraordinary, but as something humble, down-to-earth, and in many ways very simple and small.

In addition to Wilber's four orienting generalizations, I propose a fifth:

5. Mysticism refers to the inner dimension of religion. The world's great contemplative wisdom traditions typically are embedded in a larger and more "ordinary" religious or philosophical culture. Christian mysticism emerges within Christianity; Vedanta within Hinduism; Kabbalah within Judaism; Zen within Buddhism; Sufism within Islam. This generalization, however, may be more useful for Western than for Eastern religions. In the East, the line separating mysticism from religion seems fuzzier, although, even in the East, a distinction is drawn between the perfunctory performance of religious rituals and a more heartfelt inner experience. In other words, you can burn incense to the Buddha every day for years and not necessarily experience awakening or enlightenment, just as a Catholic may go to Mass day after day and not necessarily have a mystical experience or enter into mystical

consciousness. But these religious practices might help you be far more open to mystical experience than if you never bother with religious exercises at all.

The key to making sense of these differing definitions is remembering that, to some extent, they are mutually exclusive. I once asked a monk how he defined mysticism. "A mystic is someone who exhibits extraordinary phenomena," he said. "They have visions, they hear locutions, they levitate, or something along those lines." Thus, he understood mysticism almost exclusively in terms of ability. Not surprisingly, he rejected the idea that mysticism can mean nothing more than a spiritual attitude or a religious sensibility. "Everyone is not called to be a mystic," he argued. "Everyone is called to holiness." For him, mysticism is therefore reserved for truly supernatural experiences or phenomena, although ordinary people still have the opportunity to cultivate a sense of connection to God in their lives. This is not properly called mysticism, to his way of thinking; it is holiness.

THE PARTICLE AND THE WAVE

One of the most famous mysteries to perplex scientists was whether light, at its most foundational level, is composed of particles or of waves. The answer to the puzzle, it appears, is: "It depends." In fact, the properties of light may actually be influenced by those who observe it. Likewise, mysticism.

Is mysticism about specific experiences of God, or rather a more lasting consciousness of God? Is it an irresistible gift from God, or must a would-be mystic make a choice in response to God's grace and out of desire for God's love? Are all these ways of understanding mysticism the same thing, or are they really as different as a wave and a particle? Or perhaps all of these different ways of understanding mysticism reveal just the imprecision of language. Perhaps what some people call "mysticism" really should go by a different name—like holiness, or sanctification, or esotericism, or hermeticism.

Does mysticism involve something that happens as a specific event, at a specific moment and location in space and time, like Saint Paul's conversion on the road to Damascus? Or is it an ongoing state of mind, a way of seeing and thinking that may not involve particular extraordinary experiences, but rather points to a blessed and holy way of life? We are all more likely to encounter the mystery at the heart of mysticism if we remain open to all its paradoxes and possibilities.

CHAPTER 3

How Mysticism Became Christian

But anyone united to the Lord becomes one spirit with him.

I CORINTHIANS 6:17

The Christian religion is primarily about a transformation of consciousness.
This takes spiritual practice and the cultivation of wisdom. In another time,
this was called cultivating the supernatural organism, what Paul called
"a new creation." So the main thing is to be transformed into God,
what the early church called deification, theosis, divinization.

THOMAS KEATING[13]

As useful as Wilber's orienting generalizations are, they are not the only tools we have to explore the complex mystery of mysticism. History and etymology also provide important clues to understanding this recondite topic. By tracing the Greek origins of mysticism as a concept, and seeing how the meaning of mysticism has evolved in the history of the Christian faith, we can discover how this originally pagan form of spirituality took on a uniquely and specifically Christian character—and what this means for us today.

To understand the history of Christian mysticism, we have to explore the origins of Christianity, in the context of the language, philosophy, and religion of the Hellenistic world in which the New Testament was written. The word "mysticism" comes from the Greek word *mueo*, which means "to close" or "to shut." In "Mysticism: An Essay on the History of the Word," French scholar Louis Bouyer says it refers to closing the eyes, while other sources suggest it refers to keeping your mouth shut. In fact, both of these meanings make sense. Yet another source suggests the word means "to initiate into the mysteries," hence "to instruct." Mysticism thus involves shutting, closing, and hiddenness, but also initiation, learning a secret, and keeping your mouth shut long enough to listen for what's really going on.

Mysticism first emerged in the great pagan mystery religions of the ancient world. These religions encompassed a variety of independent communities that were organized around the veneration of a particular deity linked to a mythological story. For example, the Orphic mysteries venerated Orpheus, whose myth recounts how he went into the underworld in a vain attempt to rescue his beloved Eurydice. Likewise, the Eleusinian mysteries are devoted to the goddesses Demeter and Persephone, another tale with a strong underworld theme. Incidentally, this underworld theme is an important clue to understanding mysticism—even after it became Christianized.

Only initiates could participate in the ceremonies associated with the mystery religions. Initiation, as best we can tell, involved participation in one or more rituals in which the secrets of the god or goddess were revealed. Since initiates vowed never to reveal the secrets of the tradition, we know little of these ancient rites.

At least two of mysticism's orienting generalizations appear to be present in the mystery religions. The mysteries involved a specific experience—the ritual of initiation—as well as the suggestion of a particular change in consciousness that initiates enjoyed by virtue of having been enlightened by the secrets that were imparted to them. The secrets were, in all likelihood, meant to transform the faithful with a particular feeling or sense of connection with the gods, giving access to divine power.

Louis Bouyer suggests that "what the initiated must forbear from revealing... is not a doctrine, nor is it esoteric knowledge, but simply and solely the details of a ritual."[14] But the reason the rituals were secret was because they included, in a symbolic or encoded way, spiritual doctrines or esoteric knowledge designed to foster mystical experiences and/or mystical consciousness. Mysticism thus emerged through rituals oriented toward mythological gods and designed to foster spiritual experiences that led to a transformation in consciousness.

And then along came the Christians. Bouyer goes to great lengths in his essay to argue that Christianity did not borrow any secret teachings from the pagan religions, although they did borrow the *language* of the mysteries. While it is unclear just how the Greek concept of mystery influenced early Christianity, the concept of mystery as "hiddenness" that appears in the New Testament and among the earliest Christian mystics does have an entirely different flavor from the pagan contexts out of which the language of mystery emerged. The earliest Christian mystics don't talk about ritual secrets that only initiates can access; rather they talk about secrets that are *revealed*—through Christ, through the Bible, through the Christian sacraments, and eventually, through personal experiences of the presence of God.

For Christians, mysticism is thus not a static concept. Rather, it suggests something dynamic—a process, energy, or movement. It involves a continual tension between what is hidden and what is revealed. The development of this nuanced sense of the mystical was a long (and ongoing) process within Christianity.

Mysticism and the New Testament

The word "mysticism" never appears in the New Testament. That is not particularly remarkable, however, for it is not an ancient word. The word was coined in the eighteenth century, derived from the Greek word *mueo*, which appears only once in the New Testament, when Paul notes that he has "learned the secret" of what it is like to be both hungry and well fed (Philippians 4:12). This mundane use of the word clearly does not give us a lot of insight into the concept of mysticism as we know it. Of more direct interest to our inquiry is the Greek word *musterion*, meaning "mystery." Various forms of this Greek word appear in twenty-seven passages scattered throughout the New Testament. Here are some of the key concepts given in those passages:

> The secrets of the kingdom of heaven (Matthew 13:11).
>
> The proclamation of Jesus Christ is "according to the revelation of the mystery that was kept secret for long ages" (Romans 16:25).
>
> God's wisdom is described as "secret and hidden" (I Corinthians 2:7).
>
> Christians are "stewards of God's mysteries" (I Corinthians 4:1).
>
> In I Corinthians 13 (the famous "love" chapter), Saint Paul notes that, even if he could "understand all mysteries and all knowledge," if he lacked love, he would be "nothing."
>
> The Christian belief in life after death is described as a mystery (I Corinthians 15:51).
>
> In Ephesians 1:9, the "mystery of God's will" has, according to his good pleasure, been "set forth in Christ."
>
> In Colossians 1:26-27, the mystery of God is described as hidden throughout the ages, but now revealed; the mystery is "Christ in

you, the hope of glory." In Colossians 2:2, "God's mystery" is described as "Christ himself."

In the first letter to Timothy, there are references to the "mystery of the faith" (3:9) and the "mystery of our religion" (3:16), which is explained in terms of events from the life of Christ.[15]

So what does all this mean?

Certainly, the concept of mystery as it appears in the New Testament does, in some ways, mirror the spirituality of the pagan mystery religions. But there's far more to the New Testament's concept of mystery than just a subtle echo of Greek paganism. Instead of focusing on the spiritual secrets of a polytheistic god or goddess, the New Testament (of course) focuses entirely on Christ. Moreover, the emphasis in much of the New Testament is not on secrets *kept*, but on secrets *revealed*. That's the crucial difference between Christianity and the mystery religions. Christ himself is the ultimate secret that is revealed. Or perhaps it is more accurate to say that it is *through* Christ that the ultimate secret is revealed—the secret of the nature of God, the reality of God's unconditional love for us, and our invitation to partake of God's divine nature.

In Christ, not only is God revealed; his attributes and actions are as well—his mercy, his grace and love, and his plan for spreading glory and hope throughout the world. It's important to keep in mind that Christ is not just some abstract concept that is found in a book or a religious ritual. The mystery of God is Christ *in us*. Not only is God revealed through Christ, but also his presence in Christ is made known intimately to those who believe, because they abide in Christ and Christ abides in them (John 15:4).

THE CHARTER OF CHRISTIAN MYSTICISM

The third chapter of Ephesians is probably more important than any other chapter in the Bible for understanding the scriptural basis of Christian mysticism. The Letter to the Ephesians, traditionally attributed to the Apostle

Paul, is one of the shortest, but most lyrical, of the New Testament writings. Ephesians 3 examines why Christians believe that Jesus came, not just for Israel, but for the entire world—for gentiles as well as for Jews. Here, Paul speaks of the mystery that was made known to him through revelation and goes on to point out that this mystery "made known by revelation" is, in fact, Christ himself. Later in the chapter, he maintains that this "mystery of Christ" had been hidden all along "in God who created all things" (verses 3 through 9).

In its poetic description of the mystery of Christ, this chapter lays the foundation for Christian mystical theology, introducing ideas and beliefs that inspired generations of men and women who sought to unite their lives with the love of God. Indeed, this single chapter of the New Testament reveals how mysticism was a part of Christianity from the very beginning. It is the "charter," if you will, of the Christian tradition of seeking to enter the hidden, loving, and transformative splendor of God.

In the first four verses of the chapter, the author declares that God has entrusted him with a revelation of the mystery of Christ:

> *This is the reason that I Paul am a prisoner for Christ Jesus for the sake of you Gentiles—for surely you have already heard of the commission of God's grace that was given me for you, and how the mystery was made known to me by revelation, as I wrote above in a few words, a reading of which will enable you to perceive my understanding of the mystery of Christ.*

Here, "wrote above" refers to Ephesians 2:22, where Paul describes the mystery of Christ: "in whom you also are built together spiritually into a dwelling place for God." Paul makes the amazing statement that God, in the Spirit, will *dwell* in us because we, the community of believers in Christ, are "in him." We are actually immersed in Christ's spiritual presence. So the mystery that Paul is describing can be restated like this: "God is in us, because we are in Christ." Here is the spiritual essence of Christianity—Jesus is one with the father (John 10:30); Jesus' followers are, as a community, the "Body of Christ" (I Corinthians 12:27), and in that body dwells the Spirit of God. It's a dance, in which God, Christ, and Christians all are immersed in each other's presence.

The next verses lay out the main point of this chapter.

> *In former generations this mystery was not made known to humankind, as it has now been revealed to his holy apostles and prophets by the Spirit: that is, the Gentiles have become fellow heirs, members of the same body, and sharers in the promise in Christ Jesus through the gospel.*

The mystery of Christ is available to all, not just to his Jewish disciples. In other words, Paul is not so much trying to teach the readers of this letter about mysticism, but rather is pointing out how the truth of the Christian mystery (which would have been understood to his readers, since they were already believers) is not limited to just one ethnic group. Even though Paul's main point is not to describe what the mystery is, he does so nonetheless, providing valuable information for those of us who want to explore the Ultimate Mystery in our lives today. By explaining "the mystery of Christ," Paul reveals the heart of Christian mysticism.

Paul goes on to reiterate that his own calling is to spread the good news of Christ to the gentiles.

> *Of this gospel I have become a servant according to the gift of God's grace that was given me by the working of his power. Although I am the very least of all the saints, this grace was given to me to bring to the Gentiles the news of the boundless riches of Christ, and to make everyone see what is the plan of the mystery hidden for ages in God who created all things...*

Here, Paul states a central goal of Christian mysticism: to experience the ineffable splendors of the mutual indwelling of the soul in Christ.

> *...so that through the church the wisdom of God in its rich variety might now be made known to the rulers and authorities in the heavenly places.*

Paul engages in some subtle humor here. The ancient church—the community of believers who followed Christ and lived in him—was hardly in a position to instruct the "rulers and authorities" of either heaven or earth. On the contrary, in Paul's day, Christianity was a marginal religion. It was some 250 years before it became a socially accepted faith. What Paul points out here is that Christians, even if they lack any social standing whatsoever, have access to wisdom that proves to be a revelation to both human and spiritual powers (whether they pay attention to Christians or not). Paul lauds "the wisdom of God in its rich variety," suggesting that the mystery (of God's indwelling presence) cannot be reduced to a simple equation or formula.

> This was in accordance with the eternal purpose that he has carried out in Christ Jesus our Lord, in whom we have access to God in boldness and confidence through faith in him. I pray therefore that you may not lose heart over my sufferings for you; they are your glory.

The Apostle colors his subtle but important commentary with political as well as spiritual overtones. Today, in the United States, we tend to think of God as the ultimate populist—available to everyone, accessible to all. It may be impossible to set up an appointment with the President of the United States, but the God of all creation is just a prayer away. Paul reminds us that people did not always have this kind of confidence about approaching God. In the days of imperial power, God was seen as even less accessible than the emperor. But Paul depicts Christ as the great demolisher of red tape. Through Christ, God becomes accessible to everyone. This was a revolutionary idea that we take for granted today. It is also a foundational principle at the heart of Christian mysticism.

> For this reason I bow my knees before the Father, from whom every family in heaven and on earth takes its name.

Paul then tells us what he himself prays for—that all believers be mystics.

> I pray that, according to the riches of his glory, he may grant that you may be strengthened in your inner being with power through his Spirit, and that Christ may dwell in your hearts through faith, as you are being rooted and grounded in love. I pray that you may have the power to comprehend, with all the saints, what is the breadth and length and height

and depth, and to know the love of Christ that surpasses knowledge, so that you may be filled with all the fullness of God.

In a burst of mystical writing to rival (if not surpass) anything that came from the hand of the great mystics centuries later, Paul describes the breadth and depth of the mystery of Christ. Let's carefully examine his poetic language:

According to the riches of his glory: What Paul describes here is replete with the beauty, splendor, honor, and praiseworthiness of God.

He may grant that you may be strengthened in your inner being with power through his Spirit: Here's what is at stake in the mystical life—the opportunity to receive "power," but *internally*, which means growing into a dynamic spiritual life, rooted in Christ through his Spirit.

and that Christ may dwell in your hearts through faith: This powerful spiritual life isn't just some sort of inner entertainment. It means actually opening our hearts to receive the presence of Christ, who doesn't just come for a visit, but rather lives within us.

As you are being rooted and grounded in love: That Christ lives within us means we will be immersed in love, will rest on love, will embrace and be embraced by the fullness of love.

I pray that you may have the power to comprehend, with all the saints, what is the breadth and length and height and depth: This is a mysterious verse. I suspect Paul here refers to the love of Christ and/ or the fullness of God, which he goes on to mention.

And to know the love of Christ that surpasses knowledge: Paul declares that the love of Christ (which is what has just taken up residence in our hearts) surpasses knowledge (the Greek word is *gnosis*). Whatever we may comprehend or "know" in terms of God's presence in our lives will be only a tiny fraction of what is truly being offered to us in the Mystery.

So that you may be filled with all the fullness of God: This is true union with God. In other words, Paul promises that the mystery of Christ leads to a glorious end that so many mystics since have described—union with God, a beatific vision, communion with the Holy Trinity, deification, to be filled with the utter fullness of God.

Paul acknowledges that the mystery of Christ (i.e., mysticism) emerges from the "inner self," where "Christ may dwell... rooted and grounded in love." We are given the ability to grasp all the dimensions of this supernatural love, thereby integrating heart and mind in a unitive experience. "To know the love of Christ that surpasses knowledge, so that you may be filled with all the fullness of God." Yes, this is ineffable (it can't be put into words)—a knowledge beyond knowledge.

> *Now to him who by the power at work within us is able to accomplish abundantly far more than all we can ask or imagine, to him be glory in the church and in Christ Jesus to all generations, forever and ever. Amen.*

This stirring conclusion simply offers praise to the One in whom we are mystically united. But in offering this praise, Paul notes that Christ immerses us in his mystery on a level far beyond "all we can ask or imagine"—in other words, as good as you think union with God in Christ can be, it is far, far better than that.

Alfred North Whitehead once suggested that all of Western philosophy is little more than an extensive collection of footnotes to Plato. The more I read Ephesians 3, the more convinced I am that the entire sweep of Christian mysticism is, likewise, simply 2,000 years' worth of annotations on this chapter, accumulated as generation after generation has sought to explore the radiant splendor of the mystery it describes—the mystery of the indwelling presence of God in Christ, experienced in communion with other Christians, something that can be powerfully known and yet is ultimately beyond knowledge, for its true nature is love.

CHAPTER 4

The Evolution of Christian Mysticism

So we have known and believe the love that God has for us. God is love,
and those who abide in love abide in God, and God abides in them.

I JOHN 4:16

I have found heaven on earth, since heaven is God, and God is in my soul.
The day I understood this, everything became luminous in me,
and I wish to tell this secret to those I love, discretely.

ELIZABETH OF THE TRINITY[16]

The basics of Christian thought put forth in the New Testament are foundational to all subsequent Christian mysticism. In their time, these interpretations of spirituality were the religious equivalent of dynamite. They emerge out of the revolutionary concept that a flesh-and-blood human being, Jesus of Nazareth, was actually the revealed presence of God, the creator of the universe, the source of love, and the sustainer of all life. In Jesus, the mystery and hidden secrets of God were made known.

In other words, Jesus was not just a teacher or faith healer, or even a gifted prophet. He is the embodiment of God with a capital "G"—a God who, unlike pagan deities, was a God of infinite power. Jesus, the New Testament maintains, is the incarnation of the fullness of God. His followers become part of the "Body of Christ," which means we become "embodiments of God" as well.

In the early years of Christian spirituality, this notion of mystery—of the secrets of God, formerly hidden, now revealed—was applied not only to Jesus as the revealer of God, but also to the sacred writings of the Jewish people: the Hebrew Scriptures, which Christians now call the Old Testament. Some of the earliest Christian mystics—including Clement of Alexandria (ca. 150–216); Origen, also from Alexandria (ca. 185–254); and Gregory of Nyssa (fourth century)—all made names for themselves by their ability to discern the hidden secrets of God in scripture.

And what did they find hidden in the scriptures? Beyond the plain meaning of the text, they found symbolic and allegorical "clues" to the hidden activity of God.

For these early Christian mystics, the Hebrew Scriptures were encoded with hints that pointed to the coming of Christ. Some of these hints were explicit, as when the prophet Isaiah foretells the coming of the Messiah. But others were more subtle, as in the Song of Songs, a love poem that has been interpreted as mystically symbolic of Christ's love for the church.

From our vantage point today, this early Christian approach to scripture—investigating ancient writings to find evidence of God's working by discerning prophetic hints about Christ—appears quaint and naïve. To the early Christians, who did not enjoy the same scholarly understanding of the Hebrew writings that we know today, it made sense. If God's presence were perfectly revealed in Jesus, wouldn't his secrets be hidden, like Easter eggs, in the sacred writings, just waiting to be discovered? This is the line of thinking that inspired the early Christian mystics to read the Bible in an effort to find God's hidden purpose.

Out of this foundation of scripture interpretation emerged the quest to comprehend the mystery of God. In the early centuries of the church, Christians struggled to make sense of their experience of Christ as both the Son of Man (Matthew 8:20) and the Son of God (Matthew 27:43)—and also, as One with God (John 10:30). Likewise, the early believers wrestled with Jesus' promise that he would send the Holy Spirit of God (John 15:26), which pointed to "God the Father," "Christ," and the "Holy Spirit" as three different "faces" of God. This, in turn, had to be reconciled with the profound belief that God is One (Deuteronomy 6:4). Christians squared the Oneness of God with the apparent "Threeness" of the Father, the Son, and the Holy Spirit in the doctrine of the Holy Trinity, which celebrates One God in Three Persons. This complex concept was acknowledged by Christians as early as Cyril of Alexandria (ca. 378–444) as "supremely ineffable and mystical." In other words, it's a concept so mysterious, a truth so hidden, that it is beyond the capacity of human language to contain it.

ENACTING THE (CHRISTIAN) MYSTERIES

There's more to Christianity than just words, ideas, thoughts, teachings, and concepts, just as there's more to mysticism than abstract ideas. As a mystical faith, Christianity is not in the business of merely thinking and talking about Christ. Rather, it's all about *relating* to Christ, and making that relationship real in people's lives. It's about encountering Christ, experiencing his presence, and allowing him to heal and transform the lives of believers. It's no surprise, therefore, that, in the early centuries of the church, Christianity developed not only mystical doctrines, but also mystical rites—liturgical events played out in the lives of believers that anchored their mystical faith in down-to-earth ceremonies and actions, using material objects to signify and convey spiritual realities. Baptism and the Eucharist are two of these rites.

The Eucharist, also called Holy Communion, is the ritualized meal mandated by Jesus the night before he died. It was at this "Last Supper" that Christ said of bread, "This is my body" and of wine, "This is my blood." Eventually, Christians developed a rich and poetic language to describe this simple act. Unfortunately, over time, this rite also became the subject of divisions and disagreements that separated Christians from one another. What is important for our purposes here is to note that the Fathers of the Church saw Communion as a mystery—a *locus* where that which is hidden or secret (in this case, the true presence of Christ) became revealed. The Eucharist thus became an important component of the mystical element of Christianity. Nilus of Sinai (early 5th century) called Communion the "mystical bread," but also the "mystical body"—a term that eventually came to be used to describe the entire Christian people. Around the same time, John Chrysostom referred to Communion as "mystical food" and a "mystical banquet."

While Holy Communion, with its emphasis on the presence of Christ, became the central ritual of the ancient Christians, it was by no means the only mystical rite. Eventually, other liturgical acts—the initiation of new-comers to the faith through the ceremonial washing of Holy Baptism, the marking of believers with chrism (blessed oil) to signify the indwelling of the Holy Spirit, and pastoral rituals like marriage, confirmation, and the anointing of the sick—were recognized as conduits by which the grace and presence of God was realized in the lives of believers. These rituals, which all make the hidden reality of God known, became known in the West as sacraments—a word that means "consecrated act." Among the orthodox Christians of the East, however, these sacraments are called by a different name: *mysteries*.

When ancient Christians spoke of the mystical dimension of their faith, they not only acknowledged that the secrets of God had been revealed (through Christ, through the Bible, through the Eucharist), but also proclaimed that the presence of God was made manifest through these things. This led to the fullest flowering of the Christian understanding of mysticism—that it involves a conscious experience of the presence of God. Not just a nice, cozy feeling that God exists and therefore all is right with the world, but a feel-it-in-your-bones, more-real-than-real encounter with God's here-and-now presence. This experience is, paradoxically, something more profound than mere human experience. It is conscious experience—even though it's bigger than human consciousness—which means that a mystic may only be aware of just how *unconscious* he or she is of God.

NARRATING THE MYSTERIES

By the Middle Ages, Christians who underwent profound experiences of God were committing their stories to writing. Some were visionaries, like Julian of Norwich (1342–ca. 1416), who received detailed and highly symbolic visions of the life of Christ and the heavenly banquet. Others, like Francis of Assisi (ca. 1182–1226), received the stigmata, wounds in the hands and feet that echoed the wounds Christ suffered at the Crucifixion. Still others were gifted teachers who, like Meister Eckhart (ca. 1260–1328), revealed a profound sense of God's presence through their sermons and writings. In the East, Symeon the New Theologian (949–1022) underwent profound changes of consciousness through the indwelling of the Spirit, which he experienced as a presence marked by fire and light, while Gregory Palamas (1296–1359) advocated *hesychasm*, a spiritual exercise that seeks the conscious presence of God through continual prayer. By the sixteenth century, as the Middle Ages gave way to the Renaissance and the birth of the modern world, Teresa of Ávila (1515–1582) and John of the Cross (1542–1591) wrote at length about their contemplative experiences and about how the mystical life entailed an uncompromising commitment to prayer, meditation, mindfulness, and holiness.

John and Teresa lived in the tumultuous age of the Protestant Reformation, which forever changed the landscape of Western Christianity. A culture of suspicion developed among both Catholics and Protestants against the idea of personal experience of God. In the Catholic world, obedience to the church became the standard by which faithfulness was measured; in the Protestant world, obedience to the Bible played a similar role. In other words, both sides of the Reformation conflict began to promote a *behavioral* rather than *experiential* approach to spirituality. Instead of fostering a spirituality based on encountering the presence of God, Christianity (at least, in the West) became increasingly focused on behavioral markers like obedience to authority and moral rectitude as the benchmarks of a "good" Christian life.

Ironically, it is in this context that the word "mysticism" finally emerges (the earliest use of the word documented in the Oxford English Dictionary is from 1736).

Almost from the beginning, however, the word "mysticism" has carried largely negative connotations. The Oxford English Dictionary notes that "mysticism implies self-delusion or dreamy confusion of thought; hence the term is often applied loosely to any religious belief to which these evil qualities are imputed." This hostility to mysticism grew with the rise of modern science and its rejection of religious "superstition."

THE REHABILITATION OF MYSTICISM

By the end of the Middle Ages, all the various elements of the spirituality of mystery had come together in the beautiful writings of mystics who recounted their personal experiences of the presence of God, the love of God, and even union with God. Between the Reformation and the rise of modern science, however, mysticism suddenly became disreputable. Within the established churches, the spirituality of personal experience was ignored as religion became more focused on morality and obedience to authority. Then modern science, with its comprehensive rejection of all religious thinking as irrational, seemed to seal mysticism's fate.

Why, then, has mysticism refused to die?

Even though inner experiential spirituality fell out of favor in the centuries following the Reformation, people didn't stop having profound experiences of the presence of God, or even union with God. In fact, every generation has continued to produce mystics and contemplatives. Over the past few centuries, some of these figures were denounced as heretics—for instance, the Catholic Jeanne Guyon and the Protestant Jakob Böhme—while others, like Thérèse of Lisieux and Jonathan Edwards, expressed their mystical tendencies as part of their scrupulous religious observance. In the Eastern Orthodox churches, which were relatively uninfluenced by either the Reformation or the scientific revolution's critique of spirituality, mysticism continued to thrive, fueled by the publication of a profound multivolume anthology of mystical texts, *The Philokalia*, as well as the success of a popular nineteenth-century Russian spiritual book, *The Way of a Pilgrim*. Meanwhile, new and alternative movements within Christianity kept the mystical flame lit, such as the Society of Friends (the Quakers), who advocated a mystical spirituality and taught that God's "inner light" shone within all people. When Christians sat together in silence, they claimed, God could use anyone present to deliver his message.

In the twentieth century, experiential spirituality got a boost with the emergence of Pentecostalism, also known as the Charismatic Renewal. In worship marked by ecstatic singing and dancing, Pentecostals joyfully seek communion with God through the Holy Spirit, who in turn blesses believers with spiritual gifts such as speaking in tongues. A generation later, increasing numbers of Christians throughout the West began to explore the wisdom of Eastern spirituality, from the Sufi mysticism of Islam to Yoga, Vedanta, Taoism, and Zen Buddhism. This brought a new level of legitimacy to the idea that Christianity should return to its core mystical spirituality.

Ultimately, scholars and thinkers began to take mysticism seriously as a field of study. In the nineteenth and early twentieth centuries, mysticism caught the interest of theologians like William Ralph Inge and Friedrich von Hügel, and of psychologists like William James and popular religious writers like Evelyn Underhill. This revival eventually filtered into the Christian mainstream, where it united with the interest in Eastern spirituality that had emerged in the mid twentieth century.

The twentieth century also featured efforts to translate the writings of the great mystics into English—many for the first time—thereby making this wisdom available to everyone in the English-speaking world. The Vatican II Council in the 1960s launched a new effort to encourage laypeople to embrace the fullness of Christian spirituality—an effort that impacted Catholic, as well as Protestant and Anglican, circles. Finally, the arrival of the Internet and the World Wide Web made a wide range of resources available to Christian spiritual seekers, from the texts of great mystical writings, to websites explaining practices like *lectio divina* and contemplative prayer, to retreats scheduled by monasteries and convents. All of these converging streams made the widespread exploration of experiential Christianity ever more available to ordinary Christian men and women.

MYSTERY AND REVELATION

Thus we can trace the evolution of mysticism through the many shades of meaning that the words associated with it—"mystery," "mystic," and "mystical"—have taken on over the centuries. Mystery, as a religious or spiritual concept, originally had to do with religious rituals or ceremonies designed to impart secret spiritual teachings. With the transition from pagan to Christian usage, the concept of spiritual mystery kept its notion of "secrets taught," but took on a slightly more democratic notion—that of "the hidden things of God revealed." This is the predominant meaning of mystery found in the Bible.

Beginning with the New Testament and extending into the writings of the early Church fathers, Christianity proclaimed Christ himself as the incarnation of the Word of God—in other words, the revelation of the Ultimate Mystery. He is the manifestation of God in human form, the Word of God made flesh, the secret of God's love made freely available to all. Thus, from the beginning, Christianity proclaimed a message that is thoroughly mystical, which is to say, beyond the ability of language to describe or the human mind to understand fully. This mystical message became codified in teachings such as the doctrine of the Holy Trinity and of the real presence of Christ in the Eucharist.

From early on in the history of the faith, Christians performed ceremonies with a mystical dimension, embodying and revealing the hidden things of God. The Eucharist, or Holy Communion, invites partakers to a mystical experience in which Christ becomes present in the bread and wine, and, in this mystery, is united with those who commune. By the Middle Ages and into the modern era, increasing numbers of individual Christians began to write and teach others about their own unique and remarkable experiences of visions, ecstasies, miracles, and raptures, all pointing back to the heart of mysticism: the experience of the divine presence and of union with God. Many historians of Christian spirituality regard the fourteenth, fifteenth, and sixteenth centuries as the Golden Age of mysticism. In the wake of the fracturing of Western Christianity by the Protestant Reformation and the rise of modern science, however, mysticism became an object of suspicion or ridicule—a problem that remains to this day, even though, by the end of the twentieth century, mysticism was more widely accepted within Christianity than it had been for centuries.

CHAPTER 5

Christian Mysticism and World Mysticism

Anyone who loves God is known by him.

I Corinthians 8:3

Christians need to think "Nothing" when they call God "Love."
Buddhists need to think "Love" when they say "Emptiness." This will at least
wake us up to the fact that words must always fall short of the ineffable.

David Steindl-Rast, OSB[17]

What makes Christian mysticism so, well, *Christian*? What is the difference between it and all the other mysticisms out there—including Kabbalah (Jewish mysticism), Sufism (Islamic mysticism), Vedanta (Hindu mysticism), Zen (Buddhist mysticism), and shamanism (indigenous mysticism)?

On the surface, it's an easy enough question to answer: Christian mysticism is all about Jesus and the Christian faith. It is carried forward in the wisdom of people who were and are practicing Christians. Today, however, we live in an era where different faiths and traditions coexist in close cultural proximity. More and more Christians are practicing Yoga or studying Zen or learning the Kabbalah, blurring the line that separates Christian mysticism from mysticism in general. While for some this is just fine, for others—especially conservative Christians—it is troublesome. In fact, many opponents of Christian mysticism, who are usually devout and sincere followers of Jesus, attack it precisely because they see it as a point of vulnerability through which foreign ideas and spiritual practices are infiltrating the one true faith.

MYSTICISM IN THE GLOBAL VILLAGE

In our postmodern, multicultural age, people have unprecedented access to many different religious and spiritual traditions. While some may ignore this and choose to express their faith by adhering strictly to one religious path, many others experience an understandable desire to find common ground and shared values with those who come from other parts of the world. In other words, many Christians today are interested in the wisdom of Tibetan Buddhism, or Hasidic Judaism, or Taoism. This is a good and beautiful thing. The more we see ourselves as members of a single global community, the more hope we have for peace and shared prosperity.

Indeed, mysticism has become a code word for whatever it is that unites all religions, despite their cultural differences. As blogger Darrell Grizzle puts it: "Mysticism is that which enabled the Dalai Lama and Thomas Merton to meet in the 1960s and to recognize each other as brothers."[18]

Such sentiments suggest that mysticism may be the best hope for cultivating a true spirit of peace and goodwill among religions.

Some enthusiastic mysticism-boosters insist that, despite the cultural trappings that separate one religion from another, all mysticism is essentially the same. Consider this quotation from S. Abhayananda, the author of *History of Mysticism: The Unchanging Testament*:

> *Scholars may imagine that a Buddhist experiences one thing, a Vedantist another, and so forth; but one who has experienced It, whether a Sufi, Christian, or Hindu, knows that It is the final Truth, the only One. There are not different Unitys, one for each sect or denomination; there is only one One, and it is That which is experienced by Christians, Buddhists, Hindus, and Sufis alike. It should be obvious that, if there is such a thing as Unity, and if It can be experienced, then the experience must be the same for all; since Unity, by its very definition, by its very nature, is one.* [19]

Many Christians will disagree with Swami Abhayananda, insisting that Christianity presents a distinct and unique understanding of truth that is higher than the Unity of which he speaks. Others, both Christian and non-Christian, will agree with him, and may even go so far as to declare that religion is the real culprit since it creates division between people and cultures, unlike spirituality and mysticism, which unites us. Others might decide that, while it is a nice idea to assume that all mystical experiences are the same, we really have no way of knowing that this is true. For all we know, what Swami Abhayananda calls "Unity" may be nothing like the experiences of Christian mystics like Teresa of Avila or Meister Eckhart.

Jesus instructed his followers to be nonjudgmental (Matthew 7:1). This is probably a good principle to bear in mind when considering the similarities and differences between Christian mysticism and other wisdom traditions. If you prefer to think of mysticism as the source of unity, beware of the temptation to judge others who prefer to remain anchored in their own particular religion. If you prefer to focus on what is distinctive and unique about Christian mysticism (or, for that matter, any other type of mysticism), resist the urge to reject those who are eager to see similarities between the religions. Perhaps both are important. Perhaps we need both a commitment to preserve what is unique and beautiful in each particular path, and visionaries who seek to create bridges of understanding and harmony that reach across the lines that separate belief systems.

To explore this inclusive idea a bit further, I want to offer what is probably the most whimsical metaphor you'll ever come across in regard to mysticism.

MYSTICISM IS LIKE TOFU

While I believe that mysticism can be an important doorway to inter-religious understanding, I'd like to suggest a different way of thinking about it—or at least a different way of thinking about Christian mysticism. Mysticism is, in fact, like tofu. When you cook with tofu, it has a fascinating tendency to adopt the flavor of whatever you cook with it. Scrambled tofu, tofu curry, even barbecue tofu (yes, I'm from the South) all taste more like scrambled eggs or curry or barbecue than like tofu. Likewise, mysticism thoroughly and completely adopts the flavor and identity of whatever wisdom tradition it inhabits. Thus, Christian mysticism has an entirely different cultural and religious identity from, say, Vedanta or Zen.

Granted, tofu is tofu, regardless of the recipe you use it in. Mysticism is mysticism, regardless of the religious or cultural context. So in that sense, there really is an important unity of mystical wisdom that crosses religious boundaries. But if you've ever eaten plain, uncooked tofu, you'll notice that it is rather bland. If tofu's strength lies in its ability to adapt to whatever dish it's cooked in, its weakness lies in its lack of defining taste or texture of its own. Likewise, a "pure" mysticism might sound nice in theory—an experience of unity or ecstasy, unencumbered by religious dogma—but in practice, the beauty of mysticism rests in how it manifests unity in a distinct, particular way.

So Christian mysticism is more than just pure mysticism with a little bit of Jesus mixed in. It is actually a unique, distinctive, and beautiful expression of God's love and truth. Conservative Christians believe it is the *only* expression of such truth, and even more liberal Christians might insist that they think it is the *best* possible way to God. But even if you do not see Christianity as any better (or worse) than any other wisdom tradition, I hope you'll recognize that Christian mysticism cannot just be reduced to other kinds of mysticism. There are important ways in which the Christian mystery is unique among world religions.

This is why any serious exploration of Christian mysticism has to look at the nuts and bolts of the Christian religion in order to do justice to the topic. Indeed, immersing yourself in the world of Christian mysticism means something far beyond just learning to meditate: Christian mysticism explores meditation through a relationship with the Holy Trinity. This doesn't mean that it is all about thinking Christian thoughts, however. Rather, it means exploring a way of life that is shaped by the love and wisdom of Christ and Christ's followers, who Christian mystics understand to be literally part of Christ.

Take the Trinity and the Incarnation, for example—central teachings of Christianity that remain *mysteries,* which means they transcend and defy logical comprehension. No one can truly explore the splendor of Christian mysticism without embracing these great Christian mysteries. There's no way to avoid it. The mystery of a God who became flesh, or of a God whose very nature consists of loving relationships, is at the heart of what is distinctive about the Christian path.

Many people today seem to think that Christian mysticism refers to some sort of diluted or heretical form of Christianity. In other words, adding mysticism to Christianity somehow diminishes it. This line of thinking distorts both mysticism and Christianity. In fact, the witness of great mystics throughout history has been that, at its heart, Christian mysticism is just as faithful to the message and teachings of Jesus as most forms of conventional, institutional, organizational, churchy Christianity. Maybe even more so.

CHRISTIANITY AND THE MYSTICAL TRADITION

We can identify three essential elements in Christian mysticism that make it distinctive:

It is anchored in the Christian concept of God. Christianity has some unique things to say about God—not only that God is a Trinity (a single deity who mysteriously consists of three distinct persons), but also that God took on human form in the person of Jesus of Nazareth, the Christ, the anointed one. The Incarnation and the Trinity are the core of Christian mysticism, because they are the core of Christianity. A corollary of this principle is the Christian insistence that mysticism does not lead to a pantheistic merging of you and God, but rather culminates in a loving communion, where mystical unity with God occurs as an eternal loving embrace.

It is respectful of the authority of the Bible and church tradition. Catholicism insists that the Bible must be interpreted in light of tradition, while Protestants say it the other way around: tradition must be interpreted in the light of scripture. Both are essential elements in what makes Christian mysticism Christian. Granted, there is great leeway in how individuals (or different churches) might interpret scripture and tradition, but a distinctively Christian mysticism works with, not against, these founts of wisdom.

It emphasizes communion and relationship. Many of the world's great mystical traditions are oriented toward what the third-century philosopher Plotinus called "the flight of the alone to the Alone," meaning that mysticism involves a solitary quest for individual enlightenment. While Christian forms of mysticism often include this kind of personal striving, a far more dominant quality in the Christian tradition emphasizes community, from the teaching of Jesus: "love your neighbor as yourself." Christian mysticism is not a do-it-yourself project, but rather an invitation to a dance, where God is the gracious host and everyone finds joy in dancing together.

It's important to note that, throughout the history of Christianity, Christian mystics have displayed an unusual openness to the wisdom of non-Christian philosophy and religion. In other words, Christian mysticism seems, from the beginning, to have had an intuitive recognition of the way in which mysticism is a form of unity that transcends religious difference. Some of the earliest mystics, like Clement of Alexandria and his student Origen, explored their faith in the light of Greek philosophy. This led to a long tradition within Christianity of dialogue with non-Christian wisdom—an ecumenical approach that appears again and again among Christian mystics. Christian spirituality in the Celtic lands of Ireland and Scotland shows clear evidence of being influenced by the Druids. In the sixteenth century, Spanish mystics were influenced by the Kabbalah. And the twentieth century may go down in history as the great age of interreligious spirituality, with mystics like Thomas Merton, Bede Griffiths, Swami Abhishiktananda, Cynthia Bourgeault, and many others expressing their Christian faith in ways that reveal the influence of wisdom traditions such as Sufism, Vedanta, or Zen.

Granted, some Christian mystics explored non-Christian spirituality only in order to figure out ways to convert others to the Christian faith. For example, the thirteenth-century Spanish mystic Ramon Lull was interested in Islamic ideas only because he felt compelled to preach Christ to the Muslims. Others, like Merton, approached interfaith spirituality with a more open and generous spirit, hoping simply to encounter those with a different perspective in a genuine desire to deepen wisdom and understanding, and foster a better world.

While this is not a book about interfaith spirituality, I think it's important to keep in mind that, at some point, Christian mysticism can evolve into something different if it embraces values or beliefs that are at odds with Christian tradition. Ultimately, however, no absolutely clear distinction can be drawn between Christian and non-Christian mysticism. As long as we acknowledge that mysticism is, at its heart, about a deep and profound mystery that cannot be put into words, we can (and, perhaps, should) acknowledge that it is precisely in this dimension of mystery that people of different faiths and different wisdom traditions can relate to each other—not in a spirit of competition or hostility, but in a genuinely open, compassionate, and respectful manner.

CHAPTER 6

Why Mysticism Matters

You have already been cleansed by the word that I have spoken to you.

JOHN 15:3

All mystic charisms are worthless compared to the love of God.
They are as a string of pearls adorning a hungry infant
who does not heed the pearls but only wants his mother's breast.

MACARIUS THE EGYPTIAN[20]

For those who have a sense of God's presence in their lives, who enjoy a natural bent toward spirituality or a strong commitment to religion, or who simply enjoy the history of ideas, mysticism is a fascinating subject in its own right. Others without an innate attraction to the topic, however, may be asking themselves: "What's the point?" "Does mysticism really make a difference?" "How can it make life better?"

As we begin to answer these questions, think about mysticism in the context of Christianity as a whole. Christianity, in its best and highest form, is a religion that proclaims Good News (the literal meaning of "gospel"). Therefore, any mysticism embedded within Christianity is, likewise, a conduit for Good News, and this gospel is not just for those who like to meditate or ponder the inscrutable mysteries of God. It's also (and maybe even especially) for those who suffer, for those who have difficulty believing in God, for those who think that God is just some sort of angry bully in the sky. It's good news for the rich as well as the poor, for the healthy as well as the afflicted.

Like the larger Christian gospel, the "gospel of mysticism" can take different forms for different people. Sometimes, it is a kind voice of reassurance; sometimes, it is a voice that challenges and even confronts. Regardless of the various tones it may take, however, it always points to a promise to make life better and open our hearts to love. Mysticism is always a force for real, results-oriented transformation, a force for making a difference in the world.

THE PROMISE OF MYSTICISM

Based on the witness of all the great mystics over 2,000 years of Christian history, the message of mysticism can be reduced to a single paragraph:

> *God is love. God loves all of us and wants us to experience abundant life. This means abiding in love—love of God, and love of neighbors as ourselves. Through prayer and worship, meditation and silence, we*

can commune with God, experience his presence, have our consciousness transformed by his Spirit, participate in his loving nature, and be healed and renewed in that love. This new life (what the New Testament calls "the mind of Christ") will not only bring us joy and happiness (even when we suffer), but also will empower us to be ambassadors for God, to bring God's love and joy and happiness to others. There is much work to be done, and the task is overwhelming, Even our own need is very great, for we tend to resist God's love, even as we hunger for it. Yet God continually calls us back to his love and continually empowers us to face the challenge of bringing hope to our broken world.

This message is nothing new. In fact, much of it comes straight from the Bible (I John 4:16, Matthew 22:36-39, John 10:10, Philippians 2:5, and Philippians 4:13). Mysticism's promise—the promise of lives transformed by divine love—seems to some, however, to be simply too good to be true. Can we really believe that God is love? Can we really trust the love of God to make our lives better? Is the premise of mysticism simply too good to be true?

Why do we find it so hard to believe that this Ultimate Mystery we call God—the infinite force/intelligence responsible for the ongoing creation and evolution of the entire cosmos—is intimately, passionately, and personally in love with each and every one of us here on this tiny planet whirling away at the edge of a relatively small galaxy? And there's more to this than some sort of abstract love affair. God's love is more than just love from afar. The love of God flows out from him; it is poured lavishly on his creation, ready to flow into the heart of any creature willing to receive it. Not only does this transcendent being, this supreme consciousness and fountain of love, long to give itself in beauty and grace to each individual creature, but we are actually invited, in and through our creatureliness, to *participate* in the fullness of that divine love. And this is the message of mysticism.

To "participate" in God's love means to receive that love, to live in and within it, and, in a true and real way, to *be* love. Christian mysticism spirals out from a profound wisdom found in and through the story of Jesus of Nazareth. This wisdom tradition proclaims that the source of infinite love and power and consciousness is not some impersonal force, but rather an impossible-to-understand confluence of unity and community embodied in the Holy Trinity. In the faltering limitation of language, we say "one God, three persons." In this mystery, we find God the Father (the ground of being, the fount of creation, the source of sources), God the Son (Jesus, who lived and died among us, then rose from death and ascended into heaven), and God the Holy Spirit (the spirit of love and comfort and advocacy that strengthens the community of God's lovers and knits us all together into the one Body of Christ). This triune deity pours love into us in an infinite variety of ways: as the parent loves the child, as a friend loves a friend, as a spouse loves a spouse, and as artists love their masterpieces.

The love that God gives you (and invites you to embody) is meant to be expressed in three ways, as Jesus himself pointed out: to love God with all your heart and all your soul, to love your neighbor as yourself, and therefore, to love yourself (Mark 12:30-31). Just as each person of the Holy Trinity is an essential part of God, so is each dimension of this triune love an essential part of the fullness of participation in divine love. It is the nature of love to give itself away, and so God pours divine love into you so that you may more truly, fully, and wholly return that love to God, even as you love your neighbor as lavishly as you love yourself.

The amazing premise of Christian mysticism is that, when God loves you, he transforms you into love; when God loves you, he gives the fullness of his Divinity to you and, through you, back to God and to others and, indeed, to all creation. When you are called to partake of the divine nature, you are called to be loved, to love, and to be love. You thereby join in the most amazing of cosmic dances, a dance of joy and fullness, of healing and restoration, of light and rest and delight, that will give you the entire cosmos forever and ever.

Mysticism and Cynicism

Ours is a world that has decided that mysticism is actually kind of dangerous—a retreat from reality into fantasy, a thumb-sucking, navel-gazing way of compensating for how much life hurts. We've become too sophisticated to buy into all this "God is love" nonsense. Non-Christians can be particularly pessimistic about the message of the mystics and compare it, to its detriment, to the scandalous behavior that all too often characterizes Christian society. How can a judgmental and exclusionary religion be a conduit for divine love?

And so, faced with a cynicism that parades itself as realism, we turn away from what mysticism offers us. We turn our gaze away from heaven and back to earth. Ours is a world that busily (some would say frantically) offers a variety of lesser destinies. Thanks to the dominance of a strictly empirical/scientific worldview, Western society sees life strictly in terms of the verifiable—"only what can be scientifically proven is real." In other words, we live a finite mortal existence in an environment with limited resources, where we participate in biological processes for eighty or ninety years, and then we die. Life seen like this is all about limits, so we need to make the most of what little we've got. This worldview dismisses all spiritual beliefs (including mysticism) as merely wishful thinking. In other words, the mystical vision of an eternal dance of loving communion is simply too good to be true.

This pessimistic view of reality may find favor among atheists and those who insist that only what can be measured is real, but, ultimately, it's a pretty miserable way to view the world. In fact, it really only makes sense for the small percentage of human beings who live a life of material comfort and leisure—and even those who enjoy the best pleasures that the earth has to offer sooner or later discover that the limitations of that life eventually win. We always lose our health, our relationships, our very lives. Buddha said: "Life is suffering." And we know that ignoring that suffering neither makes it go away nor makes it easier to bear.

Human beings simply don't like limits, whether these are the physical limits of a life that inevitably includes suffering and death, or the ideological limits of a worldview that tells us "this is all there is." Consequently, various spiritual theories have emerged over the ages and around the world that seek to answer the question of life's greater meaning. Many of these spiritual narratives are beautiful and inspiring, although some contain their own hidden limits.

One popular idea holds that all material existence is an illusion, and that the only thing that truly exists is one, single, solitary being. You and I and everyone else are only projections or masks that this one being wears in order to create the illusion of separate entities. On the surface, this is a beguiling idea, because it basically claims that you are God (and so is everyone else). The theory begins to lose its appeal, however, when you carry it to its logical conclusion. If I am God, and everything else is an illusion, then I am all alone. What's the point of being God if you have no one to share your deity—no one to love? Sounds pretty lonely to me.

By contrast, the bold claim of Christian mysticism is not merely that we "are" God, but rather that we *participate* in God—a subtle but crucial distinction. God remains God, I remain me, you remain you, and we all love each other. We exist in each other, through each other, in union and communion, here in the beauty of the present moment—and for all of the ever-expansiveness of eternity. That, Christian mysticism dares to assert, is the ultimate promise of life. It promises the same ecstasy and joy that the all-things-are-god theory claims, but its promised bliss is grounded in relational love—a love that ultimately has no limits, either in space or in time. "Eternity," the word Christians use to describe the locus of God, transcends the physical limitations of space and time.

Christian mysticism makes this bold claim: What appears to be naïve folly in purely human terms is bracingly and joyfully possible in terms of the Divine. Possibility in God is a theme that appears frequently in the Bible. "For nothing will be impossible with God" (Luke 1:37). Nothing is impossible: not even the amazing destiny of love-in-divine-communion that Christian mysticism promises. Traditionally, this has been called the "Beatific Vision." A Trappist monk I know dismisses that term because it implies stasis. "Heaven is not a spectator sport," he insists. He suggests that a better way to describe our ultimate destiny in God is as a " Beatifying Communion." I rather like to think of it as "living in Heaven Consciousness."

And the amazing truth of Christian mysticism is that this vision, this communion, this consciousness is available to all of us—right here, right now. You can begin to live in Heaven Consciousness today.

There is a cost, however. Although you don't have to surrender your earthly life to embrace the Beatifying Communion, you do have to "die" in a figurative sense. Christianity has traditionally called this symbolic death a "dying to self." Some describe it as the death of the ego—that small, self-absorbed tendency we have to prefer control over love. When you offer God all the parts of yourself that prefer control or pride or anger to love, you begin the process of dying-to-self. It's not something that happens in an instant, and it's not always painless. But the Christian faith insists that this death leads to a resurrection. When I die to myself, I rise to Christ—which is another way of saying that I rise to new life, in love.

So is all this too good to be true? This is not just a rhetorical question. It is the question on which everything hangs. If you decide that the promise of Christian mysticism is too good to be true, then, at a fundamental level, you are deciding that life is not, ultimately, about love. But if the essence of life is not love, then what is it? One common response to this question is that life is all about power ("the person who dies with the most toys wins"). Another is that life is all about knowledge and/or awareness ("the secret of life is to know all the secrets"). Granted, awareness and ability are important keys to a life well lived, but if you organize your life around either of these principles, then you miss out on love—or, at best, experience only a limited, finite love.

On the other hand, if you dare to believe that the ultimate meaning, destiny, and purpose of life is to love and be loved in expanding, eternal divine/human communion—if you dare to believe this is true—then everything changes, literally, immediately, and everlastingly. Despair and cynicism no longer reign. Hatred, prejudice, oppression, and cruelty lose their final claim over your life; such things are nothing more than problems that must be overcome. Granted, if you give your life to love, you become responsible for cleaning up your own mess. And you take on that responsibility because you believe there is a reason and a purpose for doing so.

What I am talking about here is deeply countercultural. Few people—even those who are supposedly committed to a spiritual or religious life—accept the idea that life is totally and radically about love. We're too dazzled by the competing claims that life is all about power, or all about position or prestige, or all about knowledge, or all about bliss or fun. When you orient your life to love, however, you discover that you can attain a loving measure of all these other things as well (see Matthew 6:33). When you orient your life to anything other than love, no matter what you gain, you risk losing out on the fullness of love.

The beauty of Christian mysticism lies in its promise that, by choosing love over all the other potential blessings that life can give us, we are embracing the best possible life; a life in which all blessings can flow, but always in accordance with love.

LOVE IS THE KEY

Simply put, mysticism—at least, Christian mysticism—is all about love. To explore Christian mysticism basically means to explore love. It's an invitation to join the noblest of human aspirations. Love has inspired poets and philosophers for as long as human beings have enjoyed telling a good story. Without love, we would have no Romeo and Juliet, no Tristan and Isolde, no Elizabeth Bennet and Mr. Darcy, no Wandering Aengus and the Glimmering Girl—and, for that matter, no Song of Songs, no Jacob and Rachel, no Ruth and Boaz. Whether the topic is love won or lost, love thwarted or misunderstood, comic romance or passionate tragedy, there is nothing so fundamentally human as a good story about love. And mysticism is just that. It is the greatest of love stories. And that's why it matters.

That's why people like you and me are drawn to mysticism. For some, mysticism may be a "head trip," but for most, it's a "heart trip"—a journey into the sacred nature of love.

We are all breathing miracles, living clay with a carefully calibrated capacity to give and receive love. And no matter how that may play out on a human level—for human love, of course, can take many forms and can be joyous or heartbreaking—this thing called mysticism dares to proclaim that you, and I, and everyone else who has ever been given a beating heart and a wondering mind, have all been invited to immerse ourselves in an immediate, experiential, life-transforming relationship with the very Source of Love in its purest, most original, foundational form. Christians call that Source of Love "God" and we find God in Jesus Christ, made real and visible and accessible to everyone.

Christian mysticism is grounded in this love. The teachings of the great mystics speculate on the nature of this love, where it came from, and why we believe it is accessible to us all. Mystical wisdom about love is recorded in the autobiographies and memoirs of Christian contemplatives and visionaries who—great and ordinary, ancient and medieval, modern and postmodern, male and female, young and old, educated and not so educated—all tell about how this love surprised them, pursued them, filled their awareness with breathtaking visions and heart-rending suffering, demanded almost superhuman sacrifices, and yet overflowed with unspeakable joys.

As we discover not only the stories of the great mystics, but also our own stories, and the stories of our friends and neighbors and others who have heard the whispered call from the Ultimate Mystery, we sense intuitively that we each have something to say directly and intimately to each other. For Christian mysticism does not belong in a library or a museum. It belongs in beating hearts and meditative minds. I believe that, even though there is tremendous diversity among the great mystics of Christianity, at the heart of all their lives they are telling the same story. And I believe that we each represent, at least in potential, a new chapter in that story, a new verse in the eternal song. The great story of God's love resides in our hearts, just waiting to be given yet another new and unique form of expression.

Christian mysticism encompasses 2,000 years of wisdom that shows you how to open your heart to the possibility of receiving this love, to conducting your life in a manner that is both honorable and worthy of it. Through this wisdom, you learn how your mind and heart can perceive and receive the overtures of this love as it comes to you in an infinite and unpredictable variety of ways. In other words, the writings of the great mystics include instructions on how to live a mystical life—a faithful life, a holy life, a life in which we strive to become saints even while we humbly learn to accept that, ultimately, we have no control over just how "mystical" our experience or our God-awareness may be. When you become an acolyte of mysticism, you learn how to pray, to meditate, to contemplate, to read the Bible and other sacred writings in a divine way, to serve and to sacrifice, to open your heart with hospitality for the world even while you somehow realize that you are, ultimately, the citizen of another country.

That's why mysticism matters.

CHAPTER 7

The Mystical Paradoxes

You cannot see my face; for no one shall see me and live.

EXODUS 33:20

Blessed are the pure in heart, for they will see God.

MATTHEW 5:8

Think without thinking.

FRANCISCO DE OSUNA[21]

Paradox, physicist Neils Bohr tells us, explodes our everyday linear concept of truth and falsehood by positing two qualities that exist on a single continuum. "The opposite of a correct statement is a false statement," he claims. "But the opposite of a profound truth may be another profound truth." Paradox thus points us to the mysterious place where two or more profound truths pull against each other in a tension that cannot be resolved by the clever machinations of the rational mind. Mysticism is all about paradox. It's all about the ways in which God and faith always seem to be pulling us in two directions at once. In the words of the French Orthodox theologian Jean-Yves Leloup, "God has no name and God has every name. God has none of the things that exist and God is everything. One knows God only through not knowing. Every affirmation, like every negation, remains on this side of God's transcendence."[22]

Paradox is not always warmly received by those who want their faith to be watertight and easy to control. If you have invested your heart and soul in the idea that God makes everything neat and tidy and your job is simply to obey the rules, then you will have no room for paradoxical statements in your spirituality. After all, if the goal is an unassailable faith, then seemingly contradictory truths must be eliminated.

But for those who regard faith as a relationship rather than a belief system, paradox is not nearly so threatening. When faith is large enough to encompass "unknowing" rather than mere certitude, paradox can be a source of joy and wonder rather than fear or doubt. A spiritual paradox may provide evidence that God is bigger than our limited human capacity for reason and logic. Is the kingdom of heaven within or among us… or not of this world (Luke 17:21; John 18:36)? Are we justified by faith apart from works… or is faith without works dead (Romans 3:28; James 2:26)? These seeming inconsistencies may pose a challenge to some, but a source of delight to others—not because they introduce an element of chaos into the landscape of faith, but because they point to an ultimate mystery that is beyond human control, beyond what passes for "common sense."

Saint Paul made a common-sense observation when he noted: "When I became an adult, I put an end to childish ways" (I Corinthians 13:11). The spirituality of paradox represents precisely the kind of mature faith to which Paul is alluding. When my faith offers me equivalent truths that pull me in different directions, I see this as an invitation and a challenge. Rather than pretending that these inconsistencies or seeming contradictions don't exist or don't matter, I feel encouraged to approach the mysteries of God in a spirit of humility, recognizing that no one will ever reduce God to the level of human reason. In saying that mysticism is about paradox, I'm not suggesting that Christian mysticism is a series of word puzzles or locks to be picked. I'm simply pointing out that, again and again, mysticism requires you to take a step back and look at the truths of your faith from a larger, more inclusive perspective. Doing so, in many cases, brings you to the very threshold of mystery. At that place, on the frontier where human reason shades off into divine unknowing, you may find a resolution to the paradox, or at least a sense of acceptance that can help you assent to the apparent contradictions in your spiritual life. But if God remains inscrutably beyond the farthest reaches of the most brilliant human mind, sooner or later we can expect to stumble across paradoxes that simply cannot be resolved. These insoluble paradoxes are the core of faith. They invite you, like Zen *koans*, to surrender the hubris that lurks beneath your apparent understanding and control. A God you cannot comprehend is a God you cannot manipulate. This, I believe, is a God of true grace, a God worthy of worship.

One reason I like the word "paradox" is that it is a first cousin to that most religious of all words, "orthodox." The prefix "ortho" means "right" or "correct;" the prefix "para" means "beside" or "alongside." What links the two is the root word "dox," which can mean "opinion" or "teaching" (as in doctrine) or "praise" (as in doxology). The praise/teaching meanings merge in a spiritual way when we consider that both of these concepts point us to God—a God whom we praise and from whom we learn.

Thus, an orthodox statement is simply something that is settled and generally accepted by the larger Christian community: God is love; we are called to repentance; the Holy Spirit is with us always. These are the ground rules by which the Christian faith operates in the world. Meanwhile, a paradox does not negate orthodoxy, but rather exists "alongside" it. Paradox represents the breathing room in which the ongoing guidance of the Holy Spirit occurs. The paradoxes of faith invite you into a deep unknowing—that place beyond the reach of human reason, not *pre*-rational, but *trans*-rational—where God wishes to meet you without the pomp and noise of your finite, gotta-be-in-control mind getting in the way.

The Mystical Paradoxes

Some of the paradoxes that characterize Christian mysticism are central to Christianity as a whole; others are uniquely the province of mystical spirituality. Some are easy to resolve; others are like tenacious vines that simply refuse to yield, even when we hack at them with the blade of human reason. To some, these inconsistencies and logical disconnects are evidence that Christianity is irrational or unworthy of belief. From the perspective of the mystic, however, these open-ended places are the exciting launch pads from which Christian mysticism spirals off into supra-rational and trans-rational dimensions.

Mysticism is the quest for God.

You cannot seek God unless God has found you.

Christian mysticism celebrates the passionate love that flows between humanity and God, which means that, for each of us, it represents a personal romance with our maker. And love is all about seeking a beloved, right?

Looking for true love is a central fact of being human. It's the stuff of fairy tales, date movies, and romance novels. We understand how love sustained Jacob day after day when he had to work fourteen long years for Rachel's hand in marriage. We want every love story to have a happy ending, and we sigh with disappointment when—as with Romeo and Juliet—it doesn't work out.

Christianity teaches that human beings are, by nature, meant to love and be loved by God. This can lead to endless bliss and ever-unfolding joy in a heavenly communion that can begin here and now and will embrace all of eternity. But this outcome is by no means automatic. God is a very polite and rather shy lover, and he never forces himself on you. If you want his love, you have to declare to him, and to yourself, and indeed to the world, just what it is you seek.

Of course, this declaration of love can take different forms. Many seek God simply by following the program laid out for them by their church: they read the Bible, they worship every Sunday, they tithe, they volunteer in programs to care for the needy or otherwise make the world a better place. These are all worthy pursuits, and mysticism is not opposed to any of them. But for some, ordinary religious observance often represents only the beginning of the search. A variety of contemplative practices are available to those who feel called to enter into the deeper mysteries of faith.

For mystics, seeking God is a lifelong, and pretty much full-time, pursuit that proceeds even in the midst of down-to-earth activities like working or cleaning the house. For the contemplative, this quest for divine love is a daily concern. But God, being the shy and polite God that he is, never just pops up in your life merely because you say a lot of prayers or meditate for a half-hour a day. God is God, not a formula, not the sum of an equation that will always behave predictably. So the experience of seeking God is always open-ended, uncertain, and mysterious. What will happen if you devote your life to prayer? Who knows? Pray and see.

Augustine once said that you can seek God only because God has already found you. The point is that, even your seeking—which seems and feels as if you are taking the initiative—is actually already, on a very deep level, a *response* to God. The seeking may, paradoxically, be evidence of the finding—or, should I say, the having been found. I once had a boss who was fond of quoting a rather clichéd phrase: "Success is not a destination, it's a journey." Seeking God is pretty much the same.

Mysticism is about experience.

Mysticism cannot be limited to experience.

Missouri is called the "Show-Me" state, a curious and obscure nickname that, according to legend, originated when Missouri congressman Willard Duncan Vandiver declared: "Frothy eloquence neither convinces nor satisfies me. I am from Missouri. You have got to show me." Mystics would be at home in Missouri.

It may be only a short jump from "seeing is believing" to "experiencing is believing," but that jump takes us to the heart of the mystical approach to spirituality. Most mystics may not be as skeptical as Vandiver, but neither are they credulous. Mystics want their faith to be born out of firsthand knowledge. They want their relationship with God to be grounded in their own experience and awareness, and not be just a by-product of what they have been told. When theologian Karl Rahner mused that the Christian of the future must be a mystic, he was referring to precisely this deeply felt encounter with God that transcends mere ideas or ideology.

Religion without experience is abstract and overly mental—what in popular jargon is known as "being stuck in your head." Not only is such an attitude a religion of ideas rather than intuition, it's also a religion built around submission, for, without direct experience, religion must rely on its ability to keep people in line through threats: "If you disobey, you will go to hell." Religion without an experiential dimension is religion without spirituality, whose purpose is little more than moralistic control of people's lives. This is what Karl Marx rightly derided as the opiate of the people—religion as a set of teachings designed to make people docile and submissive, while keeping them locked in fear-based beliefs.

By contrast, mysticism argues that only experienced religion is authentic. There's a difference between *knowing about* God and *knowing God*, and this distinction is the key to understanding the difference between stuck-in-your-head religion and truly mystical spirituality. Think about the difference between knowing that you have grandparents and actually taking the time to relate to them, interact with them, and become intimate with them. Ours is an age that recognizes that experience matters more than just abstract ideology. That is why evangelical theologians like J. I. Packer and John Piper, who would probably never describe themselves as mystics, nevertheless argue that experiencing God is at the heart of the Christian way.

But if religion divorced from personal experience is inauthentic, an entirely different set of problems arises when we focus too much on experience—the most obvious being the sheer unreliability of human understanding. We are just as good at deceiving ourselves as we are at hoodwinking one another. Having an "experience"—whether feeling one-with-God or seeing a UFO—in and of itself proves nothing. The experience may be a self-created illusion, or perhaps merely the result of not having enough sleep. It could be drug-induced, the product of wishful thinking, or evidence of mental illness. If we insist that unusual or supernatural phenomena can be instigated by angels, logic demands that we also at least consider that unfriendly spirits with an interest in fooling us could just as likely be responsible. A vision of God that comes from a heavenly messenger sounds like a bona fide mystical experience, but such a vision could just as easily come from a less benevolent source—and be little more than an egotistical excuse to feel proud of our own spiritual "advancement."

Not only are experiences subject to a wide variety of interpretations, there is no consistency in what a "mystical experience" looks like. In the annals of Christian history, mystics have had visions, heard angelic voices, been caught up in ecstatic consciousness, and experienced flashes of insight or intricately detailed dreams. No two mystics have walked the same path as they forged their relationship with God. How, then, can we define mysticism as experience, when it is based on such a wide variety of phenomena? And what about the experience that never happens? Many sincere and well-meaning people, including dedicated practitioners of meditation and contemplation, have no sense of ever "experiencing" God at all, or perhaps have only the subtlest intuition or a vaguely comforting sense that God is present in their lives. Can we really say that such people are not mystics? Is mysticism only for the elite? Do some people receive mystical gifts, but other, "lesser" folks do not? This flies in the face of the teachings of Christ, who consistently tells us that the life of faith is not about who is the greater or more powerful, but rather about who is most willing to love, care for, and serve others. So, while it appears that experience, in some form, is central to the mystical life, it is also true that mysticism is bigger than mere experience.

God is immanent.

God is transcendent.

When we ask whether mysticism is fundamentally about experience or about something beyond experience, we are looking at the God/human love story from the human point of view. Let's turn this around and try, as best we can, to think about this from God's perspective.

God is greater and more vast than the entire cosmos. But God is also present in the smallest of places—intimately involved in the dynamics of the entities that make up particle physics and string theory. So, while God is infinite, in the words of author John Ortberg, he is closer than you think. Paul tells us that, in God, "we live and move and have our being" (Acts 17:28). God is in us, and we are in God. This is the doctrine of *immanence*—which declares the indwelling or inherence of God. God is closer than you think; God is closer to you than you are to yourself.

A generation ago, the English writer J. B. Phillips penned a book called *Your God Is Too Small*, warning his readers not to pigeonhole God or box him in, and pointing out the psychological distortion possible when we see God as immanent. The problem with seeing God as immanent, Phillips claims, is that, by doing so, we can too easily reduce him to some sort of cosmic butler who is there to serve our needs. Indeed, when we consider the purity of God and set his divinity beside the sufferings and imperfections of the cosmos as we know it, we can see why Christianity has always insisted that there is a fundamental "otherness" to God. While immanent, God is so much greater than all things and so far removed from the cosmos that it's silly to talk about him in human terms at all. God has no limits, God has no duality, God has no imperfection. This is the doctrine of *transcendence*, which confirms that God surpasses the realm of matter, energy, and human consciousness.

So which is it? Is God immanent and personal, or transcendent and infinitely far away? Can we touch the face of God, or must we remain blinded by a veil that separates us from the Ultimate Mystery? Is spirituality about finding intimacy with the God who is present, or standing in awe of the God who is so vast that we cannot consciously know him?

The answer is yes.

**Mysticism involves significant, life-transforming events
and changes in consciousness.**

A mystical experience may seem as insignificant as the Butterfly Effect.

Why are some lovers of God granted truly earth-shattering encounters
with the divine presence, while these awe-inspiring experiences seem
beyond the reach of so many others? Why do some people have gifts for
spiritual healing, and some not? What are we to make of stories about how
some mystics did extraordinary things—Teresa of Avila levitating, or Ther-
ese Neumann thriving for extended periods of time eating nothing other
than her daily Communion?

I suppose I am like most in that I find stories of truly extraordinary
mystical experiences both thrilling and inspiring—and maybe even just a
bit intimidating. Even if I never have visions as vivid as those of Julian of
Norwich, or perform charismatic miracles like those attributed to Teresa,
it enlivens my faith to believe that these phenomena are possible. But is
it accurate to equate Christian mysticism only with rare, extraordinary
events? Must a spiritual experience be truly *supernatural* before it can be
regarded as *mystical*?

Many people of faith have said to me: "I'll never be a mystic." When
I hear this, I usually find that they see mysticism in terms of miraculous
or extraordinary events, and assume that they themselves will never have
such awe-inspiring experiences. Many of those who feel this way are truly
humble and down-to-earth people—just the kind of people that Jesus
praised as being close to the kingdom of heaven. This strikes me as a pretty
strong criticism of mysticism. If a person has to choose between being holy
and being a mystic, I for one certainly hope that holiness wins the day.

The idea that mysticism involves only supernatural experiences is,
in fact, as limited as saying that God is only transcendent. In fact, some of
the most renowned mystics are those who have few, if any, extraordinary
or supernatural experiences. Take Thomas Merton for example. Merton
had some powerful experiences of God's presence in his life, but a skeptic
could explain most of them away as little more than profound insights.
The same can be said about Caryll Houselander, or Brother Lawrence, or

Thérèse of Lisieux. The truth is that, sometimes, great mystics are marked, not by the supernatural light that illuminates their minds, but by a combination of very simple, almost ordinary, experiences of God's presence in their lives. These encounters, in turn, can inspire a profound and passionate commitment to holiness, or to a life devoted to serving the poor, or to some other significant calling that embodies the subtle insights and experiences received from God. In other words, mysticism incorporates humble as well as exalted encounters with the Ultimate Mystery.

The Butterfly Effect is a concept related to chaos theory, which holds that seemingly insignificant phenomena can have amazing consequences. The classic way of illustrating this is to suggest that a butterfly in Brazil can, by the disturbance in the atmosphere caused by its wings, set into motion a chain of events that results in a tornado in Texas. We do not know how to measure the relationships between such tiny causes and huge effects. This is also true of mysticism. A single act of compassion or forgiveness can help prevent a terrible crime or a suicide. The decision to say a prayer or spend an hour reading the Bible can lead to an insight that can literally change a person's life.

With this in mind, consider God as a force for "holy chaos." A subtle, gentle, if-you-blink-you'll-miss-it sensation of God's presence may be all the mystical experience you need (or can handle). Perhaps most mystical encounters with God operate under the principle that less is more. Perhaps those who have dramatic mystical experiences are simply less well attuned to God's presence to begin with. Unlike those who can quietly discern God's voice in the midst of mundane life, some people need to have their minds blown in order for God to get through. If we can accept that mystical experience comes in all shapes and sizes, then we must also recognize that mystical gifts touch far more people than any of us realize.

You can do nothing to "earn" the mystical life.

If you are passive, you will be thwarting the action of the Holy Spirit.

Christian mysticism is all about grace. In other words, the experience of, or encounter with, or awareness of God that constitutes the heart of mysticism is always given, never earned.

From a quiet sense of God's presence, to an awe-inspiring shift in consciousness, to a dramatic dream or vision in which Christ comes to you with specific information about your vocation—whatever may transpire in your unique relationship with God, one thing is certain: it's not your doing.

Grace is a free gift. You cannot earn grace any more than you can earn God's love. Accepting Christ as your savior or being baptized or going to Communion or reading the Bible or doing good works or refraining from sinning—none of these can earn God's favor and love. You enjoy the blessing of God's grace because he gives it to you, not because you deserve it.

The same holds true for the nature of your relationship with God. Whether you are clearly conscious of God, or continually search for him as if lost in a fog; whether you have amazing moments of joyful union with God, or seem to be forever lost in the dark night of the soul—it doesn't matter. God is the architect of every person's unique journey into him. You cannot force God into giving you an extraordinary experience of his presence, any more than you can force God into loving you more than he already does.

God relates to each of us in the manner that is best for us. Those who enjoy mystical wonders need them, on some level. Likewise, those who only experience God through a sense of absence are receiving from him exactly what they need. So it makes sense simply to recognize that God is in charge, not you. Your job is to sit back and see what he has in store for you. Right?

Wrong.

When the Apostle James said "Faith without works is dead," he wasn't just suggesting that you can't grow in your faith if you don't take responsibility for your actions. That's part of what he was saying, but it goes beyond that. The "works" that keep faith alive aren't the things you do to try to earn God's love and respect (or mystical presence). They are rather all the things you do *in response* to the grace and love that God has freely given to you, even if you aren't consciously aware of it. Mysticism is not about making God love you, or making God give you his grace or blessings. God's gift is always freely given. But once that gift has been given to you, it's up to you whether you unwrap it, whether you accept it. Your actions, your efforts to live a contemplative life are what make the grace of God come alive within you.

What kinds of actions are essential to the mystical life? Spiritual practices that dispose you to receiving God's presence. Not spiritual practices that summon or mandate God's presence, but rather practices that create *within you* the ability to receive the gift. Contemplative spiritual practices do not change God; they change only you. Just as it takes exercise and a healthy diet to stay fit, it takes spiritual exercises like *lectio divina*, daily prayer, meditation, contemplation, participation in a faith community, and serving those who are in need to dispose yourself to the mystical life. If you don't do these things, God can still overwhelm you with the mystery of his presence. But when you engage in a spiritual practice, you clear a space within yourself where God can act—in whatever way he sees fit.

Mysticism is the "flight of the alone to the Alone."

Christ is present "where two or three are gathered" in his name.

Plotinus described mysticism as the "flight of the alone to the Alone." Although he wasn't a Christian, Plotinus' philosophy had a strong influence on early Christians. Augustine, arguably the greatest theologian of the first millennium, was well versed in his thought.

Plotinus was a student of Plato who interpreted Plato's teachings in the light of the philosophy of his day. His deeply mystical philosophy spoke of the cosmos as an "emanation" from the One, and saw the goal of all creaturely existence as a return to that primal unity. Human existence originated in the One and our destiny, according to Plotinus, lay entirely in returning to that source.

While this is not the message of the gospel, Plotinus' shadow has loomed large over the history of Christian mysticism. Ever since Plotinus, mysticism has been, in large part, the province of individuals who renounced worldly wealth, social standing, and other material benefits in their quest for union with God. Many of the earliest Christian mystics lived as hermits in the deserts of Egypt and the Middle East. The ideal of the hermit—a person living in solitude, for God alone—is found in Christian writings throughout the ages, and is exemplified by mystics like Julian of Norwich, Richard Rolle, Thomas Merton, Henri LeSaux, and Matthew the Poor. In solitude—in a flight of the alone to the Alone—these contemplatives found union with God.

There's an entirely different, and more distinctively Christian, way of looking at mysticism—that stresses not solitude, but community. This paradox has its roots in the mystery of the Holy Trinity, one God in Three Persons—God who is both divine unity and divine community. Part of the nature of God is thus the web of relationships between Father, Son, and Holy Spirit. This understanding of Divinity as Trinity makes a difference in how mysticism is expressed within Christianity.

The key teaching here comes from the Bible, where Christ says: "For where two or three are gathered in my name, I am there among them" (Matthew 18:20). Although Christ encourages his followers to pray alone (Matthew 6:6), he promises his presence when Christians gather together. In other words, the Christian life is not some sort of cozy cocoon where "God and I" can snuggle together in holy privacy. Rather, the flow of love between the human and the Divine is meant to spill over in an essential flow of love between believers. This is spelled out clearly in the Gospel of John, when Jesus bluntly instructs his disciples: "If you love me, you will keep my commandments... this is my commandment, that you love one another" (John 14:15; 15:12).

Nowhere in the Bible does Jesus tell his followers to meditate, to contemplate, to recite the Psalms every day, to engage in lectio divina, or to engage in any other spiritual practice traditionally associated with mysticism. What he does insist is that we love one another. Paradoxical as it may seem, the Christian flight of the alone to the Alone must occur in conjunction with a flight of the communal to the Communal.

God is One.

God is a Holy Trinity.

Just as mysticism is both a solitary and a communal practice, Christianity understands God in terms of both perfect unity and personal interrelationship. And this is arguably the greatest of all Christian mysteries.

Christianity, which began as a sect of Judaism, insists, like its mother religion, that all things are created by One God. God's Oneness is an essential part of his nature. But Christianity also recognizes that God has three persons—not three natures or three functions, but three *persons*: the Heavenly Father, Jesus Christ the Son, and the Holy Spirit of Love. The

Father is not the Son, the Son is not the Holy Spirit, and the Holy Spirit is not the Father. Yet all are God, and God is One.

Critics of Christianity dismiss the Holy Trinity as an example of the mental wrangling early theologians had to go through as they attempted to preserve Christianity's monotheistic credentials while also explaining why the faith worshipped a heavenly creator (the Father), an incarnation of God (the Son), and an ever-present Holy Spirit sent from God. Quite a lot of arguing (not to mention some bloodshed) took place in the early centuries of the Christian era over just how to understand this. To this day, the doctrine of the Holy Trinity remains subject to ongoing debate—and philosophical speculation which is largely incomprehensible to the average person sitting in the pews.

This criticism can be turned inside out, however. Instead of dismissing the doctrine of the Trinity as a mere compromise required by history, it makes just as much sense to marvel at it as a profoundly novel and beautiful expression of how to understand the mystery of God. The Holy Trinity proclaims a spiritual reality greater than the chaos of polytheism and the loneliness of radical monotheism. The Trinitarian vision of God transcends the limitations of human intellect and answers the question of how God can be greater than the cosmos and yet still relate to us as a part of his creation. In the Holy Trinity, the infinite mystery of God the Father relates eternally and intimately to the physical universe through the embodied life of Jesus Christ and the ever-loving presence within creation of the Holy Spirit. Thus, the Trinity not only embraces the paradox of transcendence and immanence; it invites us to find our ultimate destiny and fulfillment in our becoming—in the words of Saint Peter—"partakers of the divine nature."

The Holy Trinity reveals the dynamic way in which the loving community of Father, Son, and Holy Spirit expands itself to incorporate the endless flow of love to and from God and God's beloved creation. Put another way, Christian mysticism fosters an openness to receive the gift of union with God. This union, as understood in the Christian faith, is actually a *comm*union, in which we are invited into communion/union with the Holy Spirit, with Christ, and, through them, with the infinite mystery of the Father and the fullness of the One Triune God.

Christic is fully human.

Christ is fully divine.

Next to the Holy Trinity, the most remarkable and controversial Christian teaching is the doctrine of the Incarnation, which holds that Jesus of Nazareth is both fully human and fully divine. This is the unique mystery of Christ.

Like the doctrine of the Holy Trinity, this central tenet of the Christian faith took centuries to hammer out. Some early Christians emphasized Christ's humanity, insisting that to call him "Son of God" was an honorific that had little real meaning when it came to explaining his relationship with God. He may have been specially blessed or favored by God, but was no more divine than you or I. Other Christians rejected the humanity of Jesus, insisting that, because he was divine, his holiness could never be enmeshed in the messy reality of human flesh. For them, Christ's humanity was just an illusion, a "form" he took on so that he could relate more easily with us. Eventually, orthodox Christians rejected both of these extreme perspectives and accepted the more paradoxical view—that, as a man, Christ was human in every way, except that he didn't sin; as God, Christ was as fully divine as the Father and the Holy Spirit.

While this has become a central article of faith for all Christians, for mystics, it is also an important key to understanding the relationship between the Trinity, Christ, and ourselves. Mystically speaking, Christ is the great bridge builder. He is one with God the Father (John 10:30). But he is also "one" with all of us by virtue of his humanity. When Joan Osborne sang her song "What If God Was One of Us?" a few years back, Christians could reply, "In Jesus Christ, God is *already* one of us."

Many critics of Christianity see this as some sort of two-tiered system that distinguishes between Christ and lesser mortals. This criticism stems from a profound misunderstanding of Christian wisdom, however, and totally ignores Christian mysticism. God poured the fullness of divinity into Mary's womb, and so Christ was born. Christ, in turn, pours the fullness of his divinity into each and every Christian, through the power of the Holy Spirit. We are not mere spectators of the divine nature; we partake of it.

The literal meaning of the word "Christian" is "little Christ"—and so, each Christian becomes, in a mysterious (mystical) way, a part of Christ. Just as Christ remained fully human even while he was fully divine, Christians never stop being human, even though we are invited to become part of Christ—part of his mystical body. Therefore, we share not only his full humanity, but also his full divinity.

Seek the light.

Embrace the dark.

This paradox emerges from two apparently contradictory Bible verses. In John, Jesus declares "I am the light of the world" (John 8:12). In Matthew, during his Sermon on the Mount, he says, "You are the light of the world" (Matthew 5:14). Hidden in this seeming contradiction is an important clue to just what the Christian mystical life is all about.

Christianity is not a "two-light" system. It's not as if Jesus were one light and we—the community of Christians, or little Christs—are, collectively, another. Rather, the light that Jesus says shines from him and from us is the same light. When we are united in Christ, we are incandescent with his spiritual light. Intuitively sensing this truth, Christians have been seeking the light of Christ ever since, both yearning to have it shine *on* us, and also hoping to be worthy for it to shine *through* us.

The light of Christ is true light, a spiritual light, something other than a physical energy stream to which our eyes can respond. Saint Paul explains: "For it is the God who said, 'Let light shine out of darkness,' who has shone in our hearts to give the light of the knowledge of the glory of God in the face of Jesus Christ" (II Corinthians 4:6). Thus, the light of Christ can most properly be understood as a light of knowledge, an inner enlightenment that reveals and makes plain what was previously shrouded in darkness.

The Gospel of John also uses imagery of light contrasted with darkness to express the difference between good and evil. For mystics, however, the tension between light and dark can be understood in another way—as the tension between the mystery that is revealed and the mystery that remains hidden. And since the mystery of God is never fully revealed to us, this means that God will come to us, not only as Light, but also as a divine darkness.

"If the visible light is intangible, how can the hidden Light be comprehended?" muses the fourth-century mystic Ephrem the Syrian. Another mystic from the Middle East, Pseudo-Dionysius the Areopagite, wrote around the year 500 about the "dazzling darkness," suggesting that what appears to us as the darkness of God's hiddenness is actually a spiritual light so bright that it blinds us.

Mystics throughout the history of Christianity have played with this tension between light and dark. John of the Cross wrote a lovely poem called "One Dark Night," in which he compares the soul's yearning for God to a nighttime tryst between lovers. He also wrote a commentary on the spiritual meaning of this poem called "The Dark Night of the Soul," which is now regarded as one of the greatest Christian mystical writings. His treatise has given its name to the experience of profound, ego-shattering darkness that some advanced mystics experience as they surrender themselves more and more to God's deep transforming presence.

Taken on another level, the idea that Christ is light but that God is enshrouded in darkness can lead to a holistic appreciation of both the light and dark parts of life. Ironically, spiritual people are often prone to judging their own lives—particularly when things aren't going well. When times are harmonious, pleasant, and joyful, we conclude that God is present. When we are plagued by suffering, doubt, despair, illness, or sorrow, God seems absent. The paradox of light and dark turns that simplistic approach on its head. We are more likely to feel the loving presence of God in the "light" times of our lives. But the witness of the mystics assures us that God remains present even when we don't feel that presence, even—and, perhaps, especially—in the profound shadow times. The God of darkness is a hidden God, and may feel like an absent God. On a level deeper than mere human experience or consciousness, however, he remains truly a present God.

Take delight in God.

Accept even suffering.

For mystics and contemplatives, God is just as present in the dark times of our lives as in the more joyful, light times. This leads to another paradox, one that finds God both in joy and in suffering. "Take delight in the Lord," says the Psalmist, "and he will give you the desires of your heart" (Psalm 37:4). This lovely promise offers a link between spiritual joy and personal fulfillment. Granted that your heart's desire, whatever that may be, will itself bring you delight and joy, this Bible verse suggests that opening yourself up to God's love is not merely a spiritual blessing, but will overflow to bless all of life. Delight in God leads to a delightful life.

That sounds reassuring. The only problem is that life doesn't always seem to work that way. Although blessings abound for most people—the love of family and friends, the joy of a good meal, the excitement of sport, the pleasure of romance, the satisfaction that comes with setting and achieving goals—for some, life's pleasures always seem to be just out of reach, whether because of illness, or poverty, or other challenges. Even in the midst of a joyful life, pain and suffering are never far away. Everyone will, sooner or later, face illness, injury, loss, and death—and, more painful still, will watch loved ones suffer as well. Suffering is a central part of life. In ancient India, Siddhartha Gautama was so stunned by his discovery that life is filled with suffering that he embarked on his own spiritual quest, which culminated in his enlightenment as the Buddha.

It's easy to approach faith from a narcissistic perspective, seeing God as a year-round Santa Claus who exists only to shower his blessings on those who love him; and prayer, therefore, is merely the means for convincing God to bestow his favor on us. This kind of religion rejoices in the good times, but leads to despair and angst when times are tough. But Christ beckons us to leave behind our childish narcissism and to embrace the fullness of life—suffering as well as joy. This is one of the lessons encoded in the grisly, traumatic death of Jesus: through his suffering, we are saved (made spiritually whole). Moreover, this salvation is not just some sort of promise for life after death; rather, it brings a blessing to us right here and right now—and right in the middle of our suffering, if only we are open to it. Christ does not offer to remove your suffering; he *redeems* it. In other words, he brings his presence into it and thereby transforms it from pointless pain to a smaller part of a larger, meaningful whole. A woman in the pain of childbirth can bear her suffering because she knows it leads to the joy of giving birth and welcoming her new child into the world. In the mystery of Christ, we see that all suffering has the potential to be a "birth" experience—giving birth to a newfound appreciation of God's presence and of his ability to turn anything, no matter how bad or painful, into a new possibility where divine love and presence can shine forth.

God is all-merciful.

God is uncompromising in his justice.

I think the argument could be made that the polarization within religion and politics in the United States largely runs along the fault line of this paradox, with so-called "conservatives" standing up for God's justice and so-called "liberals" standing up for his mercy. Of course, it's not entirely that simple. It seems evident, however, that relatively few people—whether in politics or among Christians—seriously try to apply both of these principles equally in their lives.

From prayer to meditation to contemplation, Christian spiritual practices focus your attention on seeking, establishing, or deepening intimacy with God. Just as a truly happy marriage must be built on love rather than a prenuptial agreement, the mystical quest for union with God gives precedence to love and relationship over rules and regulations. Yet many of Christianity's most renowned mystics would probably disagree with this position. In the writings of Christian mystics from Clement of Alexandria in the second century to Faustina Kowalska in the twentieth, you'll find a near-obsessive emphasis on obeying God's laws as the foundational requirement for anyone seeking holiness or divine union.

This obedience-to-law perspective is not particularly in sync with our freewheeling, self-centered, if-it-feels-good-do-it age. While mysticism and spirituality are popular both inside and outside the Christian faith, the classic mystical hunger to live in submission to divine law has become increasingly rare. Even among those who identify as conservatives and argue for the importance of moral regulations, too often there seems to be a selective obedience—for example, an eagerness to accept (and enforce) traditional views regarding marriage and human sexuality, combined with a willingness to ignore the far more challenging calls for economic and social justice.

Meanwhile, traditional ways of understanding "God's law" have come under increasing attack in our time. Science, psychology, sociology, and feminism have all inspired far-ranging debate that has led many to rethink old approaches to morality and holiness and wrestle with these profound social issues. For some people, this has led to a belief in ethical relativism, where each individual is required merely to follow the dictates of his or her conscience. Others react to the uncertainty of our age by adopting one of two apparently opposite but equally rigid responses—either to cynically reject traditional ideas of divine law altogether, or to retreat into an inflexible, fortress mentality that defends "traditional values" against all questioning, at all costs.

The Bible teaches that God's law is holy and just (Romans 7:12), but also that God is all-merciful (Deuteronomy 4:31). So what does it mean to say that God represents pure justice as well as pure mercy? How do these two qualities merge?

In human terms, they seem to subvert one another. Justice demands that wrongs be set right, that we are all held accountable for our actions, that those who are weak and vulnerable have their day in court against those who oppress or victimize them. Meanwhile, mercy promises forgiveness for wrongdoing, and leniency in punishment. I suspect that, deep down inside, we all want God to be just toward all those who have wronged us or offended us. But we also want God to show mercy to us and to our friends. This is human nature.

Mysticism, on the other hand, suggests turning this human impulse inside out. It enjoins you to police your own thoughts, behaviors, spending habits, and other actions with an eye to observing God's law, while trusting in God's mercy to shower forth love and forgiveness—even on those who have hurt you, or who oppose you politically, or whose moral values are at odds with your own. If Jesus could ask God to forgive those who crucified him, even though we have no reason to believe that they asked for God's forgiveness, shouldn't you ask God's forgiveness for all those whose behavior doesn't meet with your approval?

I really don't know how to resolve this paradox. But I do believe that much of what is dynamic and beautiful about the Christian life—including

Christian mysticism—is propelled by the creative tension between seeking to live a just life and seeking to be an ambassador for God's mercy.

Seek holiness.

Practice hospitality.

Here is a paradox of which most people, even most Christians, probably aren't aware. It is an extension of the justice/mercy paradox we just considered. To the extent that God stands for uncompromising justice, he calls us to live holy and pure lives. To the extent that God stands for all-embracing mercy, he calls us to live by the dictates of hospitality. Holiness is exemplified by Hebrews 7:26, where a holy priest is described as "blameless, undefiled, separated from sinners, and exalted above the heavens." By contrast, hospitality is characterized by the Parable of the Great Banquet, where a rich man invites everyone to his feast—even those who are impure or unclean (Luke 14:16–23).

Holiness is pure. Hospitality is messy. Holiness requires rigorous self-control and unwavering commitment to standards of righteousness. Hospitality, by contrast, works only when flexibility and a willingness to meet people where they are come first. Thus holiness and hospitality seem to pull us in opposite directions. Yet mystical Christianity operates under the assumption that God calls us to both: to a life of spotless holiness and all-embracing hospitality.

No one doubts that holiness is a central quality promoted in the Christian faith. Even a cursory reading of the New Testament reveals that a core characteristic of life in Christ involves refraining from behaviors regarded as "impure"—sexual misconduct, the worship of false Gods, lying, theft, even drunkenness. And while we may not worry anymore about some of the concerns expressed in the New Testament—for example, I have never been tempted to eat meat that has been offered to idols—other Biblical principles remain as relevant as ever.

Mystically speaking, holiness is more than just the quality of a life surrendered to God's grace. It is the first and essential requirement for those who wish to see God. Christ tells us, in fact, that it is the "pure of heart" who "will see God" (Matthew 5:8). Yet we all know that no one gets it right all the time, which is why Christians always have the opportunity to own up to their failings and do what it takes to set things right (in religious jargon, this process involves repentance, confession, contrition, and making amends). From the Catholic Sacrament of Reconciliation to a Southern Baptist altar call, all Christian communities acknowledge that people make mistakes, and offer tools for dealing with those blunders. The point behind holiness is to never give up striving for purity, even if it can never be achieved.

When it comes to holiness and purity, Christian mystics have tended to be even less compromising than members of the church as a whole. The Desert Fathers and Mothers, some of the earliest Christian contemplatives, demanded faultless moral behavior from their disciples, and purity of thought as well. Indeed, it was out of this quest for purity of thought that the practices of meditation and contemplation emerged.

Yet here is another paradox: the quest for purity can result in its own form of *im*purity, as individuals who desire to be holy before God can all too easily succumb to scrupulosity, obsessive/compulsive behaviors, or simply spiritual pride. Holiness and purity may be lofty goals, but there seems to be a danger in pursuing them single-mindedly.

Perhaps holiness is, finally, not just a matter of moral purity, but also a matter of gracious, joyous, and messily imperfect hospitality. When Christ enjoined his followers to "be perfect" (Matthew 5:48), he wasn't advocating moral rectitude so much as a limitless love that flows to good and evil persons alike. This includes loving the very people who offend you by their very *lack* of holiness. And I don't just mean "loving" people in the abstract. Hospitality goes beyond merely writing a check to your favorite charity or voting for the politician you believe is the most "righteous." Jesus demands more. He wants you to reach out to the homeless person who skulks around on the street corner near your office, or learn to engage in positive and charitable dialogue with those whose political values are opposed to your own, or shower yourself with forgiveness when you fail to meet your own internalized standards of "purity." For while he promised that the pure of heart will see God, he also insisted that he himself is to be found among those who are hungry, poor, homeless, or naked. Showing hospitality to those who are truly in need—no matter how pure or "impure" they might be—may, ultimately, be a far shorter route to mystical union with God than a lifetime of contemplation. In the fifteenth century, a book called *The Imitation of Christ* suggested, among other things, that those who truly want to live a Christ-like life must avoid contact with strangers. The book was written at a time when the Black Death was still all too real in the minds of most, so the author's lack of hospitality can be forgiven. But today, we need to remember that the pursuit of holiness involves more than keeping ourselves free from the stain of sin—our own or anyone else's.

Plumb deeply the Christian tradition.
Embrace all positive wisdom.

One of the practical ways that the purity/hospitality paradox plays out is in the question of how Christians ought to relate to non-Christian faiths. I have two friends who are both devout Christians who love Jesus and seek to do his will in their lives. But they are like night and day when it comes to how they express their faith, especially in relation to other religions.

One sees her faithfulness in terms of keeping herself pure before God. This means that she rejects any kind of spiritual activity, practice, or idea that has a non-Christian origin. She is uncomfortable with some forms of Christian meditation, for example, because they are too similar to transcendental meditation, which has Hindu roots. For her, there is so much splendor and beauty in the gospel and the tradition of the Christian saints and mystics that she sees no point in muddying the waters by blending Christian spirituality with elements from other religions.

The other, however, sees things differently. Not only is he a faithful and active member of a large Christian church, he is also a leader of the Atlanta Sufi community. He loves to read the Gnostic Gospels, the poetry of Rumi, and the writings of various Eastern teachers like the Dalai Lama and Thich Nhat Hanh. His faith in Christ is deepened by the delight he takes in learning about other faiths and their spiritual practices.

Think about my two friends in terms of the purity/hospitality paradox. One embodies the quest for spiritual purity untainted by any "foreign" elements. The other embodies the quest for a spirituality of hospitality, in which devotion to Christ leads to an openness toward the wisdom and insights of other faiths. Both are sincere in their faith and genuinely want their relationship with Christ to transform their entire lives into holiness and beauty. And their different perspectives represent the two dimensions of this paradox. Christian mysticism calls you to plumb deeply in the seemingly endless riches of the Christian tradition. Paradoxically, however, it also can inspire a genuine and heartfelt desire to find ways to share, and even integrate, Christian and non-Christian perspectives on spirituality.

It would be very easy, at this point, to get distracted by a debate over which of my friends is "right"—which is to say "more faithful" to the gospel. Instead, I will follow the advice of Matthew 7:1: "Judge not." Rather, I'll look at this paradox and consider how each perspective can be a powerful expression of devotion. Each approach has its limitations or "blind spots." The person who embraces all sorts of non-Christian wisdom can wind up adhering to a kind of blended spirituality that lacks any real identity and appears to be rooted in nothing deeper than individual preferences. Meanwhile, the person who eschews non-Christian spirituality out of a desire to maintain a kind of spiritual purity runs the risk of falling into a fundamentalist mentality that judges non-Christians or fears them, rather than simply trying to love all people as Christ demands.

Put another way, perhaps both the "embracers" and the "purity seekers" need to remain open to a continual process of conversion. Those who embrace other faiths indiscriminately need conversion to the virtue of stability, by which they can learn to rely on the deep roots of the Christian tradition for their spiritual identity. Those who are excessively insistent upon purity need conversion enlightened by charity, by which they can learn to relate to those who are different from themselves with a gracious openness rather than a defensive resistance and an unwillingness to learn or understand.

Love God's creation.

Do not love the world.

Christianity holds a tension between the "earth" and the "world." The earth is God's creation, and—especially in the Hebrew Scriptures—it is celebrated as a good thing, a gift from God. "I brought you into a fertile land to eat its fruit and rich produce," says the prophet Jeremiah, speaking for God. "But you came and defiled my land and made my inheritance detestable." Herein lies the crux of the paradox. What God has created—the earth, the land, nature and her bounty—is good. "God called the dry land earth, and the gathering of the waters He called seas; and God saw that it was good" (Genesis 1:10). What we do with it and to it, however, is another story. "Do not love the world nor the things in the world. If anyone loves the world, the love of the Father is not in him" (I John 2:15).

It's tempting to read the language of "not loving the world" or not being "of the world," as found in the New Testament, as mandating some sort of split between humanity and the rest of nature. It can also be seen, however, as a split between the human mind and the human body. The mind, or consciousness, is more akin to spirit, while the body is obviously part of nature. This kind of thinking leads to dualism—a distorted way of seeing the universe in which only spirit is good, while matter is rejected as fallen or evil. Dualism originated in Greek philosophy and in pagan religions like Zoroastrianism and Manichaeism, not in the original teachings of Jesus or in the Jewish culture in which he lived.

At its best, Christian spirituality can embrace a distinction between "the world" as an abstract symbol representing the human capacity for error, and "the earth" as the beautiful creation God has given us, including nature, the land, and our bodies. This is not to say that the physical universe is entirely benign. Indeed, the capacity to turn against the love of God—what in traditional language is called sin—has personal, social, and even cosmic dimensions. When we see how "the world" is so deeply embedded in nature, however, we are faced with two contrary temptations. One is simply to accept uncritically the urgings of worldly nature: "If it feels good, do it." This temptation ultimately leads to selfish exploitation, treating human beings and indeed all of nature not as miraculous gifts from God, but as instruments to be used for personal pleasure or material gain. The other temptation involves rejecting the body and nature as evil. Not only is this the error of dualism, but it ironically plays into the first temptation. If something is evil or fallen, why not treat it merely as an exploitable resource rather than as a gift from God? Once again, this paradox is an expression of the purity/hospitality issue. Rejecting the errors, addictions, abuses, and injustices of the fallen world is a function of the quest for purity, while embracing and celebrating God's good creation (even in its messy imperfection) is a form of spiritual hospitality. Both are essential to the mystical quest.

Humankind is sinful.

Humankind is invited to participate in union with God.

Now we come to one of the most unpopular and misunderstood Christian doctrines: sin. If you are secretly hoping that Christian mysticism offers a way to be spiritual without all that sin and guilt stuff, well, I'm sorry to disappoint you. If anything, the mystics throughout history have exhibited an even greater focus on sin (and its corollary, repentance) than their non-mystical counterparts.

When you fall in love with someone, *really* fall in love, you can become almost painfully conscious of all the ways you fail to live up to your beloved's expectation of who you are (or your own expectation of who you want to be). That is a fairly apt analogy for what motivates the dynamics of Christian repentance. It emerges out of love, and is oriented toward self-improvement *for the sake of love*. This is a far cry from the common misperception that repentance is merely something we mortals do to make God stop being angry with us.

For many Christians, their faith focuses more on sin than it does on God. They worry about how "bad" they are, rather than appreciating how good God is. They forget that the word "sin" means simply "mistake," and does not necessarily involve "evil." Here's a way to think about sin: whenever you make a choice that entails unloving or hurtful behavior, you have made a mistake, and sooner or later you will need to clean up the mess you've made. This makes you just like every other human being alive on the earth today.

Sin happens. We all make mistakes, and we all have that something inside us that can make us act selfishly. But let us recognize that universal quality for what it is, rather than succumbing to the ominous conclusion that "humankind is evil" (which, unfortunately, some Christians throughout history have insisted is true). Some people reject Christianity because they think it's a negative, pessimistic religion. But the problem of sin (and how to deal with it) is only one part of Jesus' overall message. Christianity also promises that those who choose intimacy with God through Christ will—in a process that begins now and lasts into eternity—actually become, in the words of Saint Peter, "partakers of the divine nature." You don't just get to "meet" God in the afterlife, as if heaven were some sort of awesome reception hall, some sort of cosmic reward for a job well done. Nor is your destiny limited to just an externalized dynamic of loving God and being loved by him (but remaining separate). The ultimate destiny for Christians, as understood by the great mystics throughout history, is *deification*—a word that basically means to become God-like. You actually become immersed in God. You become part of him. You don't become identical with God, but the union you experience between creature and creator is the closest that any two beings can enjoy. I remember a priest who used to say during Mass, "God is closer to you than you are to yourself." That is the beginning of deification, of participating in the divine nature, of finding union—or should I say, communion—with the Blessed Trinity.

A sinful, which is to say, broken and wounded and often narcissistic, humanity—destined to actually *participate* in God, the fount of ever-expansive love and delight? It's a paradox.

The fear of the Lord is the beginning of wisdom.

Perfect love casts out fear.

Again and again, Jesus tells his followers to not fear. Sometimes he says this to reassure his listeners; other times he seems to be scolding them for their timidity. As for Jesus himself, even his critics acknowledged that he feared no one (Mark 12:14). He does, however, draw a distinction between not fearing those who can hurt the body and yet fearing God, who alone has power over your spirit. The fearlessness Jesus advocates in relating to other human beings is, paradoxically, related to a deep humility and awe that we should direct only toward God.

When the Psalmist says "the fear of the Lord is the beginning of wisdom," perhaps the most important word in that verse is "beginning." Fear, or dread, or existential angst, is a force that can initiate a truly transformational spiritual journey. But if wisdom is born out of fear, it reaches its full maturity only through love. Love casts out the kind of fear that undermines our integrity and self-esteem; it purges us of seeing God as a force for punishment or condemnation. But love does not lead us to some sort of flippant place where we ignore God's call to holiness. The casting out of fear does not mean we can disregard the call to pass on to others the love that has been so freely given to us. Fearlessness is not the same as mindlessness. The love of God is not a sweet, sentimental emotion that ignores or denies such things as sin and suffering. We find fearless freedom in divine love precisely because we have known fear, and therefore know how to treat love with the respect it deserves.

Place your hope in the future when you will find conscious union with God.

Live in the present moment; that's the only place you'll ever find God.

If you're discouraged by the idea that not everyone will experience a jaw-dropping, eye-popping, mind-twisting encounter with divine consciousness, consider that pretty much everybody has peak experiences of some kind—what the twentieth century mystic Evelyn Underhill calls "unitive experiences," or experience of oneness with God and/or the cosmos. Unitive experiences do not necessarily involve a specifically religious or Christian setting; they may occur as a consequence of falling in love, or as part of the awe felt when holding a newborn baby. They may manifest as a sense of getting caught up in a majestic mountain vista, where suddenly you and the mountains become one. Or they may be grounded in a similar feeling of joyous littleness when standing beneath the Milky Way on a dark, cloudless night, far enough away from the insidious glare of urban neon that the soft luminescence of the galaxy can be seen.

Peak experiences happen. They typically are beautiful, joyous, even ecstatic. For many, even a humble experience of the beauty of nature can have a lifelong impact that changes how we see what true happiness or joy or simply feeling "alive" is like. Ken Wilber suggests that "peak" experiences are really "peek" experiences—events in which we get a sneak preview of how the highest evolution of human consciousness will unfold and what humankind will experience in the centuries and millennia to come. Wilber is interested in the evolution of consciousness, and so he sees peak experiences as harbingers of how human consciousness will evolve.

For Christians, peak or unitive experiences may not only represent hints of future evolution, they may also signify a present reality—the possibility of real, deep, lasting joy to be found in the presence of God. After all, if a work of art can evoke a sense of wonder, how much more remarkable it would be to get to know the artist who created it. So peak experiences, even when triggered by nothing more than the grandeur of nature, are hints at the beauty that lies hidden in the mystery of God.

But… life is not just about hanging out on the mountaintop. Nor do mountaintop experiences excuse you from the ordinary tasks of living. You have to keep looking for divine presence, not only in the mountaintop experiences, but also in the ordinary, mundane, slightly boring or unpleasant dimensions of life.

Remembering a wonderful peak experience can be a source of consolation, and hoping for a future mind-expanding encounter with God can be a means of inspiration that can keep you focused on the disciplines of the spiritual life. But life is not lived in the past or the future, no matter how glorious it was or how lovely it promises to be. Life is lived right here and right now, in the present moment. Which means that this is where mysticism happens as well.

Live by faith.

Live the truth.

If mysticism is about experience—such as of loving God, of feeling his love, or taking responsibility to do the kinds of things that open you up to his presence—then it seems erroneous to say that mysticism is about faith. In fact, wouldn't faith even be a hindrance to mysticism, since faith, as described in the Bible, is "the assurance of things hoped for, the conviction of things not seen" (Hebrews 11:1)? In posing this question, I'm reminded of Yoda, who, when teaching Luke Skywalker in *The Empire Strikes Back*, sternly admonished his apprentice to do the task given to him—not merely to "try." Wouldn't Christian mysticism work the same way? We are called to experience God's presence and love, not merely hope for it or believe in it.

Well, yes and no.

Mysticism is not just about experience, it is also about *mystery*, and the mystery of God cannot be controlled, predicted, engineered, or manipulated. While God in his gracious goodness may grant some sort of awareness of him to all who seek him, it may not be the kind of experience you hoped for or secretly think is necessary in order to be a "real" mystic. In fact, if you're not careful, your encounter with God's presence may be so subtle that you miss it altogether.

Just as there is no such thing as a perfect human being, so too there is no such thing as a perfect experience of God. Faith is the quality that we need because our knowledge and experience and awareness of God will never be perfect, at least not on this side of eternity. Faith is the lifeline that pulls you through the darkness—the darkness of your own sin, the darkness of the pain and suffering that characterizes so much of life, or the darkness of the mystery of God. We experience all of these shadow times, and sometimes even catch glimmers of God's presence in the dark. But there are other times when we may have only a dull sense of the darkness as, well, dark. And that's where faith proves essential.

Religious faith and spiritual experience are not at odds with one another. Experience is not a higher doorway to God that is opened for the deserving few, while faith is the breadcrumbs left on the table for those who fail to make the mystical grade. Rather, faith and experience work together just as the head and heart work together. Those who listen to their hearts but not their heads (and vice versa) can quickly do foolish things. Love without common sense can lead you to the wrong person, whereas common sense without love can lead to a life of joyless drudgery. "Use your head" and "follow your heart" are both great words of advice—especially when they are offered in tandem.

The relationship between faith in Christ and spiritual experience functions much the same way. On the surface, merely assenting to the ideas or teachings of the Christian tradition may seem like a dry intellectual exercise. But faith is more than just saying you agree to a set of propositions. It means giving your entire self—heart as well as mind, body as well as soul—to the wisdom that is offered to you. That self-giving is, in itself, an experiential act. So you can't truly have faith without it having some sort of experiential foundation. And it works the other way as well. Take Paul's conversion on the road to Damascus. By itself, it was just an amazing experience. But because Paul was able to respond by faith to what was asked of him by his encounter with Christ, it became far more than just a psychic anomaly. It became one of the most famous mystical experiences in Christian history. And, in fact, all encounters with the mystery require that element of faith. Without it, instead of being true mystical experiences, they would just be interesting spiritual phenomena. It's faith in the mystery that puts the mystery into mysticism.

Authentic Christian mysticism conforms to Biblical and church teaching.

Mysticism is following spiritual vision to greater freedom.

What makes a Christian a Christian? Well, that depends on who you talk to. Some may simply say "loving Jesus." Others may add that, more than just loving Jesus, it also means worshipping him, acknowledging him as the Son of God, and trying to live your life in a Christ-like way. Still others may say it depends on whether you think the Bible is the inerrant word of God or a collection of ancient myths, which church you belong to, or whether you believe in the Holy Trinity and the Real Presence.

Christian mysticism suffers from a similar identity crisis. Some define it loosely as an undiscriminating tendency toward "out-there" experiences. Others take a much more conservative approach, insisting that you must be a good Christian in a religious sense in order to qualify as a Christian mystic. What is at issue here is the role that Christian teachings play in the mystical life. Those with a more casual understanding of Christian mysticism are not particularly interested in Christian doctrine; those with a narrower definition of what it means to be a Christian mystic usually have a deeper appreciation of dogma.

Although our society tends to value personal freedom above group identity, for Christians the shared values of the community really do matter. Casual kinds of spirituality that are all about "doing your own thing" ultimately center, not on Christ, but on each individual. If my personal freedom matters more to me than the wisdom of the community, I might be a mystic, but it's likely that I'm not a *Christian* mystic.

But once again, there is a paradox. Christian mysticism may involve conformity with the central teachings of the tradition, but it also acknowledges, and even celebrates, the fact that subjective experience is an important part of the mystical life. Being a Christian mystic means assenting to Christian teachings, but also honoring your own experiences as long as they don't directly contradict those teachings.

But even this is tricky. Look at Galileo, who ran afoul of church authorities because he dared to promote scientific theories that contradicted church teachings. History has shown Galileo to be the wiser, an innocent victim of church authorities who placed more faith in their own dogma than in scientific truth. While mysticism is not the same thing as science, whenever a mystic has a vision or receives some sort of insight into spiritual wisdom, a real tension immediately emerges between this experience and the tradition.

Consider these two Bible verses:

Where there is no prophecy, the people cast off restraint, but happy are those who keep the law (Proverbs 29:18).

Do not let anyone disqualify you, insisting on self-abasement and worship of angels, dwelling on visions, puffed up without cause by a human way of thinking, and not holding fast to the head, from whom the whole body, nourished and held together by its ligaments and sinews, grows with a growth that is from God (Colossians 2:18-19).

The verse from Proverbs suggests that "prophecy" (some translations render this as "vision" or "revelation") is actually connected to religious law. Without vision, people lose restraint. The function of vision is thus not so much to set you free in some sort of anti-authoritarian sense, but rather to help you find a deep freedom in God that makes you obedient to his law—and, therefore, to human law insofar as it is consistent with God's law. Meanwhile, the passage from Colossians warns that visionaries, when "puffed up without cause" by a "human way of thinking," can lead you astray, simply because their pride prevents them from holding fast to the authority that comes from Christ, the "head" of the mystical body (the church).

This paradox—that Christian mysticism conforms to Christian tradition, but also involves personal experience of Christ—can be resolved only through discernment and a willing relationship with a wise and loving spiritual guide. This is not about control; it is about identity. Part of what gives Christian mysticism its identity is the recognition that not all spiritual insight is necessarily compatible with the Christian worldview or message. Truly Christian mystics are by nature humble enough to work with a spiritual guide who can help them discern when their experiences are (or are not) consistent with the overall meaning of the faith. Letting go of visions or other mystical experiences that contradict the faith may be a painful experience, but it serves a greater good—the ongoing glory of God and the health of the entire body of Christ.

Pray methodically.

Prayer cannot be reduced to a method.

Books about Christian spirituality often contain one of two very strong messages that seem to be at odds with one another. One advocates the use of methodical spiritual practices—set procedures or a step-by-step process. Saying the Rosary is one such process—reciting a series of prayers in an established sequence while meditating on key events from the lives of Jesus and Mary. The Jesus Prayer, or the Prayer of the Heart, which involves the repetition of a single short prayer (usually "Lord Jesus Christ, Son of God, Have mercy on me, a sinner") and sometimes rhythmic breathing and relaxation, is a similar Eastern Orthodox practice. Centering prayer, a form of contemplation similar to transcendental meditation, is yet another. It involves the use of a single "prayer word," similar to a mantra, to recollect the mind and allow for deep inner silence to emerge. What all these prayer practices have in common is a method, a procedure by which rhythmic and repetitive words or actions foster a subtle shift in consciousness, which enables you to relax more deeply into a state of prayerful receptivity where you are open to the presence of God.

These prayer methods have their critics within the Christian family, however. Some Protestants reject the Rosary as a violation of Christ's teaching not to use "vain repetitions" in prayer (Matthew 6:7, King James Version). Likewise, some critics denounce centering prayer because of its affinity with Eastern spirituality. But beyond the criticism of any one method is the more general objection that technique or method really has no place in spirituality. Popular Catholic retreat leader Thomas Dubay sums it up well: "Contemplative communion cannot be attained by any technique, oriental or occidental, nor by a centering method aimed at emptying the mind."[23] The logic behind this position is simple: God is a divine person, not a cosmic puppet. If the purpose behind prayer—and, by extension, spirituality and mysticism—is intimacy with God, we should avoid technical or methodical approaches to prayer or meditation that suggest that, by occupying or emptying the mind or altering your breathing patterns, you can "make God appear" as if he were a servant available to heed your call.

Does this mean you should abandon all methodical practices? I wouldn't go that far. After all, we are creatures of habit and it is in our nature to perform repetitive actions, whether they involve slowing down breathing to relax consciousness or getting into the habit of saying prayers every morning and evening. The important thing is to remember that God is bigger than you are: bigger than your efforts to contact him and bigger than your efforts to open yourself up to receiving him. Methodical prayer, like all forms of prayer, is valuable, not to the extent that it changes God— for that is impossible—but rather to the extent that it changes you. Prayer is not merely self-therapy, however: it is primarily worship and adoration offered to God. If a methodical prayer—or, for that matter, any spiritual practice—is offered for purely selfish reasons, it is hardly prayer at all. When it is offered truly as a gift for God, it shines. Methodical spiritual practices are tools designed to help you engage in your desire to draw closer to God. But the real wonder that will emerge between you and God can never be contained in a mere technique.

Become like little children.
Love God with all your heart, soul, and mind.

This paradox emerges out of two teachings of Christ that appear, on the surface, to be contradictory. In Matthew 18:3, Christ says: "Unless you change and become like children, you will never enter the kingdom of heaven," while in Matthew 22:37, he says: "Love the Lord your God with all your heart, and with all your soul, and with all your mind." Comparing these two verses, you may wonder which is more important—to have a childlike faith, or a more mature love for God?

This paradox seems to hinge on the mind. Children are much more likely to take things on faith. They do not need to be convinced to dream, to wonder, to play with possibilities. But there is a shadow side to this childlike openness: gullibility or naïveté, which can result in an uncritical acceptance of ideas or values that may not be good, beautiful, or true. Loving God with all your mind suggests making the effort to balance a childlike faith with a keen adult willingness to ask questions, to weigh evidence, and to seek the truth that may not easily be explained in a way that a small child can understand.

So what is Christ asking us to do? Be faithful and gullible, or be questioning and skeptical?

Perhaps the answer to this question lies in another comment Christ made to his followers: "Be wise as serpents and innocent as doves" (Matthew 10:16). Here, Jesus appears to be suggesting that his disciples hold different levels of consciousness within themselves simultaneously. The serpent represents the "adult" consciousness: shrewd, discerning, wise. The dove represents the "child" consciousness: innocent, simple, in the present moment. The key seems to be a matter of adopting the uncomplicated clarity of a child's mind, while simultaneously considering all the nuances that only an adult mind in its full maturity can attain. Christ appears to be calling us to have adult minds that remain childlike: to be both master and amateur, expert and humble beginner.

I suspect few of us have achieved this state of adult/child consciousness. In fact, much of the political wrangling in the church (if not in society as a whole) seems to be driven by a rift between those who are more faithful to their childlike minds and those who are more faithful to their adult minds. Let us honor them both. We need both a pure and simple childlike faith, and the discerning and wise mind that can come only out of maturity. If we can't find them within ourselves, let us at least learn how to respect them in one another. A triple paradox.

God is Father.

God is Mother.

God transcends gender.

The Nicene Creed—which for many Christians both Catholic and Protestant is the single most succinct statement of just what it means to be a Christian—begins with the words "I believe in God the Father Almighty," linking God with male language. Likewise, in the Bible, the Hebrew and Greek words for "God" are masculine, and Jesus explicitly calls God his father. Add to this all sorts of cultural imagery associated with God that is implicitly masculine—God as king, warrior, mighty in battle, a lover wooing a wayward bride—and it seems pretty obvious that God is a "guy."

But, like grass sneaking through the cracks in an urban sidewalk, some images found in the scripture paradoxically point to a more feminine understanding of God. Both biological and cultural images of God as a mother occur in the Bible. Isaiah depicts God as a mother in labor (Isaiah 42:14) and Moses compares God to a mother nursing her children (Numbers 11:12). In the story of Adam and Eve, God adopts the role of a seamstress, tenderly making clothes for his disobedient children. Jesus, meanwhile, compares God to an old widow seeking a lost coin, and even compares himself to a mother hen who seeks to gather her chicks under her wings (Luke 15:8-10; Matthew 23:37). Meanwhile, the Holy Spirit is explicitly associated with feminine imagery. Not only is the Hebrew word for "spirit" feminine, but the Holy Spirit is linked with the feminine personification of wisdom, Sophia, and with womanly traits like giving birth. Indeed, for several centuries after the time of Christ, some Christian communities viewed the Holy Spirit as feminine, and some theologians today, like Robert Hughes, are calling us to reclaim this ancient, feminine tradition.

As Christian mysticism flourished, it retained this feminine face of God. Medieval mystics like Bernard of Clairvaux, Aelred of Rievaulx, and William of St. Thierry used feminine or maternal imagery when speaking of Jesus. Likewise, Julian of Norwich bluntly said: "As surely as God is our father, so surely is God our mother." In our own day, many feminists have embraced the idea of the Motherhood of God, presenting it as a healthy corrective to centuries of overly masculine imagery for the Ultimate Mystery.

The third part of our paradox has its roots in Saint Paul's declaration that Christ is "no longer male nor female" (Galatians 3:28). Jesus may have been masculine in his earthly body, but Paul tell us here that God transcends gender. To assign either masculinity or femininity to God is to diminish the essential divine unknowability. To assign gender to God is to limit God.

From a mystical perspective, perhaps the best way to approach the question of God's gender is with a light touch and the humility that comes from unknowing. The tradition calls God the Father, but at least some voices also name God Mother.

Yet the mystics remind us that restricting God to either gender erects an artificial fence around him and projects our human biases. Because human beings are embodied (and gendered) creatures, we inevitably need masculine or feminine language to try to make God somehow more approachable. By seeing him as a father figure (or as a nurturing mother), we can relate to him better than we can through the purely abstract language about a God who refuses to be captured by any image or category of human thought.

William Paul Young's popular novel *The Shack: Where Tragedy Confronts Eternity* has sparked heated debate about his depiction of both the Father and the Holy Spirit as feminine. It seems that both those who love the novel and those who hate it point to this gender issue to explain their strong feelings. When Young spoke at the Monastery of the Holy Spirit, someone asked him why he depicted God as female. He answered that the protagonist of the novel—like himself—couldn't relate to the image of God the Father because of pain associated with having had an abusive earthly father. This simple statement highlights why we need to remain fluid and flexible in the images we hold of God. Mysticism, with its keen understanding of God as the Ultimate Mystery, allows us to do just that.

Mysticism is an intellectual pursuit.

True mysticism is mostly about the heart.

Mystics like Meister Eckhart, Augustine, John of the Cross, and Thomas Aquinas possessed towering intellects, and certainly exercised their minds in their efforts to connect with God through knowledge. Others, like Francis of Assisi, Faustina Kowalska, and Gemma Galgani, are known not for their mental prowess, but for the simplicity and beauty of their heartfelt devotion to God.

So is mysticism a matter of keen intellectual insight into the Christian mysteries, or a simpler, emotional approach to loving God?

In a sense, we've already looked into this paradox. We are called to love God with all the strength of our minds, and yet we are enjoined to become as simple as little children. And, in fact, some of the greatest mystics have rejected the entire notion that God is knowable, insisting that the mind is ultimately cast into darkness by God's divine brilliance—meaning that we can know God only through unknowing.

Yet some continue to seek God through intellectual means, following an innate desire to know, to understand, to comprehend. However, just as the quest for knowing must be balanced by the humility of unknowing, the intellectual quest for understanding must be tempered by the affective, or emotional, dimension of mysticism. Think all you want about God; just make sure that you're also opening your heart. Remember, mysticism is more than just a head trip; it's very much a heart trip as well.

This same argument can be made in reverse, however. Reducing spirituality to a lot of gooey feelings about God doesn't give you inner knowledge of him either. The Ultimate Mystery is more than just a feel-good proposition. It's one thing to feel an experiential love for God, but if you aren't discerning and mindful about the object of that love, perhaps all you are experiencing is an emotional projection of your own egoic ideals. That may feel like bliss, but it's hardly authentic mysticism.

The paradox that mysticism is mostly about the mind and also mostly about the heart can be resolved only by saying "yes" to both contentions. Mysticism is about abstract intellectual theory and feel-it-in-your-gut passion. Mysticism is visionary, and mysticism is erotic (in the best and highest sense of the word). Some mystics are more naturally "head" mystics; others are more naturally "heart" seekers. All in all, the Christian tradition seems to require both.

Practically speaking, this means balance. Mysticism is about immersion in the great stream of Christian thinking, from the wisdom of the Bible to the teachings of the great mystics themselves. But it's also about putting down all the books and retreating into silence and solitude to encounter the God who calls you to love. And then it's about returning from solitude to engage in real-world life and relating to other people in love and joy, in conflict and challenge, in suffering and trials. What you think, what you feel, and how you love are all important to the mystical journey.

**The mystical life is like climbing a mountain—
it's a lifelong journey to reach the place God is calling you.**

There's nothing separating you from the love of God—right here, right now.

Here we face the question of degrees in the spiritual life. Does the path of the mystic involve a developmental process, moving from beginner, to intermediate, to adept, to advanced student of the God-filled life? Or, on the other hand, is mysticism really just a matter of discovering that you already—always, completely, without qualification—exist right here and right now in the eternal and infinite love and presence of God?

The answer to both questions is a unified "yes." Many of the great mystics and contemplatives in the Christian tradition taught that mysticism is a process that unfolds through stages. The most common "map" of this process was first developed by the third-century mystic Origen of Alexandria, who felt that three of the wisdom books of the Hebrew Scriptures (Proverbs, Ecclesiastes, and the Song of Songs) symbolically represented three stages of spiritual growth: purification, illumination, and union. The anonymous author of *The Cloud of Unknowing* suggested that contemplatives go through a four-stage process, while Evelyn Underhill, expanding on Origen's idea, outlined five stages. The thirteenth-century mystic Marguerite Porete saw the mystical life as a journey with seven stages.

The number of stages on the path is not important. Many mystics have envisioned the spiritual life as a journey that, like any process, requires time, effort, and the passing of recognizable landmarks along the way.

But what about the mystics who suddenly experienced the unmediated presence of God, without going through all the "stages" first? What about Saint Paul, who heard the voice of Jesus even while he was still in the business of persecuting Christians? Or Julian of Norwich, who had a life-altering vision after apparently doing little more than praying for an experience of God? Jesus told a parable in which a man hired workers to work on his land, and he paid the same wage to those who worked there all day long and those who arrived at the last hour. Did he intend to imply by this that the fullness of union with God is available to anyone, at any time, not just those who "work the program"?

Of course. Just as we saw earlier that no spiritual method or technique of prayer is required to achieve intimacy with God, no linear beginner-to-advanced process is required either. To say something is not required, however, is not the same as saying it is never useful. After all, love at first sight may exist, but most people in happily-ever-after relationships go through a slow and steady process of becoming acquainted before the wedding bells start ringing.

And so it is with the spiritual life. When John of the Cross compared the mystical life to the ascent of Mount Carmel, he was not declaring that anyone with any hope of experiencing God's presence must climb the mountain in the very same manner. He was making the important point that, for many lovers of God, the journey can be quite long. When we think of this mystical life in this way, we can approach the wisdom of great mystics like John of the Cross as signposts along the path that help seekers to find their way. And one of those signposts says: "Not everyone has to follow this route; some of you can get there in the twinkling of an eye."

Robert Hughes' wonderful book *Beloved Dust: Tides of the Spirit in the Christian Life* recasts the traditional purgation/illumination/union sequence in different language—as conversion, transfiguration, and glory. But as his "tides" metaphor suggests, Hughes argues that these "waves" of spiritual experience can wash up on the shore of the soul in any order, in any sequence, in any way. Perhaps we can truly say that the mystical life will, sooner or later, call us to conversion, to transfiguration, and to glory. But as for how these experiences will manifest in any one person's life—only the Holy Spirit knows for sure.

The Ultimate Mystery is silent.

Part of being a mystic is trying to express the ineffable through words.

The contemplative life is devoted to silence. Monasteries are silent places, churches (up until about a generation or so ago) have traditionally been places of quiet reflection, and the desert or the wilderness (places traditionally associated with mystics and contemplatives) are places that invite deep solitude. Silence, it seems, is an important ingredient in mystical spirituality. This may seem odd to those whose lives are filled with electronic gadgets that continually generate sound and noise. But, when you stop to think about it, all the sonic clutter in your life functions as little more than a distraction that keeps you from attending to the unobtrusive (and profoundly silent) presence of God.

Not only is a mystery something that cannot be explained; but in spiritual terms, the Ultimate Mystery cannot even be put into words. We cannot fully and finally capture the fullness of the divine ineffability in mere human language. Perhaps our words can give us a vague sense of what we believe about God, or what our faith tells us that God has revealed to us. But, even then, words leave us with more questions than answers or lead us into paradox. Since God is so ultimately unknowable—since his light is so dazzling that it blinds us—perhaps it's reasonable to say that the Word of God is so overpowering that we can experience it only as (and through) silence.

As soon as I say that, however, another paradox emerges, for I am using words to testify to God's "meta-wordness." This is a paradox that has been part of the mystical tradition since the days of the Biblical writers (if not before). We cannot put God into words. And, it appears, we cannot stop trying to do just that. Indeed, in the Gospel of John, one of the names of Christ himself is "the Word of God." And, of course, central to Christian faith is the "word of God" as found in the Bible.

I believe it was G. K. Chesterton who said, "Anything worth doing is worth doing poorly." And this seems to be the motivation behind mystics who talk about, write about, or teach others about their experience, their visions, their insight, their speculations and ruminations about God. Of course, all their words fail—some more spectacularly than others. Some are even rejected for how their words are interpreted (or misinterpreted). Mystics like Origen and Meister Eckhart are admired for their contemplative genius, even though their teachings—their words—have been questioned by orthodox Christians as being just a little too "out there." Then there is Thomas Aquinas who, after his mystical vision on the Feast of Saint Nicholas, stopped writing because he realized that all his words were worth little more than straw.

Well, compared to the splendor of the Ultimate Mystery, he's right. But I, for one, am certainly glad that he tried. And I'm glad that Teresa of Avila and John of the Cross and Julian of Norwich and John Ruusbroec and Thomas Merton and Evelyn Underhill and countless others tried as well. Surely, all of them knew in their own way just how impoverished and error-prone and limited their words were as they tried to describe the mystery of God. And they were right. Before the Great Silence, all words fail. But even the words that fail need to be spoken.

Heaven is a gift freely given.

Hell awaits those who reject divine love.

Finally, I want to touch briefly on what Christian doctrine calls the last things: death, judgment, heaven, and hell. Death doesn't require much comment: we all have an appointment with the Reaper, hopefully after a long life well lived. But many people find troubling, and distasteful, the notions of judgment and heaven or hell. Even for many devout Christians, the idea that God will judge us and consign the unchosen to an eternity of unremitting torment seems utterly at odds with the idea that God is all-loving and all-merciful, and desires communion with us. How could such a God do such a thing?

The topics of judgment and hell, as unpalatable as they are to the modern mind, are central to the teachings of the Christian religion, and they show up throughout the teachings of the great Christian mystics. If you want to engage in this great tradition, you must come to some sort of understanding of these "final things."

The idea that God is both all-loving and all-just is paradoxical, not because it portrays him as half just and half merciful, but because he partakes of both qualities 100 percent. So whatever God's judgment may be, it does not in any way diminish God's compassion and love—and vice versa. In fact, Frederica Matthewes-Green, in her essay "Why We Need Hell," suggests that heaven and hell are not two different places or states at all, but rather one reality—the full and unmediated presence of God—that can be experienced in different ways depending on the response of the individual.

If you choose to accept the unified love and justice of God in all its glory and splendor, it may overwhelm you at first (this is what Catholics call "purgatory"). As the eyes of your soul adjust to the light, you will be brought into that glory and splendor in ways far beyond your imagining. God may dazzle you with his presence, but he also lets you choose whether you will open yourself to his glory. For those who freely choose to remain closed to God forever, that is what Christians call hell—a state of unredeemed suffering that results from rejecting the grace and power of God. God's judgment, therefore, is nothing more than absolute reality and complete self-knowledge. In that crystalline clarity, we choose what we choose. And God loves us, regardless.

So it's not God's love (or lack thereof) that accounts for heaven and hell. It's how you respond that makes all the difference. As C. S. Lewis put it: "There are only two kinds of people in the end: those who say to God, 'Thy will be done,' and those to whom God says, in the end, '*Thy* will be done.'"[24]

Taking the Paradoxes (Not So) Seriously

Perhaps one way to look at all these paradoxes, and all the ideas that go into explaining them, is to approach them all as a form of play. We tend to take our relationship with God very seriously—which is understandable, since a major theme of at least the Western religions is to order our behavior in a way that makes it pleasing to God. But if God wants us to take delight in him (Psalm 37:4), then perhaps a little bit of joy and even playfulness can be blended with our seriousness.

I'm not suggesting that the mystical life is frivolous, merely that there is more room in it for smiling than we (who tend to take ourselves too seriously) may at first admit. And this, I believe, is what paradox ultimately teaches us. We do not have it all figured out, under control, managed, and packaged. God is slippery and keeps wriggling out from our feeble efforts to pin him down. To the extent that we want (consciously or subconsciously) to be in control of our lives, we are likely to find this idea of God delighting in playful paradox rather hard to take.

And that's precisely how I think God wants it.

God tries to keep you on your toes—not because he has a twisted sense of humor and wants you to feel uncomfortable, but because he knows that the best antidote for taking yourself (and your religion) too seriously is to fill your faith with all sorts of apparent contradictions. Sooner or later, you just have to throw up your hands and say: "Okay, God, I give up. There's no figuring you out." At that point, God comes to you "as a little child," laughs in your face, and says: "That's okay, I love you anyway! Let's go play!"

Paradoxical Consciousness

One final thought on the function of paradox in the mystical life. I believe that God is paradoxical, not only because he transcends human logic, and not only because he wants us to learn to have a more childlike, playful trust in him, but also because I believe paradox can be a springboard to mystical consciousness.

We know that mysticism is all about mystery; the hardest paradoxes to crack are, in essence, profound mysteries. These mysteries/paradoxes function within the Christian tradition in the same way that koans function in Zen Buddhism. A student of Zen receives a koan from his or her *roshi* (teacher), often in the form of a question that seems rationally impossible to answer. The most famous koan, for example, is: "What is the sound of one hand clapping?" As part of the student's ongoing meditation practice, he or she wrestles with the koan, not just to find the correct or appropriate response, but—more to the point—to reach the limits of rationality and then move beyond them into the expansive place of pure presence where a new or heightened state of consciousness can be experienced.

A significant, but often ignored, declaration of the Apostle Paul is that "we have the mind of Christ" (I Corinthians 2:16). But what exactly *is* the mind of Christ? The Greek word, *nous*, offers a variety of connotations: mind, understanding, wisdom, comprehension. Plotinus spoke of the *nous* as an emanation from the divine source. This reminds me of a fascinating statement by the psychologist/contemplative Gerald May, who, in his book *Will and Spirit*, wrote: "It seems quite certain, in fact, that rather than saying, 'I have consciousness,' it would be far more accurate to say, 'Consciousness has me.'"[25] So, perhaps one of the gifts we can receive from the many paradoxes of God (and Christianity) is the opportunity to bump up against the limits of our own finite human consciousness, and thereby open ourselves up to let the consciousness of Christ, the mind of Christ, "have" us. When this happens, all the paradoxes melt away into non-oppositional, non-dual awareness. Christ does not resolve paradox; he simply transcends it.

And he invites us along for the ride.

CHAPTER 8

Christianity's Best-Kept Secret

So you have pain now; but I will see you again,
and your hearts will rejoice, and no one will take your joy from you.

JOHN 16:22

We have heaven within ourselves since the Lord of heaven is there.

TERESA OF AVILA[26]

If Christian mysticism is so important, why don't you hear more about it from the pulpit of your local church? Many ministers, priests, and other church leaders either never talk about mysticism at all, or seem to be uncertain about its role in the Christian life. One Episcopal priest told me: "I'm not sure what mysticism means anyway. My focus is on discipleship, and discipleship involves a direct and personal, as well as social, relationship with Jesus and with God." His comment suggests that, for many Christians, the language of mysticism, with its emphasis on mystery, darkness, unknowing, and paradox, can be intimidating or even threatening. What seems to be at issue here is a semantic distinction between a "direct and personal" relationship with God and the profound experiential union that forms the heart of mysticism.

There are historical reasons why mysticism has fallen out of favor in mainstream Christianity, largely aftershocks of the Protestant Reformation. But perhaps the most compelling reason has more to do with the nature of mysticism itself. Mysticism simply doesn't "preach" very well because it challenges the comfort and ease by which most of us settle into established religious observances, accepting the relatively modest demands of church membership in exchange for an abstract belief that God loves us and will care for us. Mysticism upsets this status quo.

Mysticism can shake the foundations of everything you believe or think you "know" about God. And it can be dreadfully dull, demanding a daily commitment to spiritual practices that, sooner or later, lose their appeal. Trappist monks describe their lives as "ordinary, obscure, and laborious." And while mysticism promises union with God, the price we must pay to get there (a life of daily discipline, continual self-sacrifice, and letting go of everything in our lives that does not foster love) is pretty daunting. Moreover, while we are assured that, through spiritual discipline, we will partake of God's loving presence, there's no guarantee that we will experience it consciously. So mysticism is unlikely to appeal to those who do not feel impelled to explore it.

No Silver Platter

A friend of mine recently told me a story that illustrates the ambiguous relationship between mysticism and religion. Like so many people today, he had been a spiritual explorer, checking out Yoga and Zen and other practices from around the world before settling into a more prosaic spiritual practice as an Episcopalian. While he liked the Episcopal Church, before long he began to chafe at what he thought was a rather superficial approach to spirituality. Where was the depth that he had encountered in Eastern meditation? Finally, he took his question to his priest. "It's hidden in plain sight," was the minister's response. "The Christian tradition has just as much depth as any other wisdom tradition, but no one's going to hand it to you on a silver platter. You have to go looking for it." The priest went on to recommend a few books—*The Philokalia*, *The Cloud of Unknowing*—challenging my friend to get the right equipment and start working if he wanted to climb the mountain.

Valentin Tomberg, a Russian philosopher who, in midlife, entered the Catholic faith, once wrote about the personalities of angels. He suggested that angels are always eager and ready to assist us in whatever way we need, but, because of their evolved sense of ethics, they never interfere in human affairs unless asked to. I believe this is the same dynamic that governs the Holy Spirit's relationship with us as we stand on the threshold of the mystical life. We become mystics or contemplatives only through the grace of God at work in our lives. Any effort we make to do it on our own is doomed to failure. Indeed, the author of *The Cloud of Unknowing*, a medieval manual of instruction on the contemplative life, has stern words for those who, through pride and the folly of their own imagination, try to become mystics or contemplatives without humbly relying on the guidance of the Holy Spirit. He calls these pseudo-mystics the "devil's contemplatives." Contemplation and mysticism are always gifts from God. But God will never force those gifts on anyone. God is not in the business of spiritual coercion.

It's not easy to scale a mountain. If you want to climb Mount Everest, you need to be in great shape, capable of withstanding harsh weather conditions and high altitudes, and prepared to pay for guides and assorted other expenses. You also need companions; it's not a trip you can take by yourself.

Christian mysticism works much the same way. You need to be spiritually fit to withstand the challenges of the mystical life. You must be prepared to withstand the harsh conditions of profound inner doubt, facing the pain and suffering of the world, and releasing your own sinfulness into the cleansing grace of God. You need to "pay" for your experience with a disciplined life grounded in faith. And as for Plotinus and his "flight of the alone to the Alone"? Although there may be an inherent solitude in the contemplative experience, it is a solitude that must be embedded in some form of communal experience. Every mountain climber needs a base camp; every pilot needs a ground crew; every mystic needs a spiritual director and a faith community.

The mountain-climbing metaphor fails, however, at a certain point. It makes mysticism sound too much like some sort of grand hobby, available to anyone willing to pay the spiritual price. The point of the metaphor is not to reduce mysticism to some sort of extreme sport that affluent individuals can enjoy at their leisure. Rather, it is intended to show how spiritually arduous mysticism can be, to help explain why so few people choose to respond to the contemplative call. Thankfully, not every peak is as inaccessible as Everest, nor does everyone feel a compulsion to climb it. The mystics who devote their lives to scaling the highest peaks do so because they are called to it. And they will be the first to tell you that every single step of their spiritual lives would be impossible were it not for the grace that blesses them at each point along the way.

For every person who is called to scale the highest spiritual peaks, there are countless others who are called to climb the foothills—to accept unique spiritual tasks that may seem "lesser" than the highest summits but are demanding in their own way and still promise profound joy and meaning to those who accept the challenge. And even those who are not called to climb mountains can still discern within their hearts an inner stirring to retreat into the wilderness for a day or a weekend for rest and renewal.

Here's yet another paradox of mysticism: There is only one path to follow, yet each of us must find our own way. We are all tellers of a unique tale, and yet all our stories are woven together by the Holy Spirit into one grand narrative. Ultimately, there is only one story, only one tale to tell. The worst thing you can do is to waste time trying to climb someone else's mountain, follow someone else's path, tell another person's tale. Hidden compulsions to be "someone else" can confound your spiritual life just as surely as they can complicate your career or your marriage. The path of the contemplative is at times dark and hidden in the cloud of unknowing; it requires tremendous trust and a profound willingness to be led by a Spirit who communicates with you in only the softest of whispers. This includes trusting in the singular beauty of your own path, no matter how unexceptional (or unfulfilling) it may seem, at times, to be.

The mystical dimension of Christianity is founded on the infinite creativity of God. Every one of us is called to be intimate with God and worship and enjoy him in a way that is unique and personal and can never be repeated by anyone else. What this means, of course, is that no program of mystical development, no game plan for mastering contemplation, no step-by-step process for "becoming a mystic," can ever be written or implemented. While there are books like this one, designed to evoke a desire to embrace the mystical life, and while many of the writings of the great mystics are instructional in nature, there can never be a one-size-fits-all approach to the unfolding of the splendors of mystical Christianity in your life. You can read the instructional writings of Teresa of Avila or John of the Cross and, hopefully, their words will inspire you, challenge you, beguile you, call you to enter more fully and deeply into the mysteries of God. But no one can ever give you a fail-safe prescription for becoming a contemplative. Mystics are like angels; no two are the same.

This points to personal mentoring (known in the Christian tradition as spiritual direction) as a valuable and perhaps essential component of the contemplative life. We are each unique; we each face different challenges and opportunities for our own individual journeys into the heart of God. Rather than making yourself miserable trying to conform your own walk with God to what you think you "ought" to be doing, open your heart (and your mind) and share your inner life with a loving and wise spiritual mentor so that the Holy Spirit can more easily guide you on your own personal path (see Chapter 9 for more about spiritual direction).

The mountain climbing metaphor points to a main reason why Christian mysticism isn't discussed much in Sunday morning sermons. It's not that the clergy are necessarily hostile to it. It's just that most congregations simply are not interested in immersing themselves in the Christian mysteries on such a profound and life-changing level. Imagine your priest or minister preaching a sermon that charges his flock to embrace the mysteries of God and enter deeply into silence and unknowing, to seek profound inner transformation under the guidance of the Holy Spirit. For those who do not feel called to practice contemplative prayer, a sermon like that might seem troubling—or perhaps even threatening. While every Christian is called to a relationship with God, many choose to limit their spirituality to something very gentle and simple. The radical potential of mystical spirituality is born out of silence and solitude, rather than preaching and public announcements.

Some Christians, particularly those from evangelical or fundamentalist backgrounds, may think that mysticism is somehow at odds with the gospel. When mysticism is perceived as being more about subjective feelings than objective experiences and the shared values of the faith, some believers naturally see it in a negative light. Others may assume that mysticism has more to do with Eastern or occult spirituality than with historic Christianity. Although this is a misunderstanding, it will nevertheless dissuade many devout churchgoers from exploring how mysticism can bring blessings to their faith. As I pointed out in Chapter 7, contemplative spirituality and mysticism often appeal to Christians who also feel called to learn from the wisdom of other faiths. Such interfaith exploration does not make a person less of a Christian; but to those who feel uncomfortable with any kind of religious belief other than their own, this kind of work will seem dangerous. Unfortunately, in the minds of many of its critics, Christian mysticism appears to be basically equivalent to interfaith spirituality—and equally to be avoided.

Of course, while some Christians (both clergy and lay) are hostile to mysticism, many others are either indifferent to the topic, or perhaps are curious about it, even if they have difficulty expressing that curiosity using the language of their church-based spirituality. All in all, it's a mistake to assume that mysticism and the church are somehow fundamentally at odds, and an even bigger blunder to assume that mysticism is good, and organized religion bad.

MYSTICISM VERSUS SPIRITUALITY

Many followers of Jesus equate spirituality with efforts to live a moral life, or with Bible study, or with the use of formal or memorized devotions like the Catholic Rosary, or with participation in charismatic prayer groups or evangelical revivals, or simply with regular attendance at Sunday worship services. All of these are valid and much-loved expressions of Christian spirituality, and none of them are necessarily opposed to mysticism. Indeed, all of these can be portals into a deep appreciation of the Christian mysteries. But what separates the mystical element from all the other variations of Christian spirituality is that it explicitly embraces the profound mystery that can be encountered at the heart of religious experience—and that can be apprehended only through the grace of God.

Some forms of spirituality can subtly reinforce experiences, not of God, but of the ego. Mysticism, on the other hand, concerns the more daunting task of surrendering the ego before the cross of Christ. It's about immersing your self-identity into the cloud of unknowing and the dark night of the soul. It is the hidden or "negative" path where, ultimately, all is stripped away before the awesome presence of God.

Many sincere and dedicated churchgoers seem to neither want nor need such a profound encounter with mystery. Perhaps they have not yet been called to go deeper or higher into the darkness of unknowing. Perhaps they are called to keep things simple, at least for now. Whatever the reason, for many Christians, their spiritual path simply does not presently entail an encounter with the mystery that is at the heart of mysticism. Moreover, those who *are* called to mystical spirituality need to refrain from judging or criticizing those who apparently are not. Everyone's path is unique, and the community of faith is large enough to encompass both those who are drawn to contemplation and those who aren't (or aren't yet). Remember Karl Rahner's prophetic words: "The Christian of the future will be a mystic or he will not exist at all." Perhaps the Spirit will raise up more and more people interested in mysticism for the purpose of transforming the entire Body of Christ into a more truly mystical community—but such a revolution will take place one person at a time.

Christian mysticism remains hidden in plain sight, even in the Christian churches where Jesus is worshipped and love is proclaimed. It's encoded in the Bible; it swirls around such universal practices as baptism and communion; it is potentially a part of the inner life of anyone who bothers to pray or who feels a longing to be quiet in the presence of God. It is only by the grace of God that anyone is called to the contemplative life. But no one is going to hand the mysteries to you (or anyone else) on a silver platter. It may not be hard to find, but it requires that you go looking for it.

PART II

The Contemplative Life

Be still, and know that I am God!

Psalm 46:10

It is not what you are nor what you have been
that God sees with his all-merciful eyes, but what you desire to be.

The Cloud of Unknowing[27]

CHAPTER 9

The Mystical Body

No one has ever seen God; if we love one another,
God lives in us, and his love is perfected in us.

I JOHN 4:12

The Christian is not merely "alone with the Alone" in the Neoplatonic sense,
but he is one with all his "brothers in Christ." His inner self is, in fact,
inseparable from Christ and hence it is in a mysterious and unique way
inseparable from all the other "I's" who live in Christ,
so that they all form one "Mystical Person," which is "Christ."

THOMAS MERTON[28]

Exploring Christian mysticism is like learning to drive. It's one thing to take a class on automobile safety and traffic laws. You've got to master the rules of the road before you can hope to survive behind the wheel. But you'll never be able to get your license until you sit in the driver's seat and learn how to steer, and accelerate, and brake, and become familiar enough with the experience of operating an automobile to safely and confidently take one out into traffic. No matter how good a student you may be, you eventually have to translate all of the important *theory* of driving into the *practice* of driving safely. In the first part of this book, we were engaged in the "classroom" phase of learning about mysticism. Now it's time to get behind the wheel.

Many people who are called to union with Christ take their first steps on the journey long before they ever run across words like "mysticism" or "contemplation" or "meditation." You may find, as you read the pages to come, that much of what I say seems rather basic to you. Perhaps through your own life experience, you've already begun to learn the principles of faith, prayer, growth in holiness, and other elements of Christian mysticism. Likewise, although you may never have been part of a Christian faith community, you may have picked up a general knowledge of mysticism through exposure to other wisdom and spiritual traditions. Some, however, may come to the adventure of Christian mysticism with little more than an unexplained desire in their hearts and an intuitive sense that the Christian mysteries speak to them. For them, even the "basics" of Christian spirituality represent new beginnings.

No one can reduce the mystery of the contemplative life to an easy-to-follow sequence, although many people, including some of the greatest Christian mystics, have been trying to do that since the days of the New Testament. Mysticism cannot be reduced to any kind of system. It flows among countless streams. But just because it's impossible to reduce the mystical experience to one particular sequence doesn't mean that it can't be approached or explored in a step-by-step manner. All I ask is that you keep in mind that the exploration of Christian mysticism in this book represents only one possible approach to entering the mysteries.

With this in mind, I've arranged the chapters in this part of the book in a sequential order. It makes sense to read them in the order presented, since I introduce concepts in the earlier chapters that are intended to support the subsequent material. But since the mystical life, being a dance with God, can manifest in many forms, your particular journey along the mystic way may look nothing like the sequence I present here. That doesn't make either of us wrong. It's just a testament to how rich and unique the life journey of each person who embraces the mystical adventure can be.

You may have noticed that I've used words like "contemplation" and "the contemplative life" almost as synonyms for Christian mysticism. In the pages to come, I talk less and less about mysticism and more about contemplation and the contemplative life. This is simply an acknowledgment that contemplation (also known, in Christian terms, as contemplative prayer) is the heart of the spiritual practices by which we open ourselves to the mystery of Jesus Christ. To truly embrace the possibility of moving deeper and deeper into the adventure of Christian mysticism requires spiritual practice and discipline—and of all the spiritual exercises associated with mysticism, contemplation is the summit. We'll take a closer look at contemplation in Chapter 15. For now, I just want to mention that those serious about Christian mysticism not as a hobby or a fad, but as a sustainable, transformational way of life, will find in contemplation—the contemplative life—the heart of their exploration.

THE POWER OF PRACTICE

If the mystical life is a journey, then where does it begin? For Christians, the quest commences in a way that, paradoxically, appears on the surface to have nothing to do with experiential inner spirituality at all. A person could conceivably be the most advanced mystic in the world, enjoying supernatural phenomena, breathtaking visions, glorious and unimaginable experiences of heightened consciousness, and spiritual bliss. But in Christian terms, this "spiritual master" could be nothing more than the simplest of novices. *Christian* mysticism—the journey to union with God in Christ—begins in an entirely down-to-earth and mundane way.

Christianity is an *incarnational* faith. In its fullest and truest form, it proclaims the joyful, healing, and transformational presence of God right here, right now, in the physical world—the world of flesh and bones. Another word for "incarnational" is "enfleshed." As Christians see it, you don't have to escape the world to find God. You don't have to reject your body or your physical nature to embrace spirituality. You don't have to deny the earth to embrace heaven. On the contrary, Christianity makes the bold claim that, since God in Christ became a human being, the nexus in all the universe where humanity meets divinity is right here, right now, in our mundane physical world.

This beautiful message has several practical implications. The earth and the human body are good enough for God to inhabit—whether we're talking about Christ living in a human body 2,000 years ago or the Holy Spirit dwelling in our hearts today. This means that the earth and the body are good enough for us to love, honor, cherish, and nurture. Likewise, if you want to reach out for God, seeking and yearning for his presence in your life, then you must begin right here and right now, by seeking that presence in your own heart, your own body—and in others. And this is where the importance of community comes in.

Remember the paradoxes of mysticism. No matter how spiritual Christian mysticism gets, it's also embedded in our materialist, earthy world. It is enfleshed in the way we organize our lives and relate to one another. It manifests in the social and institutional tools we have created to support one another spiritually.

In other words, the mysticism of Jesus Christ is embedded in the Christian faith. Just as Christian mysticism is concerned with making the hidden mysteries of God known, so is the wisdom of mysticism itself hidden within the most commonplace elements of the Christian religion.

Even churches that claim to be opposed to mysticism contain within their teaching and worship the seeds of the mysteries that lead to the life-changing presence of God. Christianity teaches that you don't have to climb a mountain to find God. You can find him in the open hands of a homeless beggar on the street, or in the haunting eyes of a frail old woman, lonely and ravaged by dementia, at a nursing home just up the street from where you live. And you can even find God in the church on the corner.

Luke 17:21 provides the key to understanding how the mystery is embedded in Christian community. In this verse, Jesus says one of two things, depending on the translation:

The kingdom of God is within you.

or

The kingdom of God is among you.

For those who are drawn to mysticism and contemplation, the idea of the kingdom of God (in other words, heaven) being found *within* us is particularly appealing. It suggests that the key to true spirituality is found by going within—by interior reflection, meditation, and contemplation. And indeed, all of these practices are essential to the contemplative life.

But the original Greek text of Luke 17:21 is deliciously ambiguous. While it does use a word that means "on the inside," the phrasing of the verse suggests a plural meaning—inside "all of you," or, inside the community of believers. So the paradox is that we find heaven and the key to contemplative life by turning both within ourselves as individuals, and to one another in a community of faith. The richness of Luke's message helps us enter fully and truly into the contemplative life. As aspiring mystics, we must turn both within ourselves as individuals to cultivate a deep and rich interior life, *and* to a community of faith where heaven is found within and among the family of believers. And indeed, Jesus tells us so: "For where two or three are gathered in my name, I am there among them" (Matthew 18:20).

If the kingdom of God is within you, then your strategy for exploring the mystical life will naturally include disciplines such as meditation and contemplation. As worthy as such practices are, your journey to divine union must be supported by immersing yourself in a community of fellow men and women who are trying, as best they can, to figure out what loving Christ is all about.

GO TO CHURCH

If you're already part of a faith community, feel free to skip the rest of this chapter and move on to the next. The rest of this chapter is written for those who yearn to explore Christian mysticism but who are not currently members of a church. If that's you, please take a deep breath and read on.

The first step toward the practice of Christian mysticism is to engage with the Christian religion. I don't mean just reading the Bible and the writings of the mystics, or saying prayers, or attending a retreat at a monastery once in a while. I don't mean just showing up at a church every now and then. I mean getting involved with a community of others who are following Jesus, and making this community a priority in your life: which includes showing up every week, getting to know the people there, making a financial commitment (no matter how modest it may be), and actually participating in a class or a service project or some other volunteer activity.

I know that some who read this book will insist that this is the last thing they want to do. But trying to experience the splendors of mystical Christianity without becoming part of a community of fellow seekers makes about as much sense as trying to become an attorney without going to law school. Just as the first step to practicing law is making the decision to attend law school, so the first step on the Christian mystical journey entails making a commitment to be engaged with others who practice the faith, *even when they are not mystics.*

If you are adamant that you want nothing to do with Christian community, then you are declaring to God and to your deepest self that you have no desire for Christian mysticism other than perhaps just wanting to learn about it. If you desire more than just knowing *about* Christian mysticism, and actually want a living mystical relationship with God through Christ, the first stop on the journey involves getting to know others with a similar hunger for Christ's presence in their lives.
The Franciscan friar Richard Rohr defines a Christian as "someone who's met one." It's a wonderful definition in that it neatly encapsulates the key role that community plays in the life of communion with Christ. Just as the Christian understanding of God is grounded in three persons (Father, Son,

and Holy Spirit) living in eternal co-communion, so the heart of Christianity is found in relationships, in communion, and in love. Unlike many other mystical traditions, Christianity does not narrow the goal of mystical spirituality to "becoming one with God," as if the ultimate end of mysticism is annihilation of your mortal self in an experience of cosmic divine union. Rather, Christian mysticism invites you into eternal communion with God, implying a joyful dance of ever-increasing love and delight in relationship—with God, and through God to all people (and through all people back to God).

Relationship forms the heart of Christianity, whether we are relating to God or to one another. Christianity undermines the idea, prevalent in our secularized society, that God is nothing more than a metaphor for the deepest, highest, or best parts of ourselves. While faith in Christ invites us to seek God within ourselves, we are not seeking just a *part* of ourselves. Rather, we are seeking to *become part* of something much bigger than ourselves—the God who is greater than the cosmos. We can seek this because, paradoxically, this transcendent God has been seeking us all along. We love God in response to God's love for us. Likewise, Christianity also offers an alternative to the pervasive narcissism and self-obsession of our time, by calling us to look for God not only inside ourselves, but also through each other. Meister Eckhart once cryptically remarked that "the eye with which I see God is exactly the same eye with which God sees me. My eye and God's eye are one eye, one seeing, one knowing and one love."[29] Since God is in each of us, when we gaze into the eyes of our friends and neighbors and fellow Christians, we are gazing into the Temple of the Holy Spirit.

In the fourth century, thanks to the efforts of the Emperor Constantine, Christianity became a legally acknowledged religion in the Roman Empire, which meant that more and more people became Christians, not because they necessarily accepted faith in Christ, but because it was socially advantageous to do so. Consequently, many dedicated Christians felt a calling to abandon the decadent cities and retreated into the desert, where they lived as hermits, in solitary pursuit of their single-minded devotion to Christ. On the surface, this movement of mystical individualists (known as the Desert Fathers and Mothers) seems to suggest that Christian spirituality really can be a "go-it-alone" matter. But the desert hermits who sought the contemplative life in pure solitude lasted for only a generation or so. Soon, they recognized that they needed each other and started to band together in communities for shared worship, labor, and fellowship. Those communities became the first Christian monasteries. Likewise, the Carthusians, an order of monks who live most of their lives as hermits, nevertheless gather together at appointed times for communal prayer, meals, and fellowship. So even those Christians most committed to solitary spirituality inevitably balance their isolation with an equally important love for community. No one can be a Christian in perpetual solitude. Christians need other Christians.

The social nature of Christian spirituality holds true even for those who are dedicated to following the wisdom of the Christian mystics. Because mysticism entails the cultivation of a rich inner life, a profound interior intimacy with God, it naturally appeals to introverts and perhaps even to people who regard themselves as shy or social "misfits." But just because contemplation has a strong solitary dimension does not diminish the necessity of embedding your private spiritual life in a larger context. In fact, the tradition of Christian mysticism clearly warns that those called to this path must be wary of the innate human tendency to get lost in their own inner capacity for self-deception and illusion. It is important to measure your own spiritual life against external benchmarks. And one of the most important of these is the community of fellow seekers of the love of God.

A friend of mine who is a surfer told me about the thrill of surfing—and its dangers. He described how a rip tide can easily snatch an unwary surfer and drag him away from shore. To surf safely, he said, two things are essential: a landmark on the shore to mark your location, and a surfing partner to help in the event of an emergency.

Christian mysticism may not pose these same kinds of physical risks, but it does involve spiritual risks. For example, the pursuit of mystical spirituality can lead to spiritual pride, the belief that, as a contemplative, you are somehow better than other Christians or other people in general; or to megalomania, the erroneous idea that God has called you to a "special" place or task; or to spiritual narcissism, an unhealthy and excessive self-love that interferes with your ability to love others humbly. To avoid these risks, you need spiritual landmarks and "surfing partners."

The "landmarks" for Christian mysticism are the Bible and the sacred tradition of wisdom handed down by the saints and mystics of the past 2,000 years. Your "surfing partners" consist of those who teach you, guide you, and walk alongside you on your spiritual journey. This may include a mentor (spiritual director); members of a prayer group, Bible study, Christian meet-up group, or other small community; and the members and leadership of your church (no matter how large or small it might be).

As I write these words, I am keenly aware that people who do not participate in a Christian faith community have almost always made a conscious decision not to do so. Plenty of reasons can be found for declining to join a church. Some pass over the Christian religion in favor of an interest in other religions or spiritualities (Buddhism, Goddess Spirituality, and Druidism); others reject church because they might disagree with how many Christians think about science, feminism, politics, human sexuality, or environmentalism. I don't want to minimize these concerns, and yet the good news is that among Christian communities today, you can find tremendous diversity in viewpoints and values. Frankly, no matter how liberal or conservative or academic or scientific or interfaith-minded you might be, unless you live in a truly remote area, you will probably be able to find a faith community where you can be yourself and relate to others who will either share your values or, at least, respect your right to follow your conscience. The fact that some Christian communities insist on a rigid conformity among their members should not blind you to the fact that many other, far more tolerant, options exist for Christians with unique perspectives (including an interest in mysticism).

When we criticize a particular faith community as "too superstitious," "too patriarchal," "too repressed," "too conservative," or "too liberal," often this says more about us than about the group we're criticizing. The path of Christian contemplation leads to increasing self-awareness, and perhaps a good place to begin is by considering why you do not participate in a Christian community. Are you afraid to associate with people whose views challenge your own? Or do you secretly think you are better than they are? Rejecting a church because you think you're smarter than everyone else who goes there is, frankly, a form of spiritual pride that is incompatible with the contemplative path—a path grounded in love and humility.

Conversely, if you avoid community because you are convinced that no one will accept you because of your views, perhaps you haven't made an effort to connect with other Christians who share your values.

Some avoid churches because they are scandalized by corrupt or unethical actions associated with the institution or the clergy. It is not my intent to defend or apologize for all the wrongdoing that has happened in churches over the years. But consider this: many businesses are corrupt or unethical or engage in practices that harm people; if it turns out that your employer is corrupt, this is no reason to give up on your career and live as a hobo. On the contrary, the business probably needs honest and ethical employees like you to help it overcome its problems. Churches likewise need caring, ethical, conscientious people. If you're the kind of person who is outraged by injustice, then there is a church somewhere that needs your high standards and commitment to doing the right thing. If you have been victimized in a church setting, please seek healing, which may involve professional help or support from healthy and ethical Christians who care. For the sake of the larger body of Christ, we must all help to create spiritual communities that are honorable and safe.

Ultimately, there's only one compelling reason not to participate in some sort of Christian faith community: lack of faith in Christ and the Christian message. But such a nonbeliever would not want to practice Christian mysticism anyway. If you are drawn to the possibility of achieving communion with God through Christ, then begin your mystical journey by finding (or, perhaps, rejoining) a community where you can express the religious side of the Christian life.

The Church as a Hotbed of Mysticism (Not!)

Why am I making such a strong case for participating in a faith community? It's not because your local priest or pastor or church elder is going to usher you in to the hidden secrets of Christian contemplation.

Far from it.

In fact, as I pointed out in Chapter 8, ordinary Christian churches, whether Catholic or Protestant, often seem to be the last places where you can go to explore topics such as mysticism, inner development, and contemplative prayer. Sometimes this is just an issue of semantics—the leadership of the church may be uncomfortable with the word "mysticism," but actually do encourage their membership to foster a deep, experiential, conscious relationship with God through Christ. Other communities place such a strong emphasis on social justice, outreach, and care for those in need, that inner spirituality of any kind, mystical or otherwise, never gets mentioned. Meanwhile, other churches have a tradition of Bible study, or an emphasis on personal holiness, that is in itself spiritually beneficial, but is accompanied by an implicit understanding that nothing else is necessary for Christian discipleship. The message seems to be "Follow our program but go no further."

As important as I believe it is for aspiring contemplatives to begin their spiritual journey by participating in a faith community, paradoxically I need to stress the fact that most Christian faith communities will *not* directly support your interest in the inner life. And if you're unhappy with your neighborhood church because the pastor thinks mysticism is self-indulgent nonsense, changing churches is rarely the answer. If you do switch to a different congregation, you will likely find that as far as mysticism is concerned, your new place of worship won't be any different.

Fortunately, not all Christians are opposed to mysticism—in fact, most have no idea what it is. Within any given denomination, different clergy and church leaders will have their own opinions about mystical spirituality. Especially if you are a member of a large church, chances are that someone else in the community will share your interest. But you may just as easily discover that your fellow Christians, like people in the world at large, don't share your interest in the mystical tradition, either because they are indifferent to the idea of life-changing intimacy with God, or simply because they are vaguely uncomfortable with the idea of experiential faith.

So why, for heaven's sake, must you begin with joining a church?

For the same reason that an artist's apprentice begins by learning how to clean dirty paintbrushes, or a novice in a monastery is put in charge of mopping the floors. The contemplative life rarely, if ever, begins with ecstatic visions of God. On the contrary, the first task of an aspiring contemplative is to learn how to be a humble student, a kind and considerate neighbor, and a serious student of the teachings of Jesus Christ. And the best place to learn these things is an ordinary community of Christians—in other words, a church.

Commitment to a faith community should not be driven by what you can get out of it, particularly if what you seek is a cheering section to support you in your contemplative exploits. On the contrary, church involvement is a necessary prerequisite for contemplative practice because it grounds your spirituality in a real-world, down-to-earth network of human relationships. It is very likely that no other church members will care if you meditate or not—but they will expect you to attend services every week, follow through on your committee assignments, and keep your pledge current. Church membership teaches you that the Christian community often needs you in ways different from what you may expect. You may approach the pastor with an offer to teach a class on the wisdom of John of the Cross, only to have the pastor suggest that what the congregation really needs is someone to teach teenagers about the virtues of abstinence. While you don't have to accept every unexciting task that comes your way, doing so may be a great opportunity to learn old-fashioned Christian values like obedience, humility, and perseverance—all of which are essential to the flowering of the mystical life, and all of which are far more easily learned in a communal setting than by yourself.

Likewise, participation in a church teaches you how to worship and how to pray. It familiarizes you with the great themes of the Bible and the key beliefs of the Christian faith. In short, it's a training ground for the two essential tasks of loving God and loving each other.

Finding the Right Church

Some churches are historically more congenial to contemplative spirituality than others, but each local congregation will have its own "personality."

Depending on the priorities of the clergy and the parish leadership, this will go a long way toward determining whether the church you join is a place where you can discuss your interest in mysticism freely and openly, or where you will need to exercise a certain discretion.

My first piece of advice is to start where you are. If you're already a member of a congregation, that may very well be where you belong. If you haven't been to church in a while, now is the time to dust off your Bible and your Sunday best and get back to it. The roof of the church will not cave in when you cross the threshold. Your first Sunday there, you may get some excited or bemused greetings, depending on how long you've been gone. But if you go back Sunday after Sunday, it won't be long before you feel as if you never left. Soon you'll be fending off invitations to serve on committees as if you had been there every Sunday for the past twenty years.

If you have not belonged to a church before, perhaps you can find a congregation of the same denomination you grew up in, or that your parents, grandparents, or other relatives attend. If you come from a thoroughly secular or non-Christian family, then start from scratch and just shop around for a church. Take your time to get to know the community before making a commitment to join it, especially if you have had a bad experience with church membership in the past.

Once you actually join a church, give it time. It's very easy to get bored with a church, or disillusioned by its many human and structural imperfections, or frustrated by its political infighting, boneheaded policies, uninspired liturgies, sleep-inducing sermons, and incessant pledge drives. Sooner or later, you may chafe against some of its social philosophies. But this will be true of every church you explore. The truth is that churches don't exist to meet your needs, and the spiritual benefit you get from being "churched" has more to do with the opportunities you have to give of yourself than it does with the gifts it bestows on you.

Thankfully, Christian community is not all bad news. Churches can be wonderful places for making friends, experiencing spiritual and emotional growth, finding opportunities to help those in need, or just learning more about the splendor of a faith anchored in a loving God. No church is perfect, but if you keep an open heart and mind you will encounter real blessings in your faith community.

Joining a church is a lot like getting married. You can date as many people as you want before you put on the ring, but once you've made a commitment, stick with it. In other words, if you're not currently a member of a church, explore your options. Do your homework. Examine what each denomination actually teaches. Learn the main characteristics of the church you are considering. If you want to join a church that feeds the homeless and engages in political activism, find out if the church you're considering welcomes that kind of passion.

Among the various Christian denominations and even among different congregations in the same denomination, you will find communities with markedly different priorities. Some welcome gay and lesbian individuals and couples; others see that as a betrayal of church tradition. Some emphasize raising money to build homeless shelters; others raise money to send missionaries overseas. Some fight abortion clinics; others fight urban sprawl. Some have many women in ordained ministry and leadership roles; others are adamant that only men belong in these positions. Ultimately, there's no need to stay away from church because you fear that your political or social values won't be welcome. If that is your worry, then you simply haven't found the right church yet. Of course, no matter how much you feel at home in a community, sooner or later it will challenge one or more of your deeply held beliefs. Part of being a Christian is learning how to love people even when you disagree with them—and the more bitterly you disagree, the more powerful the lesson in love.

Here is a brief summary of different churches to help you get started on your search for the place where you belong.

- **Eastern Orthodox, Eastern Catholic, and Roman Catholic churches.** Generally speaking, these churches have the most elaborate rituals, a rich tradition of history and theology, and many resources to help you pursue the contemplative life, including monasteries and convents where you can make retreats and often find spiritual directors. These churches typically are socially and theologically conservative, restricting the priesthood (ordained ministry) to men. Some religious orders, however, especially within Catholicism in the United States, have a more liberal culture and identity. Unlike most Protestant churches, these churches also foster devotion to the saints of the Christian tradition, with special devotion given to Mary, mother of Jesus. The Eucharist, the ceremony of Holy Communion, is built around an understanding that the bread and wine, once consecrated, miraculously become the real body and blood of Christ.

- **Episcopal churches.** These churches are part of the Anglican Communion affiliated with the Church of England. They are the bridge between the Orthodox and Catholic churches on the one hand, and Protestant churches on the other. Some Anglican parishes are ceremonially and theologically very similar to Catholicism, while others have more of an evangelical identity. Most Episcopal churches in the United States are socially liberal, with women priests and, increasingly, openly gay and lesbian clergy as well.

- **Protestant churches.** Because Protestantism began as a reform movement critical of Catholicism, many Protestant churches have rejected or remain wary of spiritual practices that have traditionally been associated with mysticism, but that also originated prior to the Reformation (contemplative prayer, the Daily Office, lectio divina, personal spiritual direction, and frequent reception of Holy Communion). For this reason, the teachings of many Christian mystics who came out of the Orthodox or Catholic traditions have not been embraced in the Protestant world. But Protestantism, with its focus on Bible study and personal commitment to discipleship, nevertheless can support anyone seeking an intimate relationship with God through Christ. Indeed, some Protestant leaders truly deserve to be called mystics,[30] and in our time, Protestant teachers like

Richard J. Foster and Marjorie Thompson have championed the disciplines and practices necessary for entering into contemplative spirituality. Trying to navigate the world of Protestantism can be daunting, since so many different sects and denominations exist. Some of the larger churches, like the United Methodists or the United Church of Christ, are socially and theologically liberal, whereas the Southern Baptists and many smaller or independent evangelical or Pentecostal churches are much more conservative.

- **The Quakers.** The Religious Society of Friends, based on the teachings of George Fox, is particularly friendly to mysticism. The Quakers emphasize a spirituality based on listening to the "inner light," or "that which is of God," which can be found in everyone. Each Quaker community is governed by consensus; the denomination is characterized by a strong commitment to peace and social justice. The "unprogrammed" style of worship emphasizes silence and simplicity, rather than the performance of a liturgy or sacramental rites.

- **House churches.** These are small, usually independent, communities of people who worship in each other's homes, generally without paid clergy or any commonly held church property. If you want a truly intimate and small-scale church experience, this is an option worth considering. In fact, even mainstream churches have various programs or orders that are organized around small groups meeting in people's homes, so this is an avenue to pursue even if you join a typical church. Like Protestantism in general, house churches vary widely in their personality and theological perspective, so don't assume that they are all created equal. Some are liberal, some conservative; some emphasize evangelical discipleship with no defined leadership, while others have an "independent Catholic" identity. Any particular house church may or may not be the best place for you to nurture your ongoing relationship with God, so consider all your options. Since house churches do not have readily visible public meeting spaces, you may have to search online—or ask around—to discover house churches in your neighborhood.

- **Emergent communities.** One of the newest movements within the Christian faith as a whole, emergent (also called "emerging" or "emergence") Christian communities are dedicated to discovering new and innovative ways to be faithful to the gospel today. Emergent groups can take many forms, but often they appeal to young persons with a commitment to environmental and social justice, and a willingness to incorporate elements of popular culture into their worship experience. Sometimes, what is "new" for the emergents may actually be something quite old, however, and so, through emergent communities, many Christians are discovering for the first time the long-forgotten practices of contemplative spirituality. The emergent movement represents an exciting development in the overall Christian community, as believers from Protestant and evangelical backgrounds are, without abandoning their immediate roots, finding new meaning and purpose in practices like the Daily Office, contemplative prayer, working with a spiritual director, and even gathering together in intentional "neomonastic" communities. If you choose to join a church where the pastor or the lay leadership are excited about the emergent conversation, you may find that it is a congenial community for exploring the mystical dimension of the Christian faith.

How can you tell if a community is right for you? It's a question of discernment. Certainly, praying about it is an important part of the process, and simply being aware of your own thoughts and feelings is important. If you're having difficulty deciding, turn to the guidance of a trusted mentor or elder—or even a good friend—to help you sort out your perspectives. I believe that one of the reasons so many people feel disillusioned with the institutional church is because we subconsciously expect our community of faith to be perfect, which of course is unrealistic. The perfect faith community does not exist, so finding a "good enough" church ought to be the goal of your discernment. Every church is composed of fallible human beings just like yourself, prone to errors and mistakes. Forgiveness is just as essential to happy church membership as it is to a happy marriage.

Joining Your Faith Community

Once you have found the church you want to join, what's next? You may need to go through a newcomer's class, or perhaps a formal ceremony by which you are made a member of the church. If you have not been baptized, that will be part of the process. Even if you have been baptized, there still may be a ceremonial act by which you join. This may be as informal as being prayed over during a Sunday morning service or, in the Catholic and Anglican churches especially, receiving the rite of confirmation.

Once you are a member, there's more to it than just showing up on Sunday. Get involved. Make a financial pledge (just do it); sign up for a class; show up on cleaning days; pitch in with a ministry to the homeless or some other worthy effort; find a way to contribute to worship leadership—sing, read, or assist with Holy Communion. In particular, look for ways to give to others—for example, through ministry to the sick or to those in need. None of this is particularly "mystical" or even "contemplative," but this is equivalent to a beginning pianist learning to play scales. It may not sound like music, but it is the foundation on which real music can be built.

Joining a community of faith will bring joy to your life, especially as you get to know people and make friendships that often prove to be lifelong. On the other hand, as a nonprofit, largely volunteer-driven organization, a church can make a major claim on your time and energy. Part of successful church membership is learning how to say "no" to opportunities to serve that are beyond your ability to give joyfully. I once heard a wise pastor tell his congregation it was okay to be involved in the church at whatever level is right for you. He knew that, for some, the church was the center of their social lives, so, if they spent ten to twenty hours a week on the church grounds, it was all time well spent. Others, however, may have to balance church involvement with a host of other family, social, and volunteer commitments, and therefore need to enforce strict boundaries when deciding how to invest their time.

If you are serious about pursuing contemplative spirituality, remember that it requires its own investment of your time, beyond what you give to your faith community. Lectio divina, prayer, meditation, contemplation, and study of the Bible and the writings of the mystics all take time and are most effective when practiced on a daily basis. You can easily devote three hours a day to your spiritual practice. And while you may not choose to put quite that much time into it, it's important to remember that your contemplative discipline is just one more commitment you will need to balance against the social demands of your church community.

Those who are drawn to contemplative and mystical spirituality are often introverts—who find solitude refreshing and can feel overwhelmed by large groups or too much social interaction. As Adam McHugh, author of *Introverts in the Church*, points out, churches as social organizations typically are geared more to the expectations and the needs of extroverts than introverts. If you are an introvert, bear in mind that you may have to find quiet or more intimate ways to participate in your faith community. Some churches, particularly in large urban areas, may have thousands of active members. When congregations get this big, going to church can feel like attending a performance in a super-sized sanctuary/auditorium complete with a sound system, large projected images of the minister or speakers, and (unfortunately) an overall impersonal atmosphere. Thankfully, not all churches are so large. But sometimes even a "normal sized" congregation with several hundred members can feel more "institutional" than "familial."

Some churches combat the impersonal quality of these big congregations by forming small groups that gather for a more personal spiritual experience. These groups can take a variety of forms based on their mission, their location, and their affiliation with a large church (or lack thereof). For those interested in Christian mysticism, two kinds of groups are particularly helpful: centering prayer groups and monastic associate groups. Although both of these smaller-scale Christian communities have their roots in Catholic spirituality, they are becoming increasingly ecumenical in nature, meaning that Christians of all denominations are welcome to participate.

Centering prayer or Christian meditation groups. For contemplatives, these small groups are ideal settings for communal spirituality, since their focus is on silent prayer. They sometimes follow the teachings of a particular Christian author—for example, centering prayer groups generally follow the teachings of Thomas Keating. Beginners are usually welcome at their meetings, and they sometimes offer training to help newcomers become familiar with the experience of meditation and silent prayer. Centering prayer groups are almost always ecumenical in nature—in other words, Christians of different denominations gather together in the same group. They may meet in churches, private homes, or some other location. We'll take a closer look at centering prayer and its role in the contemplative life in Chapter 15.

Monastic associate groups. If you live near a monastery or a retreat center, inquire to see if it sponsors a group of laypersons who gather there for spiritual instruction, prayer, and fellowship. These groups go by various names, including "Third Order" groups, "Secular" groups, "Lay" associates, or "Oblates," depending on the monastic or religious order that sponsors them. Sometimes they are restricted to members of the same church as the monastery (usually Catholic), but often they are ecumenical, welcoming Christians of all denominations. Since these groups are attached to a monastery, they are, by definition, different from your neighborhood church. Whereas churches offer a variety of ministries and services to meet the needs of many kinds of people, monastic associations specifically exist to support the cultivation of an inner spiritual life of prayer, meditation, and contemplation. Sometimes, they ask for a letter of recommendation from your priest or minister in order to participate. The beauty of monastic associate groups is that they give you the opportunity to receive instruction on prayer and the spiritual life from monks (or from laypersons who themselves have been students of monks), with teachings adapted to the needs of those who live "in the world."

The Liminal Christian

Throughout history, many great mystics lived on the margins of the church—sometimes literally, sometimes metaphorically. The Desert Fathers and Mothers lived on the edge that separated civilization from the wilderness. Many great monastic orders chose remote locations for their homes, settling on the margins between church and society on the one hand, and the untamed forests, mountains, or even swamps on the other. Francis of Assisi rejected a posh life as an affluent merchant's son, choosing instead to live on the fine line that separated respectable religion from a life of poverty.

Julian of Norwich lived literally on the edge—in a cell where she enjoyed solitude, but attached to a parish church where she participated in communal worship and provided spiritual direction to those who sought her guidance. Simone Weil, a Jewish philosopher who embraced Christian spirituality but refused to be baptized, never even fully entered the church, at least not sacramentally. Pierre Teilhard de Chardin, as a paleontologist, inhabited the frontier between religion and science, while Thomas Merton, Bede Griffiths, and Swami Abhishiktananda were all called to live out their faith in the gray areas between Christianity and the wisdom traditions of Buddhism or Hinduism.

So it is a common theme among mystics to express their faith and devotion to Christ in an in-between sort of place, usually between the established church and the society in which it is embedded—a place that stands in contrast to the Christian world—places like the wilderness, poverty, science, or non-Christian traditions. But living on the edge of orthodoxy did not lead these great mystics and contemplatives to be sloppy or individualistic in their observance of Christianity. On the contrary, their lives are marked by a deep love and respect for the traditional wisdom teachings of the faith, even though they remained open-hearted to people and places that seem profoundly "other" than established Christian thinking and dogma. It's yet another paradox of the Christian mystical tradition.

The fancy, Latin-based word that describes this place of "in-betweenness" is "liminal," which means "of the threshold." I believe that the great mystics often lurked on the thresholds between institutional religion and the real (or figurative) wild places of the world. As liminal figures, they were in the best position to drink deeply from the well of Christian tradition, but also to express their relationship with God in a completely authentic way. They respected the sacraments and the graces of the church, but also truly loved and befriended those who, for whatever reason, remained outside the boundaries of organized religion.

It is not easy to live authentically in these liminal spaces. Both the church and the world tug at those who stand on the threshold between them, urging them to move away from the door because "it is dangerous out there." Like all institutions, churches are committed to their own preservation and expect their members to serve the institution, no matter the cost. Likewise, beyond the boundaries of the Christian religion, there are plenty of forces that beckon those on the threshold to abandon religion altogether. The only way to remain truly centered in this in-between place is to remain anchored in meaningful relationships, beginning with a relationship with God that is grounded in prayer and contemplation.

Perhaps the in-between places that separate religion from the rest of the world are the most natural habitat of contemplatives, who feel impelled to follow God wherever God calls them—sometimes in religious settings and sometimes not. Perhaps those who discern in the call to love God and neighbors a mandate to love both "church" and "world" equally and unconditionally are the natural residents of this space. Indeed, holiness is grounded in the concept of being "set apart" for God. Contemplatives are those who are doubly set apart—from the world by their relationship with the church, and from mainstream religion by their devotion to God through the cultivation of inner silence and the embracing of the mystery of darkness and unknowing.

Many who feel a profound desire for God and hunger for the gifts of silence and solitude have ambivalent feelings toward the unexciting business of mainstream religion, with its endless committee meetings and pledge drives and cleaning days. Worse yet, they become frustrated with the often profound indifference (or suspicion) that many devout Christians show toward mysticism and contemplation. But these feelings don't release them from their need for a community in which to ground their contemplative journey. The call to contemplation includes an invitation to relate to organized religion in creative and unusual ways. You must discern—through prayer and conversation with your soul friends or spiritual director—what that means in your own spiritual life.

Your interest in mysticism and contemplation will not magically make membership in a faith community easier. In fact, it may even be a source of frustration as you try to relate spiritually to those whose religious values seem at odds with your own. For all its challenges and problems, however, the church provides a vital ingredient in the life of Christian mystical spirituality. Find the church that is right for you, and stick with it. Don't be limited by the church, but don't settle for any notion that religion and spirituality must somehow be at odds. Learning to navigate the tension between religion and spirituality, even if only within yourself, can be a crucial element in opening your mind and heart to the splendor of God's grace and presence.

THE COMMUNITY OF TWO

To finish this exploration of the importance of community, I want to briefly mention one other important dimension of spiritual relationship—the most intimate form of community: the community of two.

Ever since Saint Paul provided mentoring to his young assistant Saint Timothy, Christianity has recognized the power of personal guidance as a tool for helping believers grow in their faith. This has also been true among mystics and contemplatives. Mentoring and guidance were important elements in the spirituality of the Desert Fathers and Mothers; in fact, one of the founders of European monasticism, John Cassian, traveled from Gaul (now France) to the deserts of Egypt to receive mentoring from the Desert Fathers (even today such a trip is not casually made; in the fifth century it was an arduous and dangerous journey). *The Cloud of Unknowing*, a four-teenth century manual on contemplation, was written by a spiritual direc-tor for his young directee. Margery Kempe, writing in the early fifteenth century, describes how she received spiritual direction from the reclusive Julian of Norwich. In sixteenth century Spain, Teresa of Avila provided spiritual guidance to John of the Cross, both of whom are now recognized as among the greatest of Christian mystics; in twentieth century England, Evelyn Underhill received mentoring from Friedrich von Hügel (in his day quite renowned for his writings on mysticism, although now his directee is more widely known than he is).

The experience of one-on-one mentoring or guidance in the spiri-tual life is far more intimate than the kind of religious education or faith instruction found in most church congregations, or even in small groups devoted to prayer and spirituality. The ability to turn to an elder for advice and guidance has, unfortunately, not always been readily available to or-dinary Christians—for many centuries, serious spiritual guidance was usually available only to clergy, nuns, or monks. But beginning in the mid-twentieth century, interest in spiritual formation among lay Christians has increased, as more and more people have sought spiritual mentoring, not only from clergy, monks, and nuns, but also from other laypersons. This, in turn, has led to increasing numbers of Christians, both clergy and lay-persons, taking on the role of spiritual mentor and providing guidance to those who are interested in a deeper life of prayer. As a consequence, many churches now offer training programs to help mature Christians develop the skills necessary to provide mentoring to others.

Of course, full-time priests and ministers who have also been profes-sionally trained (and who work full-time for their churches) often provide spiritual mentoring to those who seek it. But not all priests and ministers have the time or the interest in such one-on-one guidance. Thus, personal spiritual mentoring is something that can happen in the most informal of ways, and some of the best spiritual directors may not necessarily have any official training at all. Whenever two people with a shared interest in the spiritual life come together for mutual support and encouragement, one-on-one spiritual guidance can occur. At its most informal, such personalized spiritual support can even be shared between friends who are willing to listen to one another and respond to each other's spiritual journey with thoughtfulness and care.

In other words, spiritual *friendship*, regardless of how casual and informal it may be, can be just as valuable as a more formal mentoring or guidance relationship. The Celtic Christians had a special word to describe the beauty of this type of spiritual relationship: *anamchara*, meaning "soul friend."

For anyone interested in the Christian contemplative life, working with a spiritual director or cultivating a close relationship with a soul friend can be an integral part of the journey. As beneficial as reading the writings of the great mystics or participating in a centering prayer or monastic oblate group may be, there are clear advantages to working with a wise mentor who can answer your particular questions and point out specific areas where your practice needs attention. A gifted spiritual director can be especially helpful in supporting a contemplative practice and helping you in any aspects of your spiritual life, including discerning God's will or call in your life. A mentor can help you navigate the challenges of church membership and examine practical ways to integrate spirituality into the mundane aspects of your life. If you're serious about pursuing contemplative spirituality, try to find a trusted spiritual director or soul friend.[31]

In today's consumer-oriented, instant-gratification society, it is far too easy to approach mysticism (Christian or otherwise) as if it were just another "thing" to be consumed or enjoyed. We have an ingrained cultural expectation that we will be entertained, thrilled, or pleased by all that we do and "consume." Unfortunately, this expectation now extends to religion. While it is right to find joy and pleasure in relating to God, it's important not to reduce mysticism to a mere means of inner gratification. Christian community—from spiritual direction, to small prayer-oriented groups, to the larger church congregation—can help you avoid this trap. When you embed your contemplative walk in a community setting, you are far less likely to relate to God as merely a source of spiritual entertainment.

A community, and a soul friend or spiritual director, can help keep you honest and provide you with the support you need to remain focused on the true heart of Christian mysticism—learning to become a living manifestation of the love of God.

CHAPTER 10

Kenosis and Perichoresis

Let the same mind be in you that was in Christ Jesus, who, though he was in the form of God, did not regard equality with God as something to be exploited, but emptied himself, taking the form of a slave, being born in human likeness.

PHILIPPIANS 2:5-7

God became man so that man might become God.

ATHANASIUS[32]

Christian mysticism—and, for that matter, Christian community—invites you into a real, life-transforming relationship with Jesus of Nazareth, the Christ (anointed one) of God. Many resources exist to help you create and nurture this bond. The exercises we will explore in the coming chapters—lectio divina, meditation, prayer, and contemplation—all support a deepening intimacy with Christ. But you may also encounter Jesus in other, no less important, ways. He speaks through the stories of the faith, especially as recorded in the gospels; and great works of art, church architecture, literature, hymns, and praise music also testify to him. You may encounter Christ in the sacraments of the church, Holy Baptism and Holy Communion, as well as through inspiring sermons and joyful worship. Christ is present in the lives of other people, particularly those who are vulnerable, poor, in need, or in some other way remind us of our own imperfection or brokenness. He also speaks through the lives and witness of the saints and mystics—the "heroes" of the Christian faith, both past and present, who have given their entire lives over to the service of love. In fact, Christ most surely is present whenever you experience genuine love, especially love that is freely given without any thought of selfish reward.

THE HISTORICAL JESUS, THE CHRIST OF FAITH, AND THE MYSTICAL BODY

Over the past century or so, many Christians have devoted significant energy to a quest for the "Jesus of history"—an attempt to understand, as fully as possible, who Jesus was when he walked the earth and what can truly be known about him. Often, this quest includes a critical or skeptical tendency to reject the miracles and supernatural stories about Jesus as mere mythology. For many people, this quest is both an expression of faith and a laudable attempt to keep Christianity relevant in the age of scientific thinking.

Because mysticism begins with the understanding that we can never know God fully but can only approach God through love, the focus of contemplative practice is somewhat different from the quest for the historical Jesus. Scholarly Christianity and contemplative spirituality can co-exist beautifully, but strictly speaking the quest for the historical Jesus is an academic, rather than spiritual, exercise. Mysticism seeks a relationship with Christ grounded in two other, equally important, ways of knowing him—by encountering the Christ of faith and by immersion in the mystical body. These are heart-centered approaches to Christ, in contrast (but not in opposition) to the primarily academic approach of the quest for the Jesus of history.

The Christ of faith is, in the words of Saint Paul, a mystery: "Christ in you, the hope of glory" (Colossians 1:27). He comes to you from within, where you may encounter the mystery of Christ's presence in and through your own thoughts, feelings, hopes, imagination, dreams, and love—as well as your shame, your secrets, your rage and jealousy, and all the many ways you resist love. Because God is love, Christ in you represents the coming of love into the totality of your being, but this is not a sentimental, "feel-good" love. The love of Christ is a force for healing, an agent of transformation, and a challenge to *metanoia*—a word often anemically translated as repentance or conversion, but which in the original Greek has a much richer meaning of "changing your mind" or perhaps more accurately "adopting a new consciousness." The Christ of faith is not a harsh task-master and does not place unreasonable expectations on you, but does ask you to follow him, and to take responsibility for your own limitations, mistakes, and failings. Whereas the Jesus of history is someone you can learn about but have no emotional investment in (just as you might learn about the kings and queens of England or any other historical figures), the Christ of faith demands a response. Do you love him? Are you willing to follow him? Do you agree to accept the challenge and the promise of *metanoia*, opening your mind, heart, and your soul so that Christ's Holy Spirit can slowly transform you into love, and make you a member of his mystical body? These are the questions the Christ of faith asks of you. By saying "yes," you change your life for all eternity—and you embark on the spiritual journey.

When you say yes to the Christ of faith, you are also saying yes to the mystical body of Christ. It is only by the eyes of faith, given to you by

Christ, that you will be empowered to see, and encounter Christ in his mystical body—that is to say, in the community of believers. Through the Christ of faith, your perception of the community of Christ's followers will be transformed, enabling you to see his presence among those who love him. Perhaps you are wondering why I'm discussing the importance of a relationship with Christ after the chapter in which I insist on membership in a church or some other faith community. I have two reasons for doing so. First, for all its many flaws, the community of faith (the church) remains the vehicle by which Christ's wisdom and teachings have been transmitted through the ages. To truly meet Christ, you need to encounter his mystical body. It's good to read about Jesus in the Bible, but the far more essential way to get to know him is through the lives of others who have already committed to following him, however imperfectly. But my main reason for beginning with the communal aspect of Christian mysticism is because we live in such an individualistic age. Someone could easily pretend to be a "Christian mystic" without bothering to participate in a community of faith; but hardly anyone will engage in the mysteries of Christ without paying at least some attention to Jesus. With this in mind, it seemed important to me to emphasize community as the essential starting point for the contemplative way.

As you develop your inner relationship with the Christ of faith, you will see that this hidden (mystical) bond with him depends on your outer connection with the community of faith—*and vice versa*. You won't last very long in a church if you don't continually return to the wellsprings within you to drink the refreshing waters of your own loving connection with Jesus. Likewise, that interior relationship needs to be continually supported, nurtured, and at times challenged, by your membership in the mystical body—the community of people who share your love for Christ and his wisdom.

Incidentally, the mystical body of Christ means more than just all the Christians who are alive today. All the saints, martyrs, and mystics of the past remain part of the mystical body, and although in earthly terms they have died, they continue to live in Christ. For that matter, the mystical body even includes all the generations yet to be born. "Jesus Christ is the same yesterday and today and forever" (Hebrews 13:8).

THE FIRST STEP TOWARD THEOSIS IS KENOSIS

Christian mystical wisdom points to a glorious destiny. Saint Paul instructs us to let the mind of Christ be in us, and Saint Peter notes that those who are in Christ are called to be partakers of the divine nature. These tantalizing hints in the New Testament point to what Greek Orthodox Christians call *theosis*, which in English means deification or divinization: to become God-like, to be filled with the utter fullness of God. While this sounds like the ultimate "prize" of the mystical life, it needs to be understood not as a goal, but as a promise. Mortals do not attain deification like an Olympic athlete wins a gold medal. Rather, your task is to approach Christ in confidence of his love for you, trusting that he will give you the gift of his own divinity. Like all gifts, you have no control over how the gift is given to you, when you will receive it (or, perhaps more accurately, when you will *realize* that you've received it), or even what the experience of receiving the gift will be like. But as an aspiring contemplative, what you *do* have control over is the way in which you approach Christ, in humble trust and faith for the promise. The mystical key to how we can best accept the promise of deification lies in another Greek concept: *kenosis*.

Kenosis literally means "empty." It's a rich word that carries other shades of meaning, including "futility" and "foolishness." It appears only a couple of times in the New Testament, but the most essential passage comes from the second chapter of Philippians, in which Saint Paul sings the praises of Christ: "who, though he was in the form of God ...*emptied* himself... being born in human likeness" (Philippians 2:5-7). Paul tells us that Jesus did not grasp or hoard his divine nature. For Christ, the character of his divinity is not power, or glory, or might, but rather emptiness, humility, obedience, and even death. Jesus realized that the splendor of being the Son of God meant that he could empty himself of his very Godliness.

This has powerful implications for Christian mysticism, and for anyone interested in the contemplative life.

First of all, mystical Christianity is less about attaining unity with God and more about creating the inner emptiness where you can offer God hospitality. This has implications in how you read the Bible, how you pray, and ultimately how you relate to silence, both externally and internally.

Likewise, to the extent that God does pour divinity into you, the point is not to hoard the glory of your privileged relationship with the Ultimate Mystery, but rather to immediately give it away, by lavishly loving, caring for, and serving other people. Jesus taught that "All who exalt themselves will be humbled, and all who humble themselves will be exalted" (Matthew 23:12). If you yearn for *theosis* because of your longing for communion with God, you are wise to set your heart on kenosis, emptying yourself of your fear, your hatred, your pride, your arrogance, and your sense of entitlement or self-importance, choosing instead to give yourself away and to lose yourself in love. This, truly, is the doorway into the Christian mystery.

Opening Out to the Holy Trinity

"Where Jesus is spoken of, the Holy Trinity is always to be understood," said Julian of Norwich.[33] I know a Trappist monk who believes that one of the problems with Christianity is that we tend to over-emphasize Jesus and under-emphasize the Trinity. I think he's right. As central as Jesus is to Christian mysticism, the mystery of the Holy Trinity is central to the mystery of Jesus.

"Mystery" really is the operative word here. If you try to just make rational sense of the Trinity, you may well reach the conclusion that it is little more than a fancy piece of artificial dogma—in which early Christian theologians tried to reconcile their stated belief in the oneness of God with the obvious threeness of the Father, Jesus Christ, and the Holy Spirit. I believe the Trinity "makes sense" only when approached mystically, rather than logically. Rich in paradox and functioning like a Western koan, the Trinity forces us to accept that God simply cannot be reduced to the level of human reason. Someone once said "If God were small enough to understand, then He wouldn't be big enough to worship." The Holy Trinity is mystical evidence that God is indeed far too big to figure out!

Once you let go of having to make the triune God fit into your mind, you are free to approach the Trinity with your heart instead. What the mind cannot fathom, the heart gently can embrace. The Trinity "works" because it is, first and foremost, about love. The Father, the Son, and the Holy Spirit are united *in love*, and form a community within the perfect unity of God. The communion between the Creator, the Christ, and the Spirit is splendid in that they are personally distinct and simply one, simultaneously and eternally. Julian was right: when we speak of Christ, we truly are speaking of the Trinity, so seamless is their union and integration. And yet, the Father is not the Son, for it is only in their distinctness that they have the space to love each other. And the same holds for the Holy Spirit. Perfectly one, and perfectly distinct; their mystical nature embodies the fullness of love itself.

A wonderful Greek word helps to illuminate the splendor of the Trinity: *perichoresis*, which literally means "mutual indwelling," suggesting that each person of the Trinity gracefully abides with and in each other. It comes from the roots *peri-* meaning "around" and *chorein* meaning "to move." On a poetic level, *perichoresis* evokes a lovely image—of a circle dance (think of similar words like "perimeter" and "choreography"). The Trinity is an eternal, joyful, radiant manifestation of love, loving, and being loved. Three dancers join together in one eternal dance. The love that flows between and in and among the Father, Son, and Holy Spirit is the very love that creates, sustains, and keeps the universe. It is the love by which you live, and to which you will return when you die. Becoming intimate with God means you participate in the dance.

THE DYNAMICS OF THE CIRCLE

Remember the message encoded in Ephesians 3: God is in us, because we are in Christ. As members of the mystical body, Christians actually partake in the divine nature of the Trinity. We do not merely *watch* the dance, we *dance* the dance. We join hands with Christ and the Spirit flows through us and between us and our feet move always in the loving embrace of the Father. In that we are members of the mystical body of Christ, we see the joyful love of the Father through the eyes of the Son. And with every breath, we breathe the Holy Spirit.

Christian mysticism emerges out of the ineffable truth that God and Christ are one, and that the community of Christ's followers are one with him. But just as the doctrine of the Trinity reminds us that Christ's unity with the Father does not erase their personal distinctions, so will our unique identities as lovers/followers of Christ never be erased, no matter how fully we enter into the dance. When we open our hearts to the Christ of faith, we are opening ourselves up to the endless delight of the *perichoresis*. Through the self-emptying of kenosis whereby we replace pride with humility, fear with love, and self-absorption with self-emptying, we create the space within us where the dance may occur. God comes to dwell in us because we abide in Christ. It all makes perfect sense, and yet it is beyond the mind to grasp. The dance illuminates our hearts, and to enter into it means to embrace a profound darkness marked by unknowing and paradox.

Keep in mind as you reflect on the promise of joy at the heart of the Trinitarian dance, that one of the dancers has wounds on his hands. Christ is the victorious God-man, but he is also the crucified victim. He died to remove our sins—understood mystically, this means he died to empty us of everything within us that resists the love of God, anything and everything that we cannot remove by our own efforts. The crucifixion marks the climax of Christ's own kenosis and through this the dynamics of the circle changed forever. In Christ's emptiness, you will find the grace to receive love, but also the call to embrace your own suffering as you give that love away. Although everyone's path is different, eventually everyone comes to a place of loss and suffering. With Christ as your guide, you can enter into the pain that comes to you, not in a masochistic way, but with confidence and trust—viewing your own "cross" as the means by which you will undergo your own resurrection. You cannot do this by yourself; only by the grace of God is it possible. Because God comes to you as the self-emptied Christ, you need not be afraid of him and you may follow his own life-giving example. As part of the body of Christ, you will carry your own cross. But the path leads not just to death, but also to the resurrection. And the dancers will accompany you every step of the way.

CHAPTER 11

The Path of Holiness

As God's chosen ones, holy and beloved, clothe yourselves with compassion,
kindness, humility, meekness, and patience.

COLOSSIANS 3:12

Do not think to found holiness upon doing; holiness must be founded upon being.
Works do not make us holy. It is we who must make works holy.
For no matter how holy works may be, they do not make us holy because we do
them, but in so far as we within ourselves are as we should be, we make holy
all that we do, whether it be eating, or sleeping, or working, or what it may.

MEISTER ECKHART[34]

When I first became interested in the Christian mystical life, I began to read as many of the writings of the great mystics as I could find—Brother Lawrence, Teresa of Avila, John of the Cross, Julian of Norwich, Walter Hilton, and others. I had a naïve notion that these ancient writings were basically self-help manuals that would "clue me in" to the secrets of mystical spirituality, with foolproof instructions on how to quickly experience ecstatic union with God. Needless to say, I was very promptly disappointed. What I found again and again was that many of the great contemplatives in the Christian tradition wrote about holiness far more than they wrote about their mystical experiences. Although modern interpreters of Christian mysticism like Evelyn Underhill and Bernard McGinn recommended all these historical writers, it seemed as if everywhere I turned I found discussions of repentance, obedience, humility, purification, and virtue, rather than of mysticism as I defined it.

I learned that the classical model for the Christian mystical life consisted of three stages: purgation, illumination, and union. But it seemed to me as if all the mystics were so focused on the "purgative" stage that they never got around to talking about illumination or union. However, the more I explored mysticism—the more I struggled with my own faltering and mediocre efforts at trying to live a life of "joyful penitence"—the more I began to see why the teachings of mysticism are so heavily weighted toward the purgative way.

Mysticism and Holiness

"Not everyone is called to be a mystic," says a monk I know, "but everyone *is* called to holiness." Mysticism is often equated with extraordinary or supernatural phenomena and, certainly, in its most dramatic forms, it *is* both extraordinary and supernatural. But only a very small number of Christians are destined for such a dramatic experience as the presence of God, just as only a few musicians can be as great as Mozart or John Coltrane, and only a few athletes reach the pinnacle of achievement as Olympic gold medalists.

If mysticism involves only extraordinary, singular, and rare experiences of God's supernatural activity, then any kind of desire to obtain such mystical experiences paradoxically suggests a lack of humility. Jesus made it clear that becoming humble, "like a child," is the path to heaven (Matthew 18:4). Given this mandate to be humble, how can we square that with an ambition (no matter how "spiritual") to have the most extraordinary experiences of God—experiences that most Christians, indeed most people, never will enjoy? "Humility goes before honor," insists the Book of Proverbs, which seems to confirm that the honor of enjoying mystical experiences can only truly be given to us after we have chosen the path of humility. This implies that true mysticism can occur only in the lives of those who couldn't care less if they are mystics or not.

If mysticism, understood as consisting of supernatural or ecstatic encounters with God, is only for the chosen few, however, holiness is for everyone. Moreover, it is proper, indeed necessary, for all Christians to seek the grace of holiness in their lives. But mysticism can also be understood in an egalitarian and inclusive way. By this understanding, you don't have to have supernatural experiences in order to be a mystic; therefore, everyone is called, if not to a life of extraordinary phenomena, then at least to the "ordinary mysticism" of the contemplative life. However, if you don't bother with the demands of holiness, but focus your energy on "being a mystic," you are likely to end up like the hapless person in Jesus' parable who built a house on sand. The first storm (i.e., the first challenge to your so-called spirituality that comes your way) will probably cause your spiritual house to topple.

So if you have a "high" view of mysticism and believe it is something supernatural that is given to only a chosen few, it makes sense to focus your efforts on living a holy life. Indeed, the quest for holiness is the best way to offer yourself to God, leaving it entirely up to him whether you are graced with mystical experience. On the other hand, if your view of mysticism, like mine, is more egalitarian, it only makes sense to consider that a slow, undramatic, unspectacular process of joyful transformation into the self-forgetful, God-centered life of holiness may be the only sure way to anchor your contemplative aspirations on a rock-solid foundation. It is the altar on which you humbly offer yourself to God. To seek the mystical life, you must seek a holy life.

Whichever way you approach mysticism, it appears that the great mystics of the Christian tradition got it right. All three dimensions of the mystical life—purgation, illumination, and union—are driven by grace. But of the three, it is through purgation that you are called to cooperate most actively with God's grace. Purgation is the area of the contemplative life that is the most dependent on your choices and actions. That's why the great teachers of the tradition emphasize it so much in their teaching. As John Ruusbroec said: "You are as holy as you want to be."[35]

We live in an age when holiness, like many other core elements of Christian spirituality, has become both marginalized and controversial, even within the church itself. On the one hand, many Christians seem upset with what they believe is a lack of emphasis on righteousness in to-day's church. Others, both inside and outside the church, feel that holiness has too often been used to put down those who don't fit the institutional mold. Some might argue that the call to holiness has not been particularly useful at inspiring the average person to embody the Christian "fruits of the Spirit," like love, joy, peace, kindness, and goodness. While we can't resolve or even fully examine these arguments here, we can acknowledge the place holiness holds in the wisdom of the great mystics, and use that as our starting point in exploring how mystical wisdom (including the mandate to be holy) can make a difference for Christians today—especially for those who seek to enter the divine mystery through the path of contemplation.

UNDERSTANDING HOLINESS

What does it mean to live a holy life? This is not a question we often hear, not even in many churches. For good or for ill, holiness has fallen out of favor. While some may applaud this as evidence that our society has moved beyond superstitious religious repression, and others may decry it as evidence that our culture has become lost in a miasma of narcissism and self-indulgence, I think it may have to do with a profound sense of doubt and even anxiety that arises from our attempts to integrate the spiritual/religious worldview we inherited from our ancestors with the new, emerging perspectives of our age, shaped by globalism, new communication technologies, science, and postmodern philosophy.

Part of the challenge we face as we try to understand holiness today is the fact that so many different approaches to questions of ethics, morality, and goodness have become part of our cultural landscape. While everyone may still agree that murder and theft are bad and helping others and showing deference to the elderly and handicapped are good, in many other ways, our society simply has no unified, consensual understanding of what constitutes holiness—at least in a comprehensive sense of the word. Does "being holy" entail heroic acts of virtue, like the years Mother Teresa spent serving the poorest of the poor in Calcutta? Is it possible to be holy and yet still struggle with serious imperfections, addictive behaviors, and besetting sins—the kinds of mistakes we make over and over no matter how hard we try (and pray) to do better? Is holiness just something that "great" people embody, or is it something that can be found in the little old lady who sits quiet and unnoticed at the back of the church every Sunday?

Even within the Christian faith community, there are significant differences of belief that contribute to sometimes radical differences of opinion. I heard a popular young Christian author asked, at a recent appearance on a college campus, to express his opinion about a controversial moral issue. I was impressed by his carefully considered response. He paused a moment (I suspect he was praying), and then talked about the differences of opinion concerning this particular issue within the church. Without revealing his own stance, he noted: "We Christians have to learn how to disagree well." He then went on to state that he felt it was our job as Christians to love other people, not to judge or convict them. When he finished speaking, the audience applauded.

I know not everyone was happy with this author's response to this hot-button question. Some may have wanted him to speak more definitively about it; perhaps half the audience wanted him to make a declaration on one side of the issue, while the others equally desired to hear a statement in support of the opposing side. But instead of taking sides, the speaker acknowledged the controversy, and then spoke eloquently about how love and compassion and understanding can help transform even our conflicts and disagreements. And there are plenty of conflicts and disagreements over the many divisive questions facing the Christian community today. Questions about sexual morality, about how Christians should relate to the environment, how they should relate to persons of other faiths, what our responsibilities are to those who are economically deprived or politically oppressed, and what constitutes a Christian understanding of bioethics, medical ethics, and other concerns where moral decision making must be applied to the ever-evolving and increasingly complex world of science and technology are just a few of the challenging issues faced by the faithful today. Unfortunately, it is so easy to become caught up in these contentious issues that Christians can lose sight of the many distinctive and unifying ways that the wisdom of Jesus can lead all people to holiness. A commitment to contemplative spirituality includes a call to holiness that goes beyond merely finding the "right" side of contemporary conflicts. Rather, it calls us to seek a higher perspective where even bitter disagreements might find resolution by the leading of the Holy Spirit.

Many of the conflicts at the heart of Christianity (including most of the ones I listed in the preceding paragraph) arise out of the evolving and uncertain relationship between Christian ethics and scientific knowledge. Those who seek the splendors of mysticism, however, would be wise to avoid the hard extremes that can be found at either end of this ideological spectrum—those who reject all scientific knowledge and non-Christian wisdom out of hand, as well as those who dismiss all Christian perspectives. Both of these perspectives can be rigid, unyielding, and, frankly, self-righteous. Whether we like it or not, ours is an age in which our collective spiritual wisdom must be forged in a great and grand conversation between traditional Christian values and the vast pool of human knowledge and insight that exists in the scientific community and, for that matter, in the wisdom traditions of other faiths and philosophies. In the midst of that grand conversation, we must ask: What does it mean to embrace—and to seek—a holy life?

There is no simple formula for achieving holiness, other than to seek God's grace as you grapple with the big questions of life and with your own personal process of surrendering sin and cultivating virtue. There are, however, certain steps you can take to help you determine the unique way that holiness will characterize your own contemplative walk.

THE FIRST STEP

The Hebrew word for holy is *qodesh*, which means "set apart" or "consecrated." The Greek counterpart is *hagios*, which has a connotation of "religious awe." From these words, we can recognize the first and most fundamental truth about holiness: only God is truly holy. Only God is fully set apart from the messiness and brokenness and corruption that infects human life—the stuff that leads inevitably to suffering, pain, and ultimately death. But God's holiness is more than just a type of purity. For while God is indeed set apart from the messiness of mortal existence, he also—in the person of Jesus Christ—chose to become immersed in our decidedly not-very-holy world. So holiness is paradoxical. It has a quality of being set apart, consecrated, great enough to inspire awe, and yet it continually gives itself away, undermining its own set-apart-ness and immersing itself in the very mess above which it stands. The Holy One entered the less-than-holy world in the physical life of Jesus Christ, and does so perpetually through the ongoing action of the Holy Spirit.

I believe that aspiring contemplatives can embrace the universal call to holiness by taking on a more holistic, inclusive, and comprehensive approach to holiness, gently holding on to this paradox between holiness as being set apart and the Holy One's immersion in the non-holy world. Jesus identified the two dimensions of holiness in two great commandments:

> *You shall love the Lord your God with all your heart, and with all your soul, and with all your mind.*

and

> *You shall love your neighbor as yourself.*

"On these two commandments," he insists, "hang all the law and the prophets" (Matthew 22:35-40).

Love God with all your heart, soul, and mind, he tells us (other versions add "strength"). This is the call to be set apart, to immerse yourself in God and his love, seeking purity that can come only as a gift from God. You cannot, by your own efforts, make yourself pure, any more than you can, by your own efforts, prevent the inevitable march of old age and death. Whatever purity you may have—whether moral rectitude or an innocent ability to live in love and joy and all the other fruits of the Spirit (Galatians 5:22-3)—you enjoy it, not by dint of your own efforts, but through the grace of God. Your "effort" to become holy consists primarily in getting out of your own way, cultivating in yourself a spirit of willingness, allowing God the freedom within you to give you the transforming power of his grace.

Then follows the second commandment: to love your neighbors as yourself. Notice that the standard for loving others is how well you love yourself. Jesus isn't saying, however, that if you hate yourself you have permission to hate others! Rather, encoded in this commandment about loving others is a subtle directive to love yourself as well. The implication is that you ought to love yourself—and others—with the same pure love that God has for you.

It will most likely take all of us a lifetime to learn how to obey just these two commandments. I am convinced that if every Christian, especially every aspiring contemplative, made a rock-solid, serious commitment to live according to these two directives, much of the tension and conflict that exists between Christians of different denominations, or between "conservatives" and "liberals," or "traditionalists" and "emergents," would simply disappear. When you stop judging others and start loving them instead, you create space in your heart for the Holy Spirit to enter and lead you into holiness. Likewise, take care to stop judging yourself, thereby creating space in your heart for a healthy self-love—not a narcissistic pleasure-seeking love, but a mature love that is inspired by and seeks to imitate the love God has for you.

I know a monk whose daily prayer is this: "God, teach me how to love the way you do." This, then, is the first step to living a holy life. And for most of us, it is a lifelong assignment.

The Second Step

Making a commitment to live a life of love may be the heart and soul of holiness, but as soon as we make that commitment, a new question arises: How do we know the love of God? What can we do to cultivate that love in our hearts, both as a response to divine love, and to more perfectly (or less imperfectly) love ourselves and our neighbors?

Living a life of love is the key to holiness, but it is open to so many possible interpretations that it ends up being almost meaningless. One person may have a notion of "tough love" that seems at odds with someone else's rather sentimental idea of love as "everybody's happy." Then there are the questions of the relationship between love and justice, or love and self-restraint, or love and nonviolence. How do we truly comprehend the idea of loving God and loving our neighbors?

Traditionally, Christians have turned to the heart of Jewish ethics—the Ten Commandments given to Moses on Mount Sinai—as a blueprint for the life of love. This simple and ancient moral code still inspires us with its clarity and its demands. Sadly, for many today, the Ten Commandments have become the symbol of conflict between people with different political perspectives on the boundaries that separate church and state. For others, they have become so familiar that they have lost their power to challenge and confront. We've heard them so many times that our eyes just kind of glaze over when we encounter them again.

But the Ten Commandments play an important role in the mystical quest for holiness. And perhaps the most powerful interpretation of the commandments I have seen in this regard comes from theologian Brian Haggerty. In his book *Out of the House of Slavery: On the Meaning of the Ten Commandments*, Haggerty looks at the Ten Commandments as a code of liberating directives, shaped by the experience of the Hebrew people.

At the time of Moses, when the Hebrews received the commandments, they had just been liberated from centuries of enslavement in Egypt. Haggerty suggests that, to truly understand the full meaning and power of the commandments, we need to understand them as a sort of spiritual "Declaration of Independence." The chosen people of God obey these commandments as a sign of their liberation from all human forms of oppression or slavery. Haggerty points out that most English translations of the Bible fail to convey the concept of freedom that lies at the heart of the commandments, and provides his own "restatement" of the laws:

1. You shall not worship transitory gods but shall serve only the living God.

2. You shall not enshrine any notion, ideology, or interest as God and allow yourself to be dominated by it.

3. You shall not lay exclusive claim to God's blessing or call upon God to bless your selfish purposes.

4. Show reverence for the land; regard those who labor with respect.

5. Treat the elderly with respect and deference.

6. You shall not threaten the lives of others by your aggressive or irresponsible behavior.

7. You shall not threaten another person's marriage or family life.

8. You shall not deprive other people of their freedom.

9. You shall not cause another person to be treated unjustly.

10. You shall not grasp after what belongs to someone else or seek for yourself what belongs to all people.[36]

The first three commandments teach us how to love God; the remaining seven provide an ethical framework for our love for our neighbors and ourselves. Let's look at each of these in turn.

To serve only the living God and not worship transitory gods does not merely imply forsaking the worship of false deities. It speaks to a much broader understanding of what it takes to remain faithful to God. It forbids all actions by which we place our ultimate hope and trust in anything other than the Ultimate Mystery, from whom we derive our being, our salvation, and ultimately our holiness. Examples of such transitory gods include money, the stock market, real estate, and other material goods. Some place their trust in human knowledge. Others bow before the government, employers, parents, or cultural icons. Sources of pleasure often become our gods, and there is often a fine line between worshipping something and becoming addicted to it.

Traditionally, the second commandment forbids the creation and veneration of idols. Haggerty raises the stakes by reminding us that idolatry can extend far beyond the worship of graven images. We can make idols out of political or economic systems, philosophies of life, and even our religions. As Haggerty points out, to worship an idol means, sooner or later, to allow ourselves to be dominated by it. Only in the worship of the God who transcends all idols and all ideologies can we truly be free.

The third commandment, enjoining us not to take the Lord's name in vain, has been debased in our culture to mean "don't swear." Indeed, swearing is impolite and often may arise from a heart shaped more by anger than love, but it is only the tip of the problem that this commandment addresses. To "not lay exclusive claim to God's blessing or call upon God to bless our selfish purposes" reminds us that we love to be in control. We try again and again to shape God in our own image, usually by insisting that he behave the way we expect him to (in accord with our own favored way of interpreting the Bible). We have a long and sorry history of trying to use God to justify our own selfish aims, with just one glaring example being how Christians as recently as the nineteenth century insisted that the Bible justifies slavery. This commandment reminds us that, whenever we try to use the name of God to promote hatred, oppression, judgmentalism, or social privilege, we are using the Lord's name in vain.

The fourth commandment, traditionally "remember the Sabbath," challenges us to balance work with rest, labor with leisure, and—perhaps most important for aspiring mystics—activity with contemplation. Haggerty injects a social and political dimension to this law by linking respect for laborers with respect for the land. Rather than taking a legalistic view of "keeping Sabbath" (which Jesus continually ignored, landing him in trouble again and again), Haggerty recommends honoring the spiritual dimension of this commandment: Respect the gifts of nature and human toil to create wealth, and do so by creating space for rest and rejuvenation.

The fifth commandment, "honor your father and mother," can be understood in the broader sense of treating all the elderly with kindness and respect. I would add to this a moral imperative to care for those who are handicapped or disadvantaged. Striving to honor the most vulnerable members of society is an important component of working to respect the dignity and worth of all people.

The injunction not to kill is perhaps the most transparent of the commandments. But Jesus added another dimension to it by suggesting that "killing" someone in the anger of your heart is, morally speaking, as great a failing as actual violence. Haggerty expands on this by suggesting that threatening others, through either vicious or negligent actions, is also a kind of "killing" that is forbidden under this commandment.

The commandment against adultery has become strongly associated with sexual acts outside of marriage. While integrity in sexuality is certainly an important aspect of Christian life, Haggerty reworks this commandment by taking the focus off of a narrow rejection of sexual wrongdoing, and expanding it to a prohibition against anything that can destroy marriage or family bonds, including emotional infidelity, breach of trust, or the poisoning of another's relationship, for whatever reason.

Likewise, Haggerty turns the self-explanatory "Do not steal" into a more sweeping prohibition against anything that threatens another's freedom. To deprive people of their rightful property, he claims, undermines their freedom to use or enjoy what belongs to them. His perspective on this commandment suggests that, anytime we impinge on other people's individual sovereignty, we steal from them, depriving them of dignity, identity, and freedom. This theft is contrary to the will of God.

The ninth commandment prohibits lying, which Haggerty describes as "causing another person to be treated unjustly." Here, he forces us to face the reason why lying is contrary to holiness. It is, he points out, a fundamentally unjust act that destroys relationships, trust, and possibly even entire communities. Whether it is a stated untruth or a passive deception, lying undermines the bonds of honor and goodwill that hold relationships and communities together.

For Haggerty, the last commandment against coveting another person's belongings extends not only to other individuals, but also to society as a whole. This has powerful environmental as well as social implications. Like the prohibition against stealing or dishonesty, however, this commandment challenges us to let go of any action by which we secretly place our own interests above those of others.

The Ten Commandments should not be regarded as a rule book that provides concrete, relevant guidance for every possible ethical challenge we face. As concise ethical statements that challenge the human family to surrender dysfunctional self-interest in favor of a more expansive and generous commitment to family and community, however, they make a powerful statement about love. True spiritual love elevates us out of egocentric, "me-first" morality, demanding instead that relationships and bonds of trust and goodwill define our understanding of right and wrong.

If you are like me, even these simple ethical guidelines may leave you feeling humbled (if not ashamed) at your own inability to live a truly holy life. It's tempting, when faced with our own stubborn sinfulness, to decide that the quest for holiness is for others, that we lack what it takes to achieve holiness. The truth is, we *do* lack what it takes—all of us, even those who manage to "look" holy. And this is where grace comes in. You cannot earn God's love and favor—not by being holy, or super-religious, or, for that matter, by being a contemplative or a mystic. Thus, you're faced with the paradox of being called to live according to uncompromising ethical standards while, at the same time, being loved and accepted *just as you are* through God's grace. The quest for holiness is not something you do in order to make yourself perfect; it is something you do in response to the fact that God already loves you so perfectly.

The Third Step

Together, the two great commandments of Jesus and the Ten Commandments of Moses provide brilliant general principles for ethical action. If you accept these two sets of commandments as the summation of your call to holiness, however, you run the risk of seeing holiness as merely a function of your human effort. But holiness is not primarily about your efforts; it's primarily about God's grace. Your efforts to become holy can be offered only in response to that grace. To help underline this spiritual truth, let's consider a third set of standards from the New Testament given in Galatians 5:22-3:

> The fruit of the Spirit is love, joy, peace, patience, kindness, generosity, faithfulness, gentleness, and self-control.

Paul's enigmatic comment describes the contours of a holy life, not in terms of what holiness *does*, but in a more existential sense of what holiness *is*. As there is no law against the fruit of the Spirit, so the qualities of holiness are not achieved by following rules. Rather, the characteristics of a holy life come to us through a variety of channels, including observance of the commandments, commitment to prayer, striving for emotional maturity and integrity, and—most important of all—reliance on grace.

Notice that love, the mandate of the two greatest commandments, takes its place as the first fruit of the Spirit. All the other fruits describe what a loving spirit looks like. A corollary to this is the famous "Love Chapter" in Corinthians often read at weddings, but useful far beyond its popular association with matrimony. It says, in part:

> Love is patient; love is kind; love is not envious or boastful or arrogant or rude. It does not insist on its own way; it is not irritable or resentful; it does not rejoice in wrongdoing, but rejoices in the truth. It bears all things, believes all things, hopes all things, endures all things (I Corinthians 13:4-7).

Ask yourself: Am I living a truly loving life? A truly joyful life? Am I marked by peace, by patience and goodness and kindness? Am I shaping my quest for holiness with faith and gentleness? Is self-control (moderation) a factor in my spiritual life?

Of course, no one can truthfully say he perfectly embodies the characteristics of love. The purpose behind these questions is not to shame you into discouragement or despair, but rather to remind you that, ultimately, holiness can come only through God's grace—and your humble willingness to ask for and receive that grace in your life. In a very real way, holiness is not something you "do" so much as it is something you *allow*—by getting your ego and your small-minded self-interest out of the way long enough to let God's love and joy and grace flow gently through you.

THE GIFT OF GRACE

Each of these Biblical descriptions of holiness functions as both a challenge and an inspiration. God loves you enough that he will not settle for second best in either your behavior or your character. While the commandments provide useful general guidelines to the parameters of holy or Godly behavior, ultimately you are called to a holy character, as Paul describes. Christians understand that all good things are gifts from God; therefore, the fruit of the Spirit is only yours by grace. Like all gifts from God, it is given to you, not for your pleasure or satisfaction, but for your well-being and your ability to love and serve others.

Thus, these gifts are rarely if ever given to us in an easy or instant way. The characteristics of holiness are slowly shaped and formed in us over time, just as all the characteristics associated with mystical spirituality—a contemplative outlook, the ability to meditate, an ongoing desire for God and the things of God, and a humble acceptance of our limitations tinged with sadness over our sinfulness—are all shaped and formed in us over time.

In other words, it is a mistake to assume that you must "master" the purgative way before hoping to enter into the splendor of illumination or union with God. Each of the three ways is a lifelong process. Purgation is never finished while you live and breathe on this earth. Like all aspects of mystical spirituality, holiness is a process.

CHAPTER 12

The Journey that Isn't a Journey

Draw near to God and he will draw near to you.

JAMES 4:8

All the way to heaven is heaven.

CATHERINE OF SIENA[37]

So far, you've anchored your commitment to Christ in a faith community; you've integrated yourself into the life of grace through worship and study, and you've begun, at least, to apply the virtues and values of Christ to your own life in an ongoing process of learning to love like God loves—what the tradition has variously called repentance, sanctification, or growth in holiness. Maybe it's not a perfect alliance, but, by integrating yourself into the outward forms of the Christian tradition, you have set the stage for focusing on a sustained cultivation of the inner life.

Now what?

In the next few chapters, we'll turn our attention to practices specifically associated with the contemplative life—including devotional reading, prayer, meditation, and contemplation, all exercises that can open us to receive the light of mystical wisdom. These spiritual practices are not just an extension of church piety, but rather an offering of your mind and body to God that makes you available for transfiguration into love. If community life and the quest for holiness constitute a type of contemplative boot camp, then these practices that we'll consider are like the first (and never-ending) assignments for a soldier who has made it through basic training. Now, we actually begin the journey—the one-day-at-a-time journey of contemplation.

The Contemplative Life as a Journey

One of the most common metaphors used for mysticism—indeed, for spirituality in general—is that of a journey. Perhaps the most obvious example of this is John Bunyan's *The Pilgrim's Progress*, a deeply symbolic and allegorical tale of a person called only "Christian" who journeys through the trials and tribulations of life as he perseveres toward the final goal: the Celestial City. Although Bunyan was writing in a general way about the life of faith and very likely did not consider himself a mystic, his work falls into a genre of writing that appears throughout the history of Christian mysticism.

Early mystics like Origen and Gregory of Nyssa found inspiration in Biblical tales of journey and pilgrimage—particularly the stories of Moses and the exodus of the freed Hebrew slaves who journeyed from Egypt to the Promised Land. In the Middle Ages, Dante explored mystical spirituality in his sprawling poem-epic *The Divine Comedy*, which describes a journey through hell, purgatory, and heaven. This allegorical journey is often understood in terms of climbing or ascending a ladder, a staircase, or a mountain, as seen in the titles of several major mystical writings: *The Ladder of Divine Ascent* by John Climacus, *The Stairway of Perfection* by Walter Hilton, and *The Ascent of Mount Carmel* by John of the Cross.

From the earliest Christian mystics onward, the *inner* process of transformation—the blossoming of inner beauty that characterizes the mystical life—has also been understood as a journey. Origen saw three of the poetic writings in the Hebrew Bible—Proverbs, Ecclesiastes, and the Song of Songs—as emblematic of three stages on the mystical path. The first, as symbolized by Proverbs, involves growth in virtue and living a holy and ethical life. Ecclesiastes embodies the second stage, in which we learn to live in a proper relationship with the natural, physical world and those who live in it. Finally, the Song of Songs represents the summit of the mystical journey, in which we ascend into the pure contemplation of God.

This three-stage model of the mystical life was embraced by other authors and, by the time of Pseudo-Dionysius in the sixth century, it had more or less stabilized as the threefold path of purgation, illumination, and union. In other words, the mystical life consists of growth in holiness, growth in awareness of the presence of God, and finally, participation in the divine nature (II Peter 1:4). We achieve each of these "stages," not by our own efforts, but entirely through the gift of God's grace.

Other mystics and contemplatives over the centuries have put forth other descriptions of the mystical path. In his wonderful anthology of essential Christian mystical writings, Bernard McGinn points out that, since every human being is unique, we all chart our own course toward God, even when we have the benefit of a supportive faith community and tradition to guide us along the way. In addition to the classic threefold path, McGinn notes that other mystics envisioned a journey with four, six, or even seven stages of transformation. Evelyn Underhill, in her study of mysticism published in the early twentieth century, expands the traditional threefold path to a five-stage journey: conversion, purgation, illumination, dark night, and union. More recently, American theologian Robert Hughes recast the traditional language into three "tides of the Spirit": conversion, transfiguration, and glory.

But not all mystics use the metaphor of a journey, nor do all consider it particularly useful. Instructive here is the Irish poet, philosopher, and mystic John O'Donohue, who said: "There is no spiritual program." In other words, we ought to be wary of linear models of mystical development that present the contemplative life as a nice tidy progression from point A to point B to point C. As O'Donohue notes: "When time is reduced to linear progress, it is emptied of presence." In other words, if you are so hypnotized by the notion of a journey, you can too easily dismiss your past as worthless and regard the present as merely an instrumental moment useful only for launching you into the future, which in turn is valuable only insofar as it beckons you to the next "stage." This model reflects the human insistence of being in control, which is at odds with the deep contemplative mandate to surrender our controlling into the love of God.

Hughes suggests that, as an alternative to a linear understanding of the three-stage journey, we use the metaphor of waves crashing on the beach to describe the various dimensions of spiritual growth and development. Water flows, dances, and cascades. Waves do not move in straight lines; they advance and recede according to the overall thrust of the tides. Hughes suggests that we think in terms of "tides of the Spirit" when talking about the journey of faith. This metaphor can help alleviate the temptation to think of the mystical life as a "ladder" involving prerequisites and an orderly, predictable sequence of development.

So again we enter the realm of paradox. Mysticism is a journey; and it's not a journey. It's a climb up the mountain; it's a transformation that happens right here, right now—no movement necessary. Since paradox is at the heart of mystical experience, the journey/not-journey becomes yet another key to unlocking the depth of the Christian mysteries.

Therefore, rather than try to describe various stages of "the mystical journey," let's try to think of these descriptions as a map, remembering that "the map is not the territory." Furthermore, as spiritual adventurers, we may sometimes throw the map away and explore terrain that has not yet been mapped out. And sometimes we may even find that the map is a bit outdated.

Let's start by looking at some of the elements that are often part of the contemplative or mystical life—some of the features on the map. Although many mystics and contemplatives follow the traditional model of purgation, illumination, and union, remember that the inner life is organic, and simply cannot be reduced to a universal model or outline. The manner in which you—or anyone else interested in the mystical life—may actually explore or experience the mysteries of Christian spirituality may be nothing like anything anyone has experienced before.

Ultimately, the particular contours of your relationship with God are between you and the Holy Spirit (and, perhaps, your spiritual director). The structure I have chosen for the next three chapters comes from a medieval manuscript of spiritual instruction for monks, written by Guigo the Carthusian (also known as Guigo II) to guide monks on the spiritual path. I assume most people reading this book today are not monks and never will be, but I think this wisdom remains relevant even for those of us with "secular" lives. After all, every journey—even a journeyless journey—has to follow some sort of map to begin with, even if the itinerary changes once the journey has begun. Contemplation requires not that we know where our destination might be, for ultimately that knowledge is God's alone. All the contemplative life asks of us is that we be willing to move forward in faith, one step at a time.

CHAPTER 13

Lectio Divina

Finally, beloved, whatever is true, whatever is honorable, whatever is just, whatever is pure, whatever is pleasing, whatever is commendable, if there is any excellence and if there is anything worthy of praise, think about these things.

PHILIPPIANS 4:8

Let all my world be silent in your presence, Lord, so that I may hear what the Lord God may say in my heart. Your words are so softly spoken that no one can hear them except in a deep silence. But to hear them lifts him who sits alone and in silence completely above his natural powers, because he who humbles himself will be lifted up. He who sits alone and listens will be raised above himself.

GUIGO II[38]

Lectio divina is a Latin term that means "sacred reading." It describes an ancient monastic practice that employs a particular method of reading—an approach to reading the Bible or some other worthy text, like the spiritual writings of a saint or mystic. Lectio divina is a unique approach to reading that enables you to open up the time you spend with the written word so that your reading becomes a doorway to meditation, prayer, and contemplation. The method is easy to learn, yet a powerful tool for opening up to the presence of God, mysteriously hidden in your life, and especially in your interaction with sacred scripture or other contemplative writings.

Lectio divina, or lectio, is a nexus where the wisdom of the Bible encounters, and is immersed in, the complementary wisdom of silence—the portal to the mystery. Although the practice of lectio is not as well known as meditation (which, as you will see, has for Christians an intimate connection with sacred reading), it is nevertheless the single most foundational spiritual exercise related to Christian mysticism. Indeed, if you decide to engage in only one practice from this book, I hope it will be lectio. If you want to engage in Christian meditation or in contemplative prayer, begin with lectio.

Lectio opens you up to allow God to lead you where he chooses. Prayer, meditation, and contemplation are powerful disciplines of the mystical life precisely because they are outgrowths of this practice. As disciplines of silence, meditation and contemplation function like a house in which you will live out your journey into the mystery of Christ. Lectio, by contrast, is the foundation upon which that house is built. I remember when I first became interested in rock music. I wanted to learn everything I could about it—who the best musicians were, how rock and roll evolved from earlier musical forms like folk and the blues, and how technology was influencing the evolution of rock sound. It seemed that a natural extension of my love for the music was a desire to learn as much as I could about it. Eventually, that interest even extended to reading biographies of my favorite musicians, playing my own guitar and bass, and keeping an eye on what my favorite critics were saying, while being careful not to let their opinions sway my own perspective on which bands made the best music.

This natural hunger to learn more about our favorite things also holds true for religion and spirituality. In fact, one of the most important gifts you can receive from a faith community is the opportunity to learn more about the history and philosophy of the Christian tradition. This may come to you through the actual study of Christian doctrine or Biblical theology, or in more down-to-earth ways—through absorbing the ideas and values of the faith, by participating in Christian worship, or by getting to know the great stories of the life of Christ or the heroism of the saints; stories that help to define what it means to be a follower of Jesus. The joy you take in worship and in prayer, the choices you make to cultivate a willingness to be holy, and the actions you take to build fellowship and community with other Christians all come alive for you when you make the effort to learn about your faith. When you study the scriptures and learn the history of the faith, when you learn about the great heroes of the faith (saints, martyrs, and mystics), and apply their lessons to your own life, you make the experience of being a Christian more rewarding, more challenging, and ultimately more satisfying.

However...

As valuable as this knowledge is, be careful not to reduce the Christian mysteries to mere intellectual exploration. You can become so caught up in trying to understand the Trinity or some other exercise in theological hair-splitting that you lose sight of the profound invitation to love that lies in and beneath all the words. In other words, as joyful as it is to learn *about* God and Christ and the faith that bears Christ's name, be careful that these mental gymnastics don't become an obstacle to actually *becoming intimate* with this God you are so busy studying.

This tension between studying God and getting to know him forms the backstory to this chapter, in which we will look at a way of reading the Bible and other sacred texts that is significantly different from traditional methods of study. For contemplatives, this essential difference is the key to relating to the words of wisdom at the heart of the tradition as containers in which the silence of God can be discerned.

For most of my early childhood, my family did not participate in a church community. We were nominally Christian, but made no effort to seek out a church until I was in the sixth grade, and met a teacher at my school who was married to a Lutheran pastor. Soon we joined the Lutheran Church, marking the first time in almost twenty years that my parents regularly attended church, aside from weddings and funerals. But even during those years without formal religious observance, my parents always kept an old King James Version Bible on the coffee table in our living room. I don't ever remember anyone actually reading it; on the contrary, once when I was a toddler I was reprimanded for touching it! But even if it was off-limits to me, the Bible always had a place of honor in our home. It was the one firm symbol of our religious identity, no matter how dormant that faith may actually have been.

As a teenager, I became friends with a number of evangelical Christians—who not only owned Bibles, but also actively studied the scriptures. For them, believing in Christ meant more than just going to church on Sundays; they read the Bible, marked important passages, made notes in the margins, and mulled over how the words of scripture could be applied to their daily lives. At the recommendation of some of my evangelical friends, I bought a "chain-reference" Bible, which features references on every page pointing to other verses that address the same or similar themes. This focus on studying the Bible—analyzing it, dissecting its message, seeking to grasp intellectually the full meaning of the text—is a distinctively modern phenomenon. Among Protestants today (but increasingly among Catholics as well), Bible study has become an essential, core element of what it means to be a serious, devout follower of Christ.

I'm not suggesting that ancient Christians didn't study the Bible; of course they did. Before the advent of the printing press, however, few people had access to, let alone owned, a copy of the Bible. But even more to the point, before the coming of modern ideas of scholarship, research, historical criticism, and other aspects of the academic pursuit of knowledge, nearly all those who wrestled with the words of scripture did so to acquire a spiritual, rather than an intellectual, understanding of the text. In other words, for most of Christian history, reading the Bible was not an exercise in "figuring out" Christianity, but rather a practice for encountering God through the medium of the written word.

Of course, many Christians who engage in all the mentally stimulating processes of serious Bible study will insist that, for them, an intellectual approach to sacred scripture is very much an exercise in drawing closer to

God. Although these Christians may feel spiritually nurtured when they study the Bible, however, the ancient spiritual practice of lectio divina suggests that, in terms of fostering intimacy with God, there are approaches far more valuable than mere study and analysis.

Some Christians would even claim that approaching the Bible as if it were a textbook chokes off any sense of the divine presence rather than nurturing or inviting it. And indeed, a strictly academic reading of the Bible may stimulate the brain, but doesn't necessarily transform the heart. When it comes to the divine mystery that is at the heart of Christian mysticism, more is required of us than just a cognitive understanding. Knowing about God does not necessarily lead to the powerful transformation that lies at the core of Christian mysticism.

THE KEY TO THE MYSTERIES

If merely studying the Bible is an exercise that is, by itself, spiritually incomplete—or, even worse, spiritually meaningless—what is the key to true mystical intimacy with God? The great Christian mystics insist that the key to the threshold of the divine mystery lies not in filling our minds with words, no matter how holy or edifying they may be, but rather in bathing our minds, our awareness, our consciousness in *silence*.

Mystery lies at the heart of all our thoughts, images, experiences, notions, ideas, and speculations about God. Nothing reveals God perfectly; indeed, everything that reveals God also conceals God. Our experiences of God's closeness conceal his transcendence. Our sense of God's judgment masks his mercy. Our intuitive grasp of God's fatherhood blinds us to his maternal care. The paradox at the heart of mysticism emerges from the paradox of being human. That which is infinite cannot be squeezed into a finite container, no matter how grand and noble and beautiful that container may be.

If we talk about how God is present in our hearts, we proclaim ourselves as containers of God. But we are finite, and God is infinite. We can ponder God's presence throughout the cosmos, but even the entire expanding universe is finite when compared to the infinity of God. We trust certain modes of authority to reveal God to us—the Bible, the church, the wisdom of the great saints and mystics of the past. Yet we must not forget that all these are finite containers holding—or attempting to hold—an infinite God. All conceal even as they reveal.

My point is not to undermine the authority of the Bible or its value as a source for Christian wisdom. But I think either ignoring the Bible, or approaching it merely as a textbook to be studied, functions as a way to ignore the depth of the mystery to which the sacred text invites us. Without denying the insight and information that may be gleaned from studying the Bible, the contemplative tradition offers an entry into scripture that, spiritually speaking, invites us deeper into the Christian mysteries.

For those who are eager to encounter the divine mystery, the Bible—and indeed, all worthy spiritual writing, not just that which has been canonized as sacred scripture—is best engaged in a spirit of silence, of meditation and reflection, and, most important of all, in the context of prayer in order to realize its power to transform us. And this is precisely the function of lectio divina.

A New Way of Reading

The actual process of lectio divina is deceptively simple—so simple, in fact, that the medieval contemplative who wrote the classic instructions for it, Guigo II, did so in a text that is barely twenty pages long. The key to lectio is not just in learning a four-step process, but also in rethinking your entire approach to the meaning and purpose of written words and how we use them. Lectio does not change the Bible, but it does change how we approach it. Therein lies the secret of its power.

The written word is a tool and, like all tools, it serves as a means to an end. Reading is a means to learning something new, to gathering

information, to being entertained, to staying in touch with friends. The ability to read is such a profound blessing that we consider literacy to be the primary indicator that separates those who are educated from those who are not. The power to read is essentially a means by which we maintain (or seek to expand) control over our lives. We read to attain something we may not otherwise have—more knowledge, more pleasure, more mastery, more skill, more data, more fun, more love and social contact. All of this is very good; clearly, the ability to read is a true blessing.

However, everything that reveals God also conceals him. Thus, one of the challenges we face when we read a sacred or saintly text is the very hiddenness of God (Isaiah 45:15). Reading a spiritual text in the "normal" way of reading for personal mastery or control can sometimes have the unintended consequence of pushing God farther into hiding.

Hence the need for lectio divina. Lectio turns the normal goal of reading—for attaining mastery and control—on its head. When you practice lectio, you do not seek to control, but rather to yield. You do not seek to master, but rather to serve. Whereas you usually read to discover new ideas or enjoy entertaining stories, sacred reading presents an opportunity to turn yourself over to God and let him be the master, the one in control, the one wielding the power. Whereas you usually read with the subconscious intention of helping yourself, lectio leads you to ask the question: "How can I be of service (to God)?"

Lectio divina is simple—so simple, in fact, that it hardly appears worthy of serious attention. It involves reading a passage from the Bible or some other sacred text completely and wholly as *an act of slow, deliberate prayer*. It is a practice for formation, rather than a means of gathering *in*formation. As a spiritual exercise, lectio divina involves opening your heart and soul in order to be formed (and transformed) by the Spirit of God.

In his essay on lectio divina, Guigo describes sacred reading as the first step in a four-part spiritual process:

Lectio: prayerful, slow, heart-centered reading of a sacred text

Meditatio: deliberate pondering of the message in the text

Oratio: responding to God's message with honest, sincere prayer

Contemplatio: allowing the prayer to dissolve into wordless, silent contemplation, while simply resting in the divine presence, beyond the limitations of human thought

Lectio is a subversive activity, because it invites you to surrender your willfulness and control to the leadings and promptings of the Holy Spirit. Thus, it runs counter to the mainstream values of our "can do," Type-A, gotta-stay-on-top-of-things culture. In the intentional slowness of lectio, you are reminded that Christian spirituality emphasizes God's action and your response—not the other way around. Thus, lectio is a practice in which you slow yourself down, creating space in which you can gently learn to seek, and discern, God's presence hidden in the sacred text and in the subtle stirrings of your heart and mind.

By opening up to the divine presence through the written word, you simultaneously open yourself up to the deeply relational nature of Christian spirituality, which is indeed the heart of the contemplative path. The Christian mystery is not so much about finding the "God within," although that is a crucial element of Christian spirituality and mystics throughout the ages have encouraged us to recognize the presence of God within us. Even more important than that inner gaze, however, is the ultimately paradoxical nature of the divine encounter within lectio divina. This occurs when you read and seek an encounter with God within the word that comes, not from within, but as a gift from outside us (in this case, mediated through the writings of authors who lived many years ago). Finding God in the word given to us does not mean God is not to be found within. But that works the other way around as well. When we encounter God within us, Christianity reminds us that God comes to us through the gift of other people (including the prophets, evangelists and mystics from ages past). Through lectio, you are given the opportunity to celebrate the mystery of encountering the God who is both intimately one with you and simultaneously, paradoxically, wholly transcendent and "other" than you.

Lectio

All you need to engage in the practice of lectio divina is something worth reading. Traditionally, lectio was specifically a practice for pondering sacred scripture, and anyone who recognizes that Christian mysticism is ultimately about following Christ will devote at least some of their time for lectio to the writings of the Bible. But there's nothing that says you can use *only* the Bible when practicing lectio. The writings of the great mystics can richly reward you when you approach them in the slow, meditative style of lectio. If your schedule permits, try to engage in lectio divina twice a day: scripture reading in the morning, and the writings of one of the great mystics in the evening. (For a list of texts you could use in your lectio practice, see Appendix B.)

Once you've selected your text (or texts), set aside enough time to read the material slowly and deliberately—ideally, in a quiet place where you feel comfortable reading and praying. Set aside at least twenty minutes to allow not only for lectio, but also for the subsequent steps of *meditatio*, *oratio*, and *contemplatio* (half an hour to an hour is ideal). It's critical not to rush. Lectio can be a powerful and transformational practice even if you read only a sentence or two! Remember, the goal is not to amass knowledge or information. You can always supplement your lectio practice with other time spent in more informational spiritual reading. The goal of lectio is simply to create a space where God may encounter you via the medium of the sacred word.

To begin, read a sentence, or a few—but no more than a paragraph or two. Then stop. Go back and slowly reread the passage, and perhaps even a third or fourth time, at as unhurried a pace as possible. If you find yourself analyzing the text, gently let it go. Don't rush to figure out the text; just keep an open mind. Let the text read you. Be open to discerning a particular word or phrase that speaks to you with particular meaning or relevance.

When you encounter such a word or phrase, stop reading. That is your signal to move on to the reflective, meditatio, stage of the practice. In meditatio, ponder thoughtfully what this particular word or phrase means to you, and how God may be using it to communicate with you. Eventually, you may feel inspired to engage in your own verbal, prayerful response to God's word. This is the oratio stage. Pray honestly, simply, sincerely. Remember, you pray not to make a good impression, but simply to be intimate with the One who loves you. Eventually, the words will drop away and the wordless silence will embrace you as you simply sit in God's presence (contemplatio).

And that's all there is to it. It's simple—but deceptively so, especially for Westerners who are used to processing an endless stream of information. Setting aside your mind's tendency to analyze and dissect all that you read is not an easy task. Indeed, lectio divina can be a source of humility in your life as you come face to face with how unwilling you are to embrace silence and unknowing—an unwillingness that may appear again and again in your quest to become deeply contemplative. As you seek to engage in the deep silence and openness of lectio, you will inevitably catch yourself indulging in your mind's analytical chatter. When that happens, simply return to reading silently and attentively, focusing on the words in front of you rather than the words that arise in your mind. And, yes, this refocusing is something you will have to do again and again.

One way to let go of your analytical mind during lectio is to make sure that you have plenty of time for more traditional forms of Bible study in addition to your lectio time. It can be very fruitful to read the Bible or other sacred texts in both a contemplative and a scholarly way. Just set aside different times for each approach; do not try to blend contemplative and scholarly reading. Commit to one approach or the other when you sit down with your text. When you make time to explore both a mystical and a scholarly approach to the Bible (or other spiritual texts), you can discover profound and multi-layered wisdom within the writing.

Meditatio

The second stage in the lectio process is *meditatio*, or meditation. This is perhaps the single most misunderstood element of this spiritual exercise.

In the popular mind, the heart of mysticism is meditation. This comes from the influence of several generations of Eastern spirituality on Western culture. Eastern spirituality—from the yogi reciting a mantra to the Zen Buddhist's relaxed attention on breath—has become the cultural standard by which many Westerners understand meditation.

In the Christian tradition, however, meditation is not an exercise in moving beyond thought. It is, rather, a gentle process of pondering and reflecting on a holy text or a point of doctrine (like the Incarnation or the Trinity). This process of meditation (which, in the exercise of lectio divina, comes after reading and before prayer) occurs during the pause in which, having read the sacred text, you stop to mull over its meaning and its relevance in your life. This type of meditation, far from seeking to move beyond the cognitive mind, actually involves calm thinking—a meditative thought that moves best when it moves slowly. Just as sacred reading requires you to slow down and lay aside your illusions of being in control, sacred meditation asks you to slow down the normal high-speed chase in which one thought seeks to overcome another in the chattering, endlessly frenetic arena of the mind.

This frenetic chatter is what Buddhists call "the monkey mind." Eastern meditation is about peacefully quieting, or at least ignoring, the monkey mind. In the Christian tradition, however, meditation is not so much about silencing the mind as it is about seeking a middle ground between the extremes of letting the mind chatter away and attempting to get it to shut up. In this middle ground, allow your mind a serene freedom, but with the understanding that it remain focused on a point of faith or an insight of wisdom consistent in tone with the gentle, unrushed, God-focused activity of lectio.

Meditation thus serves as a bridge between the word that is read and the final resting point of wordless contemplation. It is a fulcrum point between the word silently received and our response, gently offered to God in prayer (oratio). As such, it need not be a long or involved process. After a few minutes of lectio, you may spend only a minute or two in meditation, pondering the text that you've read and reflecting on how its message can inform your prayer—your efforts to open your mind and heart to God. Prayer, in turn, leads to contemplation (contemplatio), which is the point at which you really do seek to gently shush your monkey mind and just be in God's presence.

CHAPTER 14

The Heavenly Conversation

*What should I do then? I will pray with the spirit, but I will pray with the mind
also; I will sing praise with the spirit, but I will sing praise with the mind also.*

I CORINTHIANS 14:15

*Just as no one comes to wisdom except through grace,
justice and knowledge, so no one comes to contemplation except by
penetrating meditation, a holy life and devout prayer.*

BONAVENTURE[39]

The Christian mystical life can be compared to a long-distance romance. God makes his presence felt in our hearts, but remains shrouded in mystery, and can seem distant, absent, or cloaked in the darkness of unknowing. We look forward to the day of complete and total union with God, but we recognize that such fullness of joy may not come until after we pass the threshold of death. In the meantime, we have to "make do" with the joys of a relationship in which God is both revealed and concealed. Part of this "making do" involves the imperfect, but nevertheless joyful, process of prayer.

When you communicate with someone over a telephone line, you cannot touch, caress, or embrace the person with whom you speak. Indeed, even hearing that person can sometimes be difficult because of static or interference on the call. Sometimes when the phone rings, you are irritated at the interruption; at other times, you wait impatiently for the call. Sometimes, a ringing phone can be a cause for joy; at other times, it can be an ominous harbinger of bad news.

The same can be said of prayer. Sometimes prayer is easy—you're eager to open your heart and mind to heaven, effortlessly making time and joyfully entering into the silence where you hope to taste the good presence of God. At such times, it's easy to make a commitment to pray regularly, perhaps once or twice a day. But then will come other times, when you may feel duty-bound to set aside time for prayer and see it as more of a bother than anything else. Sometimes prayer can inspire you to cry; sometimes it makes you writhe in shame. Prayer can evoke feelings of wonder, of delight, of joy, of quiet love, of embarrassment, of self-consciousness, of humility. The silence at the heart of prayer can feel like a delicious moment of respite in an otherwise frantic life, or it can feel cold and impersonal, an unforgiving barrier that separates you from the love and acceptance you crave so deeply. Prayer can feel like the most important thing you could ever do, or it may leave you wondering just how stupid you really are.

A Christian mystic is a person of prayer. To be a Christian contemplative is to be a person of prayer. Even if have only a passing interest in Christian mysticism and contemplation, this could be evidence that God is inviting you to find transformation and healing in the practice of prayer. At the heart of the Christian mystery is the call to intimacy with God, and prayer is the tool by which we respond to that call.

The Centrality of Prayer

A Christian mystic prays as surely as a lawyer litigates and a doctor treats illness. For that matter, the practice of prayer is common to all Christians, including those who have little or no interest in mysticism. Given the tremendous diversity that has come to characterize the various denominations and branches of Christianity, prayer, grounded in devotion to Jesus Christ, may well be the only common denominator that unites Christians from across the spectrum of the faith. Those who are illiterate or learning-disabled may not be able to read the Bible, but they can still lift their hands and eyes in prayer.

In the preceding chapter, we considered how sacred reading is related to the practices of meditation, prayer, and contemplation. In fact, taken as a whole, the entire four-part practice of lectio divina is a form of prayer. Reading the Bible or other sacred texts is a tool for listening to God's word for you; meditation is the means by which you seek to unpack or digest that word; prayer, as understood here, is responding to the sacred word with your own thoughts and feelings; which leads to contemplation, the quiet resting in God's presence as the culmination of the first three movements in lectio. Even though each stage of the process is unique, it all encompasses the quest for communication with God. Therefore, it is all prayer.

Indeed, conversational prayer—a spontaneous sharing of your thoughts and feelings with God—is the task of oratio. But conversational prayer is not the only way to pray. Meditation and contemplation, both focused practices aimed at achieving mental clarity and the experience of consciousness beyond the ordinary, everyday mind with its practical concerns, are important Christian forms of prayer. Prayer can also take highly structured and even ritualistic forms, as in the Daily Office, the Jesus Prayer, and the Rosary. Anything you do to foster an experience of communication with God—disclosing your own thoughts and feelings to God, or listening for God's word for you—is a form of prayer.

Christians don't need to be mystics in order to pray; but they do need to pray in order to seek a mystical life.

Don't Stop

Prayer works best when it is regular and frequent. The Apostle Paul understood this when he bluntly instructed his readers (and yes, that includes us, 2,000 years later) to "pray without ceasing" (I Thessalonians 5:17). But what, really, does that mean?

Saint Paul's words can be interpreted in a number of different ways. For example, the Desert Fathers and Mothers, who lived solitary lives, understood their commitment to prayer in a very specific way. Their routine entailed reciting all 150 Psalms, *every day*. It takes more than four hours to read or recite the Psalms out loud. While four or more hours of recited prayer every single day may not literally be praying "without ceasing," it's still quite a commitment.

Eventually, the solitaries of the desert moved toward monasticism, a more communal (and sustainable) way of life for those who wanted to follow Christ without compromise. Monks and nuns live in communities, but in such a way as to preserve, as much as possible, the emphasis on silence and solitude that characterized the spirituality of the desert. One of the benefits of communal living is the opportunity for shared, corporate worship—the chance to pray with one another. And so, from the beginning of their history, monasteries have placed central importance on this idea of praying without ceasing.

Monasteries structure their common schedules around a daily regimen of prayers, canticles, readings, and silence that comprises the "Daily Office" (the official daily prayer of the community). Following Psalm

119:164, which notes "seven times a day I praise you," the earliest monks established a daily program of seven "offices" or communal prayer services. Although interspersed throughout the day and balanced with labor, lectio divina, and other claims on their time, nuns and monks rely on these seven regularly scheduled prayer times as their way of "praying without ceasing."

Another means of praying without ceasing was developed among Greek Orthodox monks and mystics. Known as the Prayer of the Heart, this practice involves a simple prayer—"Lord Jesus Christ, Son of God, Have mercy on me, a sinner"—that is synchronized with the rhythm of breathing, so that disciplined practitioners can literally recite it as continuously as they breathe. Another Western spiritual practice developed by the Carmelite friar Brother Lawrence, "the practice of the presence of God," aims at cultivating a God-focused state of mind that anyone can enjoy, even while doing mundane chores like washing the dishes. While these forms of prayer begin to push the boundary that separates oratio from contemplatio, they do signify some of the many ways that Christians throughout history have sought to follow Paul's instruction and make intimacy with God an unceasing aspect of their lives.

Christian mysticism invites us to think about ceaseless prayer in a variety of ways. Certainly it can (and should) include a daily regimen of prayer, whether conversational prayer, recited prayers like the Daily Office, repetitive prayers like the Jesus Prayer or the Rosary, or a daily practice of God-centered silence. Lectio divina and prayer naturally complement each other, and a balanced diet of sacred reading, formal and conversational prayer, and informal/wordless prayer can be a deeply satisfying anchor for a contemplative life.

MAKING PRAYER A PRIORITY

Prayer, like lectio divina, is a central discipline for anyone who wishes to integrate the wisdom of the mystics into their lives. And prayer, like lectio divina, needs to be a regular, daily practice—not just something done "when you feel like it." For many people, however, this is surprisingly difficult to attain.

If you already have a rich and satisfying prayer life, you are truly blessed. Others, who sincerely desire a sense of God's presence in their lives or who simply wish to be more focused in their spiritual journey, often feel "stuck" when it comes to prayer. Alas, it seems that prayer is easier to talk about (or think about) than to do.

Here are some of the attitudes, thoughts and feelings that you may experience as potential obstacles to a truly satisfying and intimate prayer life:

I just never can find the time to pray.

Prayer discourages me. I feel as if I'm just talking to myself.

When I pray, strong feelings, whether positive or negative, emerge and I'm not sure what to do with them. Frankly, I find prayer to be rather unsettling.

I feel ashamed of my sins. I don't think I'm worthy to pray.

I don't know what to say to God. After all, he already knows everything I need!

Perhaps you can think of other obstacles that have held you back in your quest for a deeper prayer life.

These objections are all variations on a single theme: As much as we want to be closer to God, we also resist it. In the words of Marianne Williamson, made famous by Nelson Mandela: "Our deepest fear is not that we are inadequate. Our deepest fear is that we are powerful beyond measure." I believe we can make a similar statement about spiritual seekers: "Our deepest fear is not that there is no God. Our deepest fear is that God *does* exist and wants to become an intimate part of our lives, changing us forever." When two people fall in love, often their relationship can be troubled by one or both of two fears: the fear of loneliness or abandonment ("Please don't leave me") and the fear of engulfment ("I need my space"). But when

it comes to relating to God, I think that the fear of being engulfed is for many people the greater of the two. It manifests in our "not having enough time" to pray, and in other excuses we make to avoid a daily practice of seeking intimacy with God.

Prayer, therefore, is like physical training or even military combat. It requires that you make enough effort to move through resistance, and it requires profound courage to see you through the scary places it will take you. Thankfully, the gospel promises grace to those who believe; indeed, without that grace, a disciplined prayer life remains ultimately unattainable. Without the grace of God who loves you, your resistance will overwhelm your desire. Without the grace of God beckoning you and calling you into relationship with him, prayer too quickly gets lost in the hectic pace of life. Grace is the secret ingredient that can, finally, lead you to overcome your resistance. Indeed, grace helps you to see how all the supposed obstacles to your life of prayer are ultimately of your own making.

Here are a few points to consider as you seek to make prayer a high priority in your life:

> **Don't go it alone.** We are all social beings, and we are far more likely to embrace a new discipline and stick with it if we don't try to do it all by ourselves. This is one of the reasons why participation in a commuity of faith is so essential. Having others to turn to for advice, encouragement, accountability, and instruction can make all the difference in following through on your commitment, particularly when the novelty wears off and the going gets rough. Likewise, a spiritual director can be an invaluable help in dealing with some of the difficult feelings that can emerge in prayer—like doubts that God doesn't exist or doesn't care, or overwhelming feelings of sadness, guilt, or anger that can emerge.

> **Start small.** If you're out of shape and want to do something about it, you don't begin by running twenty miles each morning. Physical training has to be tailored to your current abilities;

as your strength develops, your regimen can gradually become more challenging. So it is with prayer. If you have difficulty finding time to pray, start by making a commitment to pray for one minute a day. Master that before you stretch out to five minutes, or ten minutes, or beyond. Even for seasoned contemplatives, twenty to thirty minutes twice a day is usually enough. And not everyone needs to, or can, devote that much time to prayer. A trusted friend or director can be of great help in discerning just how much daily prayer time is right for you. Even if your heart longs to give an hour every day to God, take it slowly at first. It's better to establish a daily routine that becomes as anchored in your life as brushing your teeth. Once your everyday pattern is established, you can start to stretch out the amount of time you give to prayer.

Establish a routine. Essential to a successful daily discipline is a sense of routine. Ideally, your prayer routine will fit in with your overall commitments: for example, if you need to leave for work every morning at 7 AM, plan your morning so that you have enough time to shower, dress, and eat, then get up fifteen minutes earlier and devote those first few minutes to your spiritual practice. If your schedule permits, try to establish time for regular prayer along with the regular practice of lectio divina. In addition to finding a set time for prayer, select a specific place— ideally a quiet corner in your home where your family or roommates will not disturb you and you can avoid distractions like the computer, TV, or telephone. Put a Bible or cross or crucifix in your prayer space so that it is clearly a center for fostering intimacy with God.

Experiment. The prayer types we'll be examining later in this chapter are only part of the overall "toolbox" for contemplatives. No one has to master all the many different methods of prayer that have evolved over the centuries. You may find that your devotion to God is nurtured more by the Rosary than by the Daily

Office (or vice versa). Some are naturally more comfortable with recited prayers; others chafe at anything that doesn't come spontaneously from the heart. Try to pray in different ways, and get to know how your prayer life shines.

Pray as you can, not as you can't. Because prayer is all about fostering intimacy with God, every person's prayer life will be unique. The way God communicates with you and the way you respond to God will be yours alone. This makes it a colossal waste of time to try to impose expectations about the "right" way to pray on your prayer life. If all your friends love the Rosary, but you have a clearer sense of God's presence when you take a long walk in the forest gently sharing with God whatever's on your mind, give thanks for your uniqueness. When others are pulling out their beads, head for the woods.

Remember, it's all about God, and it's all about love. A disciplined prayer life is a commitment that requires a certain maturity to get through the dry periods. During those dry spells, it may feel like anything you do to pray goes wrong. It's important, therefore, to remember that most of what's "wrong" with your prayer life is a reflection of your own human limitations, if not your inner poverty and brokenness. But don't be a masochist about it. Prayer is about God, and God is love. At least some of the fruits of the Spirit (love, joy, peace, kindness) should color your prayer experience, at least some of the time. If your prayer life is joyless, burdensome, and feels like continual drudgery, talk it over with a trusted friend or director. Sometimes an arid prayer life is a sign of being called more deeply into contemplation, but it can also be a signal that something else is out of joint. Don't give up on your walk with God or grow cynical; don't lose faith in the mystery of love. Keep your eyes on the prize. Focus on the God who is Love, even when prayer becomes difficult. With your heart set on love and the caring support of a prayer partner, even the longest dry spell can be a time for growth.

Printed words in a book cannot teach you how to pray. Ultimately, all you can bring to your prayer—your time offered to God—is yourself. Far more important than your thoughts or your eloquence is, simply, your heart and your soul. You need to be willing to offer yourself to God, and to dispose yourself to the possibilities that lie just beyond the reach of your senses or your rational mind. Even faith is optional in prayer! Some of the best prayers emerge out of profound doubt and questioning. But a certain flexibility of mind and heart is probably necessary. If you are arrogant, either in your unbelief or in your conviction that you have a rock-solid knowledge of God, your prayers will fall flat. Humility and an open-hearted vulnerability, coupled with a willingness to let God take the lead, is probably the most helpful attitude to embrace. Prayer is not about impressing God (as if we could do that); it's about getting real with God.

Some people love to fill their prayer space with sensual aids—candles, incense, icons, or recordings of Gregorian chants playing softly in the background. None of this is necessary, however, and sometimes these things can be more distracting than reinforcing. If you like those sorts of things, great. But they are neither necessary nor always helpful for prayer.

RECITED AND SPONTANEOUS PRAYER

In the 1970s, the controversial theologian Matthew Fox insisted: "Prayer is not saying prayers." I think he was on to something, but I think a more accurate statement would be: "Prayer is more than just saying prayers." Prayers that we recite—the Lord's Prayer, grace before meals, devotional supplications found in inspirational books—are the "training wheels" of the Christian spiritual life. In other words, they teach us the language and the rhythm of intimacy with God. Prayers that we read and recite are designed to set us free to enter, eventually, into unscripted intimacy with our divine lover.

This is not to suggest that formulaic prayers are unnecessary or inferior. On the contrary, just as great musicians practice their scales throughout their careers, mystics rely on the most childlike forms of prayer even as they move deeper and deeper into the splendors of wordless contemplation. The Daily Office, which began as a prayer regimen for monks, is now available to all Christians. Those who embrace these beautifully written, but entirely formulaic, prayers find in them a continual source of spiritual nourishment and are inspired by them to more spontaneous ways to seek intimacy with God.

While it is possible to recite formulaic prayers without sincerity or authenticity, this does not mean that praying in such a way is necessarily futile. Some of the great mystical writers wrote at length about the spiritual treasures available in the humble recitation of the Lord's Prayer. To a dedicated contemplative, even the most familiar prayer represents a new opportunity to be fully present and completely mindful with each word that is prayed. If you recite a prayer in a rote or mindless manner, you always have the opportunity to take a deep breath, slow down, and recite the same prayer, again, only this time with mindful attentiveness to the beauty and the power of the words.

At its best, prayer—even a simple, memorized prayer like the Our Father—is like healthy digestion. It requires that you take your time to "chew" the words and "digest" the thought. When you rush through your prayers, you simply set yourself up for spiritual "indigestion." On the other hand, when you recite a prayer in a mystical way, you slow the process down enough so that each word can be fully "chewed," broken apart and savored both consciously and subconsciously as you make your way through the prayer. No one experience of praying will ever be perfect. But, to the extent that you slow down your engagement with the prayers you say, you will be prepared for deeper and more intimate forms of prayer. In learning to recite formal prayers mindfully, you will be preparing yourself to share with God the truest and most hidden thoughts and feelings that emerge from deep within you, offered up spontaneously, in your own words— or even in sounds and gestures that, inspired by the Holy Spirit, are "too deep for words" (Romans 8:26). Just as recited prayers eventually lead to conversational or spontaneous prayer, "from the heart" prayers eventually shade off into the post-verbal experience of wordless prayer, which takes you to the spiritual frontiers of contemplation.

Formal Prayer

Formal prayers are those recited from the Bible, from sacred texts, or from traditional writings. There are several kinds:

Basic Prayers. Every Christian should know the Lord's Prayer. Catholics and others with a devotion to Mary should know the Hail Mary. Various other Bible passages, hymns, traditional prayers, and nuggets of wisdom from great saints or mystics, can all be memorized and recited from the heart. One of the earliest Christian monks, John Cassian, recommended regular prayer of this verse from the Psalms: "O God, come to my assistance; O Lord, make haste to help me" (Psalm 69:2 Douay-Rheims Version). My wife and I love to recite this prayer from Julian of Norwich: "God, of your goodness, give me yourself, for you are enough for me. I may ask nothing less that is fully to your worship, and if I do ask anything less, ever shall I be in want. Only in you I have all." These simple prayers are easily memorized and can be recited at any time throughout the day. These recitations can also be used to begin or end periods of time set aside for lectio divina, meditation, or contemplation.

The Rosary. This popular Catholic devotion combines recitation of memorized prayers (particularly the Lord's Prayer and the Hail Mary) with reflection on various key events in the lives of Jesus and Mary. Part meditation and part prayer, the Rosary can be a powerful tool for slowing down the monkey mind and discerning God's silent presence.

The Jesus Prayer (Prayer of the Heart). Entire books have been written about this simple prayer and its power to transform your life. Indeed, *The Way of a Pilgrim*, the work of an anonymous Russian Orthodox author concerning this prayer, is a classic of mystical literature. Several variations of the prayer exist, the most common being: "Lord Jesus Christ, Son of God, have mercy on me, a sinner." When you entrain the prayer to your breathing—inhale as you pray "Lord Jesus Christ, son of God"; pause; exhale as you recite the rest of the prayer—and repeat it slowly and gently as you breathe, this prayer is arguably the best tool for achieving Saint Paul's ideal of prayer without ceasing. The Greek Orthodox spiritual tradition of *hesychasm* is anchored in the use of the Jesus Prayer, and its repetitive nature is clearly reminiscent of the mantras found in Eastern forms of meditation. Like the Rosary or centering prayer, this practice can help foster an experience of acquired contemplation.

The Daily Office. Also called the Divine Office or the Liturgy of the Hours, the Daily Office is a form of communal prayer used in monasteries and in Catholic, Orthodox, Anglican, and some Protestant churches. Different churches and monasteries have their own forms of the Daily Office, which usually consists of between four and seven "offices" or services of prayer to be prayed at appointed times throughout the day. Each office includes scripture readings, Psalms and other canticles, hymns, antiphons, and prayers. Because it is designed as a communal form of prayer, even if you recite it in solitude, you are on some level participating in the larger praying community of the church. We know from the gospels that Jesus prayed the Psalms. So, by joining in the Daily Office, you are joining in a tradition of prayer that extends back to the origins of the faith. The Daily Office is a complex form of prayer; different readings, Psalms, and canticles are assigned to each day, and the days themselves are influenced by the season of the church year (Advent, Lent, etc.), as well as the days on which the lives of saints are commemorated. While it can be daunting to learn to pray the Office, once you become familiar with it, it's a lovely tool for anchoring a daily practice of prayer.

CONVERSATIONAL PRAYER

Sooner or later, recited prayers may begin to feel stiff and overly formal. This is not necessarily a sign to abandon them, but rather to stretch out and begin to pray without a script, offering to God your uncensored thoughts and feelings, and even the "space" between your thoughts and feelings.

Conversational prayer is prayer that comes from the heart, in your own words. Ultimately, it works best when it's spontaneous and unrehearsed. Having said that, it's helpful to consider categories of prayer that are traditionally associated with this kind of extemporaneous reaching out to God.

> **Adoration.** God is love, and therefore infinitely lovable. So what better way to express yourself to God than by offering words of love? This is easier said than done, however, if you have images of God that are less than loving: God-as-angry-father, God-as-implacable-judge, or God-as-indifferent-creator. Of course, God is beyond all our images of him (whatever reveals God conceals God—even our ways of thinking about God), so if you become aware of ways in which you perceive God as unloving, you will find tremendous healing in choosing a more kind and compassionate understanding of him. Learning to trust God and to pray words of love to him can be an important part of coming to know God as love.

> **Confession.** No one is perfect. Everyone makes mistakes. And everyone is capable of making unloving choices, even with full knowledge and consent. Facing the God of infinite love means facing your own unloving choices, behaviors, and dispositions as well. While coming face to face with your own sinfulness may seem to encourage shame or guilt, the Christian tradition is less interested in you feeling sorry for yourself and more interested in you honestly confessing your faults to God as a key step toward healing your brokenness and embracing a new (or renewed) life of love.

Thanksgiving. The Benedictine monk David Steindl-Rast calls gratefulness "the heart of prayer." Meister Eckhart suggested that if all we ever prayed was a single prayer of thanksgiving, that would be enough. Counting your blessings and acknowledging God as the ultimate source of all that is good in your life is essential, not only for your spiritual health, but also for your mental health. Gratitude creates the space in our hearts for love, peace, joy, and hope; praying our thankfulness can be a powerful tool for learning to live in gratitude.

Petition and Intercession. Petitions are prayers made on your own behalf; intercessions are prayers in which you appeal to God on behalf of someone else. Some people think that prayer is primarily about petitions and intercessions—about asking God for blessings, for healing, for favors, whether for yourself or for others. For contemplatives, however, prayer is about far more than just crying for blessings—prayer is primarily about establishing, or strengthening, a relationship with God based on trust, love, and intimacy. Although petition and intercession remain important ways to communicate with God even for contemplatives, those who truly seek to embrace the divine mystery will understand such "asking prayer" to be only one part of an overall prayer discipline. Even when contemplatives do offer petitions and intercessions, their requests extend far beyond seeking material benefits. Mystics pray for healing, for strength, for confidence and faith, for comfort, for spiritual blessings (as well as material needs), and for a sense of God's presence and guidance in their lives. And while cynics may argue that there's no scientific evidence that prayer has any impact on external reality—if you're dying of cancer, will prayer really make a difference?—from a Christian spiritual perspective, this kind of skepticism is pointless. You can never know the difference between praying and not-praying, because each individual and each circumstance is unique. Furthermore, prayer assumes that God knows what is best, and that the answer to your prayer may come in ways that you don't necessarily expect or want. Moreover, whether or not prayer changes external circumstances (like a cancerous growth), it always changes the internal circumstances of your heart, your soul, and your trust in the goodness and love of God. In all these ways, intercessory and petitionary prayer remains invaluable—even for those whose faith is unsure.

Lament and Complaint. Things don't always go well in life. Bad things happen. Disease strikes; divorce breaks up families; crimes occur; jobs are lost; loved ones die. It's a terrible mistake to assume that prayer should always be positive—as if we have to reassure God that we have everything under control and there's nothing to worry about down here. On the contrary, prayer can be its most effective when you are broken, hurting, angry, scared, lost, or confused. The key is to bring these feelings to God, dark and shadowy though they may be, without censorship or self-editing. When you lament, you share with God just how bad things are for you; you express your frustration, particularly for God's perceived absence or inaction. God is big enough to take on your sorrow and your anger. In fact, your spiritual life is impoverished if you do not offer these parts of yourself to God.

CHARISMATIC PRAYER

Charismatic prayer literally means "gifted prayer," and refers to prayer inspired directly by the Holy Spirit. According to the New Testament, charismatic prayer is given "in the spirit" and expressed in the "language of angels" (I Corinthians 13:1). The fancy word for this is *glossolalia*, or speaking in tongues, referring to the lovely but unintelligible "prayer language" that characterizes charismatic prayer. The New Testament identifies the miraculous ability to speak or pray in an unknown language as one of the miracles associated with the presence of the Holy Spirit. While at least one story in the Bible suggests that speaking in tongues includes the miraculous ability to speak a human language unknown to the speaker (Acts 2), the concept of the "language of angels" implies that at least some forms of glossolalia involve utterance that is not related to any earthly vocabulary, grammar, or syntax. Critics of glossolalia insist that these unintelligible words and sounds have no rational or logical meaning—in other words, they're little more than vocalized nonsense—while proponents insist that such speaking or praying *in the spirit* has an objective meaning that is hidden (dare we say mystical?). Whichever you choose to believe, it is clear to those who pray in tongues that this method of prayer is deeply liberating, in that it frees the mind from having to be in charge of the prayer. By allowing the syllables to flow forth—often in a beautifully melodic song—the person who prays in tongues is free to let the experience manifest on a level higher or deeper than rational thought. Praying in the spirit is all about praying in love and joy, at a level beyond what mere words can hope to express.

Not everyone has the gift of tongues, and the New Testament discourages believers from going out of their way to seek it. If you don't have a natural ability to pray in tongues, follow the Bible's advice and seek the "higher" gifts of growth in wisdom and love. If praying in tongues and singing in the spirit is a part of your spiritual experience, be aware that there is a profoundly mystical dimension to this form of prayer. Because charismatic prayer functions at a level beyond normal human reason, it can serve as a doorway to the deepest and highest form of prayer: contemplation.

Beyond the Language of Prayer

The four-step process of lectio divina leads from sacred reading to meditation to prayer to contemplation. Eventually, your thoughts fall away before the deep and profound silence that characterizes the presence of God. Sooner or later, you discover that your words, no matter how eloquent and meaningful they may be, are like distracting noises in an otherwise restfully quiet cathedral. You cannot hear even your own words, let alone any "word" from God, if there is too much noise interfering with your prayer. Words need to be expressed in at least a relative degree of silence in order to be heard and understood. Eventually, your interest and focus in prayer will turn from your words—even if they're offered spontaneously—to the silence that lies behind and beneath and before them.

Because prayer ultimately leads to contemplation, however, do not think of it as merely an opening act—the hors d'oeuvre before the meal. Whether formal or conversational, prayer that involves words and thoughts is not only a necessary prelude to contemplation, but also a necessary companion to an ongoing contemplative practice. When you fall deeply in love with someone, you can enjoy many quiet hours together. But that does not mean that you no longer need to talk or listen to what each other has to say. On the contrary, a deeply contemplative spirituality needs prayer as surely as a beautiful diamond needs a golden setting in order to be fully appreciated.

Prayer is not just a means to some mystical end. Saying the Rosary or the Jesus Prayer often enough will not somehow qualify you for supernatural experiences or extraordinary levels of consciousness. Prayer is an end to itself, and functions as its own reward. But it's also a way for God to prepare you for his deep silence and to foster within you the fruit of the Spirit, such as love and joy. Through the discipline of prayer, you are invited to an ever-unfolding adventure in loving God.

Learning to pray is a lifelong process you will never complete, no matter how many years you devote to prayer or how deeply intimate your relationship with God becomes. You will encounter dry spells, fear of meaninglessness, and unremitting doubt that will threaten to overwhelm your feeble efforts to connect to God through your words and thoughts. To keep it meaningful, integrate your prayer into all areas of your life— your work, your relationships, your creative endeavors—and anchored in a community of faith. By embedding your prayer in the reality of human relationships, you make it easier to love God and to love your neighbor simultaneously.

CHAPTER 15

Prayer Beyond Words

The Lord is in his holy temple; let all the earth keep silence before him!

HABAKKUK 2:20

Meditation is the mother of love but contemplation is its daughter.

FRANCIS DE SALES[40]

As traditionally understood, Christian meditation differs from Eastern spirituality in that it's a "thinking" form of meditation. Disciplines like Yoga and Zen typically involve techniques that focus on silencing, or at least ignoring, the cognitive chatter of the mind. Christian meditation, by contrast, is a way to relax and open up your mind, to ponder gently and expansively the stories and doctrines of the Christian faith. This is an important bridge between the word of God as you read it in a book, and the word of prayer that you offer up to God.

This does not mean that Christian mysticism lacks an appreciation for the deep interior silence that Eastern seekers encounter during their meditation practice. On the contrary, immersion in the silence that lies beneath and beyond thought is as important to Christian mysticism as it is to any other mystical tradition. The spiritual practices associated with contemplation (also called contemplative prayer) take you to the most silent places in your soul, just as surely as Zen meditation takes Buddhists to their own silent temple within. Since Christian spirituality is *relational*, however, its goal is not for you to achieve self-enlightenment or self-realization, but rather to enter into ever-expansive loving communion with God. Thus, for Christians, even your explorations of silence will have a fundamentally relational character. To enter into the silence, seek it not merely in the solitary practice of meditation, but in the context of prayer—the relational act of responding to, seeking, and nurturing intimacy with God. This is what contemplation is all about.

Whether you seek to foster contemplative prayer by your own initiative ("acquired contemplation") or await it as something miraculously given to you by the grace of God ("infused contemplation"), it represents that ineffable point where the words of your prayer shade over into ever-deeper strata of silence. Contemplation is, therefore, the summit of Christian spiritual practice, just as surely as lectio divina is the foundational practice of the inner way.

Approaching Contemplation

As prayer is the heart of Christian spirituality in general, so contemplation is the heart of the mystical life. What begins with lectio is completed in contemplation—the point at which thought is laid gently aside; the point at which the present moment becomes the moment of presence. Time spent in contemplation is time dedicated exclusively to God and love and emptiness and unknowing. In contemplation, you come most fully to that place where you brush up against the mystery of God—the frontier within you where your thoughts and opinions and beliefs suddenly become tiny in relation to the vast, awe-inspiring silence of the dazzling divine presence. And in that awesome place, you are invited to think little and love much. Contemplation has been neatly defined by the nineteenth-century saint John Vianney who describes his prayer life in the simplest of ways: "I look at God and God looks at me." This is the heart of contemplation.

Contemplation is, in fact, silly. "Silly" is a rich word that comes from the old German *selig*, meaning "blessed," and also "foolish." I Corinthians 4:10 speaks of being "fools for Christ's sake." Contemplation is time wasted foolishly for God and for God's love—foolish because you can't control it, master it, program it, or figure it out. All you can do is enter into it, be present to it, and offer yourself to the unknowing. Contemplative prayer is a potential portal into an ecstatic experience of mystical union, although that's rather like saying a lottery ticket is a potential windfall of a million dollars. For most, the rewards of contemplation are gentle, humble, and even ordinary. And while most lottery tickets bring no reward, even a fretful and distraction-laden half-hour of contemplation is never wasted, for God is present even in your suffering, your doubts, your distractions, and your fidgeting.

More than anything else, Christian contemplation is a discipline of prayer. Unless you recognize this, its mystery and its inexplicable nature will remain lost to you—time spent in contemplation will seem to be time wasted rather than time set on fire with a love that cannot be measured or mapped. Contemplation does not replace the other forms of prayer we have considered—scriptural prayer, the Daily Office, the Jesus Prayer, or spontaneous conversational prayer. Indeed, one mistake that novice contemplatives sometimes make is to immerse themselves so totally in the practice of contemplation that they abandon all other forms of prayer. This is like launching a boat into the open sea without bothering to bring a compass or a GPS. Contemplation needs to be "anchored" in an overall prayer life just as a successful journey needs to be guided by useful and effective navigational tools.

THE SILENT TEMPLE WITHIN

Contemplation is one of those words with a murky history. It comes from the Latin verb *contemplare*, which means "to observe" or "to notice." The word is also rooted in the word "temple," however, relating it to sacred space, or a place set aside for spiritual matters. In its pagan usage, *contemplare* involved the reading of auguries—a divination technique in which people sought guidance from the gods or other spirits. Once Christianized, contemplation lost its association with divination, and came to signify the prayerful practice of attending to the presence of God. While this may suggest devotion in an actual temple—in other words, a church—it also evokes a more spiritual sense of seeking the presence of God in a gathered community of believers, wherever they may be (Matthew 18:20)—or perhaps most significantly, in the solitude of your own heart (I Corinthians 3:16). Thus, for Christians, contemplative spirituality consists of the effort to spend time "in the temple" of silence with God. In contemplative prayer, therefore, you listen in receptive silence, and hold yourself open for the purpose of fostering the experience of God's presence within you—a presence promised by scripture (John 14:17).

Some of the earliest Christian mystics, who abandoned a comfortable life to seek God in the deserts of Syria and Egypt, entered into deep silence to pray—a practice written about by spiritual teachers like Evagrius Ponticus. This wordless prayer is not just a relic from the ancient world, however. Evidence of contemplation as a central Christian spiritual activity is also found in the Middle Ages (see *The Cloud of Unknowing*), after the Renaissance (John of the Cross), and into the modern and postmodern eras (Thomas Merton).

In the twentieth century, a new era of contemplative spirituality dawned when many Christians discovered the rich practices of the Eastern wisdom traditions. Some Christians even began to write about contemplative spirituality using terminology and imagery drawn from Eastern sources. Thus, the Benedictine monk John Main wrote about "Christian meditation" (redefining meditation as a practice of interior silence, in contrast to the traditional Christian understanding of the word) while Trappist monks like M. Basil Pennington, Thomas Keating, and William Meninger borrowed the language of Thomas Merton to teach a method of contemplation under the name of "centering prayer." By the early twenty-first century, some uninformed Christians ironically began to attack centering prayer (and contemplation in general) for its so-called "Eastern influence," dismissing it as a syncretistic innovation. These objections do not take into account the long tradition of authentic Christian contemplation that stretches back into the early centuries of the Christian faith. Even though many Christian contemplatives (myself included) believe that Christians can find their faith enhanced and nurtured by respectfully learning from other wisdom traditions, the practice of contemplation is so thoroughly Christian that it is appropriate even for those who only feel comfortable engaging in orthodox Christian spiritual practices.

Contemplation ushers you into the prayer of wordless intimacy, of moving beyond thought in a natural, gentle, and authentic way. Various methods of contemplation have been practiced by Christians at different times and places throughout the history of the church. In its purest and richest form, however, contemplation does not require a method or a specific exercise. As many mystics have taught, pure contemplation is pure grace—a gift from God, not the fruit of human endeavor.

The process of moving from praying-with-words into the silence of contemplation can be compared to moving from time spent in a lush, verdant garden into a more austere landscape where life is sparse and marked by at least some measure of suffering. It's easy to fall in love with the garden—and, by extension, with prayer that anchors itself in the sweetness of experiencing (or even merely imagining) divine love and heavenly bliss. But, just as not all landscapes are lush with vegetation, not all prayer is automatically suffused with an experience of joyful connection with God. Sooner or later, you will feel led to leave the garden and move into the wilderness. Sooner or later, you will need to take several deep breaths and face the "harsh terrain" within you—the untamed chatter of your mind, your murky passions and the self-serving desires of your deep subconscious, and the shadow dimensions of your psyche.

Some of these wilderness places may be dry and arid, like a desert; others may be thick with nearly impenetrable vegetation, like a rainforest; still others may be stark and uncaring, like the endless gray of the postmodern urban landscape. But, just as Jesus retreated into the desert to fight the demons and ultimately experience the loving care of the angels, so you will travel your own path into the barren unknown when you embark on the spiritual life. You must walk this path because others have walked it before you, because Jesus walked it, because spiritual maturity mandates that you learn to discern the presence of God, not only in joy and happiness and abundance, but also in emptiness, in unknowing, in the shadow places, and even in the midst of the roiling frenzy of your own soul.

BECOMING A CONTEMPLATIVE

Strictly speaking, contemplation involves no method or technique of prayer. Over the centuries, various spiritual teachers have in fact developed methods or techniques for fostering inner silence. But contemplation itself can never be reduced to a mere procedure. Contemplative prayer is not so much about mastering silence or achieving a desired state of consciousness as it is a gentle, unforced opening-up of your mind and heart—a simple gesture of allowing yourself to sit in the uncreated presence of God. In other words, contemplation is not something you achieve; it is something you allow. You open yourself to spend time with God, just as you allow yourself to spend time with anyone you deeply love.

To enter into contemplative prayer requires nothing more than a commitment to spend time in silence, with the specific intent to offer the time to God. Time spent in contemplation is time spent listening gently for God's soft whisper. But this is more easily said than done.

We live in a particularly noisy world, increasingly defined and dominated by technology, and therefore by the noise and stress that technology brings into our lives. From machinery to music, from telephones to traffic, from broadcast media to mental chatter—ours is a world filled with persistent, ever-present, and often simply frantic noise. As a result, silence feels foreign and awkward, if not anxiety-provoking, for so many people. Even the best-intentioned Christians face many obstacles to contemplative prayer: a busy life, an active mind, a nervous body. These can all contribute to forces both external and internal that conspire to prevent us from simply sinking into the silence where God's presence may be discerned as a "still small voice" (I Kings 19:12).

For this reason, contemplation is not something that you can do just once or twice—or even just once in a while. Contemplative prayer, like any other endeavor designed to foster genuine intimacy with another person (or, in this case, with God), has to be a frequent and regular part of the relationship. The communion with God we seek through contemplation can be found only within the context of a recurring—ideally, daily— discipline. Since contemplation is the culmination of the practice of lectio divina, easily the best way to foster a daily practice of contemplative prayer is to devote time each day to lectio. Even if you rest in contemplative silence for only two to five minutes at a time, this regular practice can be far more valuable to your spiritual transformation in Christ than an occasional thirty-minute marathon of silence.

When you enter into silence—whether for half an hour or just for half a minute—you always face the temptation to fill this time with "stuff," with words, with thoughts. You want to tell God all about your needs, and the needs of others. You may feel inspired to sing God's praises and express in creative ways just how much you love and adore him. However you are drawn to do it, you are tempted to fill the time you give to God with wordy distractions.

Unfortunately, this all-too-human urge to clutter up time spent in contemplative prayer with endless mental static is simply a way of trying to control the agenda. Thankfully, God is loving and forgiving; he waits patiently for you to let go of your need to control, whether that takes you five minutes, five hours, or fifty years. God waits for those times when you breathe through your distractions and simply let them go, allowing the silence to wash throughout your consciousness like a cleansing wave of crystal water.

Sometimes, even often, you may not discern God's presence during the practice of contemplation. Even when you give up trying to think your way into controlling your prayer time, you nevertheless may feel continually distracted by the state of your emotions, by spontaneous mental imagery, or by your endless capacity to daydream yourself out of focused silence. Despite all the ways in which you can fail to pay attention to the silence within you, however, grace still leads you into occasional moments of unexpected wonder. Sometimes, you may notice the Uncreated Presence within and beyond the silence that rests quietly beneath your mental clutter. Sometimes, your time spent in contemplation is rewarded with a quiet sense of resplendent joy and profound experiences of heavenly love. For most who walk the path of contemplation, these times are unpredictable, and less common than we hope—and appropriately so. God comes to you to be in relationship, not just to make you feel good. So contemplation ultimately nurtures you at a level far deeper than emotions or conscious awareness.

THREE FORMS OF CONTEMPLATION

Contemplation is not only the single most essential element of mystical spirituality; it is also the Rosetta Stone that unlocks and clarifies the meaning of all other spiritual exercises. Through contemplation, you are brought to the threshold of the mysteries, and then ushered in deeper, and then deeper still. Contemplation takes you beyond the place where your mind can understand and your tongue can recount. And you never outgrow the invitation to go deeper.

In her book *Practical Mysticism*, Evelyn Underhill describes three forms of contemplation:

Discernment: Experiencing the immanent presence of God in and through nature (including in your own heart); sensing the artist by gazing upon the artwork.

Recognition: Knowing that God truly transcends all created things, thereby entering the "cloud of unknowing" where you seek God, not in any created object, but in the mysteries of your own being and consciousness.

Acknowledgment: Accepting the limits of even your own consciousness and spirit to reveal God to you, and so learning to wait in the silence and darkness, trusting that, even beyond all human experience, God will come to you without any effort on your part. This marks the transition from "active" to "infused" contemplation, and completes the transformation of contemplation from an exercise in seeking spiritual fulfillment to a fully God-centered act of loving response to the Mystery.

While Underhill's distinctions are certainly not the only way, or even perhaps the best way, of understanding the different ways in which we can experience contemplation, they do illustrate that contemplative prayer is not something that you master, that you work at until you get it right. It is a lifelong (and beyond) process of ever-unfolding possibilities that move you deeper and deeper into encounter and intimacy with God—an encounter that occurs beyond the limits of your thoughts, ideas, mental images, and ability to "know" the ways of the Spirit.

To climb halfway up the mountain is *not* to reach the summit, even though the view from that mid-point of your journey may be spectacular. When you embrace a spirituality that calls you into silence and beckons you to let go of your discursive awareness, you will have no choice but to see your journey through to the end (that is to say, to the very heart of the mystery).

CENTERING PRAYER

While it is important to bear in mind that contemplation is far more than a mere method or technique for entering the silence, this does not mean that learning to contemplate (to enter the silence) in a methodical manner is unnecessary or ill-advised. Aspiring contemplatives may find considerable benefit in practicing a spiritual exercise designed to help foster inner peace and a disposition for silence. Centering prayer is perhaps the most popular such method commonly practiced by Western Christians today.

The Trappist monks who developed this technique were concerned that young Christians were turning to Eastern techniques like Yoga and Zen to find something that was already part of their own Christian heritage. So they began to hold retreats on the practice of contemplation, calling it centering prayer—a term inspired by Thomas Merton, who spoke of contemplation as prayer "centered entirely on the presence of God."

Centering prayer is a method of relaxing into the natural silence that persists beneath the thoughts and images of normal consciousness. To do this, you choose a single word—a prayer word—and repeat it silently, slowly, and gently as a way of centering (and recentering) your mind on the silence whenever distracting thoughts or images arise. Once you are centered in the silence, you can set the prayer word aside, returning to it to help you find the silent center again when distractions re-emerge. After a set period of time (ideally twenty minutes), your prayer time culminates in a slow recitation of the Lord's Prayer or a similar chosen prayer—perhaps the prayer of Julian of Norwich.

At first, centering prayer can be maddening to those immersed in our bottom-line-driven, goal-oriented, pragmatic and utilitarian society, because it feels as if you're doing nothing. Although the attention you give to the silence is profoundly relaxing and can lead to feelings of well-being, serenity, and even euphoria, it can also lead to feelings of restlessness, or to an emotional release that taps into hidden wells of anger, grief, or sadness. Because of its profound orientation toward silence and toward the places in your consciousness that take you beyond rational or cognitive thought, it can leave you feeling empty rather than spiritual, meaningless rather than God-infused.

Here it is important to balance your experience with the collective wisdom of the larger Christian community, particularly those who have embraced the contemplative life before. Christian mystics have had much to say about feeling discouraged in prayer, struggling with a sense of God's absence, dealing with feelings of meaninglessness, or questioning their commitment to God and to the spiritual life. The tradition encourages perseverance through those times when prayer and contemplation seem frustrating rather than edifying. This is because contemplation invites you to a place of mystery—a place beyond the safe zone where you can rationally interpret what is going on inside you. If you choose to enter this place of mystery, you open yourself up to the frontier of wonder and hiddenness that many mystics have explored before you. To enter that place requires surrendering all the objections of your practical, rational, used-to-being-in-control, egoic consciousness.

If you seek to embrace God even beyond the limits of your mind, you must first come to peace with the fact that your mind will scoff at this and see it as a silly, stupid, impractical endeavor. Only by clinging to the wisdom of those who have gone before can you gently turn aside the protests of your ego and persevere into the cloud of unknowing, where loving the hidden God is more important than holding on to your limited human mental images of him.

OBJECTIONS TO CONTEMPLATION

Because contemplation takes us to a place where the human ego is asked to surrender control to the leading of the Holy Spirit, it may not be surprising to consider that some people find this practice threatening. While many Christians today are unfamiliar with contemplation, a small minority have decided that contemplation is a bad thing, and are outspoken in their objection to it. These objections usually take one of two forms:

Contemplation is not in the Bible.

Contemplation is too much like the spirituality of Eastern non-Christian religions like Hinduism or Zen.

While it is true that contemplation is not directly mentioned in the Bible, the Bible contains numerous passages that encourage a spirituality grounded in silence, solitude, and stillness. Nowhere does the Bible forbid seeking God in silence and stillness. If we assume that Christians can lawfully use only tools and practices that are mentioned in scripture, then modern medicine, computers, and automobiles must all be forbidden!

Even if they accept that there is no scriptural injunction against contemplative prayer, however, many Christians reject it because they believe it blends Eastern practices with the Christian faith. Some of this confusion may have to do with the origins of centering prayer, which was seen at first as a Christian alternative to practices like transcendental meditation and Zen. The earliest proponents of centering prayer often used Eastern terminology to describe the practice—for example, calling the prayer word a mantra. It's sad that a form of prayer designed to provide people with a Christian alternative to Eastern spiritual practices is now rejected by some expressly because of its similarity to those practices! The real problem here is not the infiltration of "foreign spirituality" into Christianity, but rather the judgmental attitude of those who are too quick to jump to conclusions about spiritual practices with which they are unfamiliar.

In truth, centering prayer is anchored in ancient Christian practices that go back to some of the earliest Christian mystics, among them the Desert Father Evagrius Ponticus and the fifth-century monk John Cassian. It draws on teachings found in the fourteenth-century manuscript *The Cloud of Unknowing*. These ancient and medieval Christians were uncompromising in their love and devotion to Christ and to the teachings of the Christian faith. Centering prayer keeps their wisdom alive for new seekers of the contemplative path today.

Although the purpose of contemplative prayer is to foster greater intimacy with and devotion to God, some object that the darkness and unknowing inherent in the process hides God as much as it reveals him. True enough. Contemplation is the prayer of paradox, for in it you relax your mind to listen for a God whose light comes to you as darkness and whose word comes to you as silence. Thus, contemplation is the prayer of mystery, for it forces you to sit still and silent in the center of the mystery, where God is a question more than an answer, where God responds to all your questions by asking deeper questions still.

This is not to suggest that contemplation may not have ordinary benefits and blessings; often it does. Many who engage in a sustained, daily practice of contemplation discover not only a deeper sense of well-being and serenity in their lives, but also a heightened awareness of God's continual presence, and of his love flowing to and through them—particularly in their dealings with others who may suffer, or who are wounded or in some manner of need. Such subtle blessings cannot be reduced to a simple formula, however. ("Sit in silence an hour a day for a year and you will suddenly feel God's presence all the time.") God is in control here, and he will not be reduced to an equation. Contemplative prayer is a spiritual practice, not a magical spell.

When you engage in contemplation, you join in solidarity with the long tradition of Christian contemplatives who have come before—and who will come after. You pray along with Francis of Assisi, Thomas Merton, Evelyn Underhill, Julian of Norwich, Teresa of Avila, John of the Cross, Meister Eckhart, Bernard of Clairvaux, Thérèse of Lisieux, Brother Lawrence, the anonymous author of *The Cloud of Unknowing*, and countless others. Indeed, the renowned mystics who are known to us because they were great writers or teachers represent only a tiny fraction of the great contemplatives in Christian history, most of whom were lovers of God in obscurity and are now known by name to God alone. When you embrace the prayer of deep silence, you join in their communion—a communion that transcends the normal limitations of time and space. For all the contemplatives throughout Christian history (and extending into the future), silence is praise and stillness is a song of love. When you surrender your thought to enter into the dazzling darkness of the unknowing of God, you reach the full flowering of your yearning to be, in the words of Saint Peter, "partakers of the divine nature."

Is Contemplation for You?

If you want to integrate the wisdom of the Christian mystics into your own spiritual life, chances are good that, sooner or later, a daily practice of time spent in contemplative silence will be a central part of your relationship with the Ultimate Mystery. But not everyone is called to contemplation. Or, perhaps more accurately, not everyone is called to contemplation *now*.

The anonymous author of *The Cloud of Unknowing* suggests that if you are interested in contemplation you must experience two things to discern if you are truly ready to engage in this form of prayer. First, you must feel a growing, daily desire for this kind of prayer, a desire so strong that it impinges on your daily prayer. If you aren't already praying daily, you are probably not ready for contemplation. Christian contemplation emerges from a mature prayer life. Just as toddlers crawl before they walk, aspiring mystics must be immersed in simpler forms of prayer before moving to the more demanding practice of contemplation.

Just as important as this inner longing for contemplation, however, is feeling a sense of joy or enthusiasm concerning your relationship with God, not just during prayer, but also when you are merely thinking about your spiritual practice.

Every Christian is called to pray, but not every Christian needs to, or should, engage in contemplative prayer (at least, not now). If the thought of entering into sustained periods of silence on a daily basis strikes you as daunting or overwhelming, then don't do it—or at least, limit your time spent in silence and focus instead on more foundational practices such as sacred reading or verbal prayer. Don't try to force contemplation. Trust your heart and focus on other spiritual disciplines like sacred reading, the Daily Office, or regular time devoted to conversational prayer. Share the dynamics of your inner life with a trusted spiritual friend or director, and be mindful of the subtle ways the Holy Spirit may call you in the future—including, perhaps, a call to enter silence more fully when the time is right.

Contemplation emerges naturally out of a mature spirituality. Thus, people who do not feel a sense of longing or joy related to contemplation should aim their spiritual commitment toward those practices that *do* appeal to them. Lectio, meditation, conversational prayer, and the Daily Office can all, in themselves, foster a more intimate sense of relationship with God—which is to say that they are all means by which you can enter into a mystical dimension of Christian discipleship. Furthermore, a sustained, disciplined practice of lectio and prayer can "till the inner soil" to prepare you for an eventual transition into a deeper experience of contemplation.

So if you lack the longing and the enthusiasm for contemplation today, you may simply not be ready for it. It takes self-awareness and more than a little humility to recognize that sometimes your reach exceeds your grasp. It is possible to have a cursory interest in mysticism and contemplation and yet not be spiritually ready to immerse yourself in it. Many people may feel uncomfortable, or not prepared, to engage in a daily practice of sitting still, breathing deeply, and letting go of all extraneous thoughts. Silence may appear to some not as an intriguing mystery waiting to be explored, but rather as a source of fear and uncertainty. Such unease is often a sign that a person is better off pursuing some other form of prayer.

Another important point to consider, however, is that feeling "not ready" for silent prayer could be a mark of humility rather than a sign of not being ready. Paradoxically, humility signifies readiness to do the work of contemplation, even if the nature of humility is to assume one is not worthy! Here, as in every place along the spiritual path where discernment is necessary, the wise counsel of one or a few trusted peers or a mentor will be invaluable.

The wisest of spiritual guides recognize that contemplation, like prayer in general, can manifest in many different ways. Thomas Merton, in his book *The Inner Experience*, wrote about what he called "masked contemplatives"—ordinary men and women who, although they may never have a formal practice of contemplative prayer, nevertheless cultivate a spirit of openness, of wonder, of resting in God in a place deeper than thought. This kind of masked contemplation can happen at any time throughout the day and need not be linked to any particular exercise or practice. Merton gives us an important reminder here that we should never put limits on the action of the Holy Spirit or judge others because they fail to "fit in" with what we consider to be a normal expression of spirituality.

CHAPTER 16

Wood, Water, and Wine

In returning and rest you shall be saved;
in quietness and in trust shall be your strength.

ISAIAH 30:15

The fullness of joy is to behold God in everything.

JULIAN OF NORWICH[41]

An old Zen Buddhist tale recounts the story of a young student of meditation who approaches his teacher with a question: "Roshi, what did you do before you were enlightened?" The old master thinks for a moment and then says, "Mostly I just chopped wood and carried water," referring to the normal chores of his agricultural existence. "And now that you have received enlightenment, how do you pass your time?" continued the student. The teacher smiled and said, "Well, I just chop wood and carry water."

This story carries two lessons for those who follow the Christian path of contemplation. First, it highlights the sheer ordinariness of the spiritual life. Perhaps the young student was hoping to hear about a daily regimen of meditation, chanting, study, and other "spiritual" pursuits. It must have been a surprise to hear the master speak instead about everyday household chores. Likewise, for most people, the concept of "Christian mysticism" probably brings to mind images of monks in contemplation or nuns in ecstasy, rather than more humdrum activities like balancing the checkbook, dealing with rush-hour traffic, or mowing the lawn. And yet, those tasks are exactly what ordinary Christian spiritual seekers and contemplatives are called to do.

The second lesson in the Zen story is perhaps even more important. The roshi is, in effect, cautioning his student against expectations that the spiritual life will quickly or automatically change him in radical or remarkable ways. While Christian spirituality may not use the language of enlightenment in the same way the Buddhists do, the parallel is clear. Before I fell in love with God, I washed the dishes and folded the laundry. After I fell in love with God, I washed the dishes and folded the laundry. Before I experienced a call to the life of contemplation, I lived an ordinary life—and after receiving that call, my life remains as down-to-earth as ever.

A daily practice of lectio divina, prayer, and contemplation can, in subtle ways and over time, change your attitude toward life, help you see the evidence of the Holy Spirit in the most unlikely places, and even propel you, when you least expect it, into moments of profound joy—even ecstasy. There can be moments when everything falls away and you taste the sweetness of union with God. But daily Christian spiritual practice will also take you through periods of boredom, restlessness, and questioning: "Why am I doing this every day? It seems so meaningless." God, in his wisdom, can give you the gift of feeling his absence just as easily as the gift of feeling his presence. Anyone who is serious about exploring the Christian mysteries will, sooner or later, receive both of these gifts.

Aspiring mystics and spiritual seekers place such a strong emphasis on the need for direct, personal experience with God that we run the risk of rejecting mere faith as somehow second-rate. People who merely *believe* in God without actually having experiences of his presence are somehow missing out, or so we think. But perhaps we're missing an important detail: in our quest for spiritual experience, perhaps we have traded "belief in God" for "belief in experience." In the words of the French mystic Francis de Sales, "There is a great difference between being occupied with God, who gives us the contentment, and being busied with the contentment which Gods give us."[42]

The longer I study the wisdom of the Christian mystics, practice the disciplines of the Christian life, and compare notes with my brothers and sisters in Christ who are journeying along this path with me, the more convinced I am that experience is only part of the mystical story. When meditation and contemplation lead to the cloud of unknowing, perhaps this points to the fact that God loves you enough to shield you from mystical experiences, most if not almost all of the time. In fact, a mystical relationship with God would soon implode if you were shouldered with the burden of continual, or even regular, experiences of ecstasy.

This is not to say that you must go through life with no sense of God's love or presence or activity in your life. Rather, I think the hidden point behind the Zen story is that, while, on the one hand, nothing changes as a result of embracing the mystical life, on the other, everything changes. You do the same chores, perform the same tasks, enjoy the same pleasures, and struggle against the same sins. And yet, you do all of this in the light of your disciplined commitment to seek intimacy with God. It is a light that subtly informs who you are, regardless of whether you are bored or energized by your spiritual exercises on any given day. And the light of your daily practice is the light by which you can see, if not the face of God, then at least the subtle traces of his presence in your life and in your soul.

Five hundred years before Christ, the Greek philosopher Heraclitus said: "You cannot step into the same river twice." This koan-like insight into the impermanence of existence can serve as a clue to the question of how to live a truly contemplative life. "See, I am making all things new," promises Jesus toward the end of the New Testament (Revelation 21:5). If we take him at his word, then we can never step into the same river twice because of the bracing action of God in the universe, creating new possibilities and new realities every moment of our lives. What this means, of course, is that, even on days when you can barely stand the thought of slogging through a half-hour of meditative Bible reading, and praying to God about the boring details of your life, and sitting in silence that feels like little more than a continual struggle against your incessant mental chatter—even on those less-than-exciting days, God is present, hidden in the mystery of your own inability to see, your own willful refusal to see, your own need to be ordinary and restless rather than ecstatic and joyful. And every moment may be the one in which, suddenly, the scales fall from your eyes and the tiniest and most undramatic things in your life become radiant and luminous with the presence of divine love. Living a contemplative life means, in large measure, living in continual expectancy of receiving an unexpected kiss from God—on good days as well as bad.

HUMBLE WISDOM FROM AN ANCIENT GUIDE

One of the wisest guides for living a Christ-centered life is Benedict of Nursia, the monk whose *Rule for Monasteries* became the standard for governing monastic communities in the Western church. Even though most Christians today would never even think about living in a monastery, Benedict's rule is surprisingly adaptable to life "in the world," largely because of the common-sense advice that lies beneath the specific instructions for managing an intentional community of monks.

At first glance, Benedict's writing can strike the reader as surprisingly *un*spiritual in its focus. He comes across as mostly concerned with mundane issues like how the community is organized and which Psalms will be prayed each day. He seems unconcerned with questions like how to pray, how to meditate, or how to contemplate. Benedict is utterly down-to-earth and his writing reflects this. And Benedictine monasticism has been shaped by his "chop wood, carry water" approach to spirituality ever since. Indeed, the motto of Benedictine spirituality is *Ora et Labora*, which means "pray and work."

The utter simplicity of this motto corresponds beautifully to the two great commandments of Jesus, commandments we first considered in Chapter 11 (Matthew 22:37-40):

> *Love the Lord your God with all your heart, and with all your soul, and with all your mind.*

> *Love your neighbor as yourself.*

The first commandment calls us to prayer; for, as we have seen, prayer is the heart of fostering or deepening a loving relationship with God. The second calls us to work; because, as the Lebanese poet Kahlil Gibran said, "work is love made visible." We work because we love. And we love because it is essential to a truly spiritual life.

Out of the love you seek to share with God comes the call to live a truly spiritual and contemplative life, a life that, in turn, can foster within you the splendor of mystical consciousness. Likewise, it is through the love you seek to share with your neighbors that you have the opportunity to anchor that contemplative spirituality in the most humble, down-to-earth, and ordinary of ways—by embracing the effort required to truly serve and care for one another, no matter how laborious, tedious, or exhausting that work may be.

The Christian mystics understood that you cannot separate the commandment to love God from the commandment to love others. To live a contemplative life, you cannot ignore either one of the two great directives. Although some may orient their lives more toward one than the other—there will always be deep contemplatives as well as social activists—even if you do, you are still bound to observe both in some way. In other words, you cannot truly love your neighbor as yourself unless you are fully grounded in the love of God. And you cannot fully experience the love of God unless you are engaged in loving your neighbors. Perhaps we need to love our neighbors in order to recognize God's love in our life, as it is only through God's love that we are able to love our neighbors at all. Richard Rohr sums it up nicely in his book *The Naked Now*: "When you honor and accept the divine image within yourself, you cannot help but see it in everybody else, too, and you know it is just as undeserved and unmerited as it is in you. That is why you stop judging, and that is how you start loving unconditionally and without asking whether someone is worthy or not."[43]

So the life of a Christian mystic is the life of love and, therefore, the life of work—whether that's exciting and creative work, or dull and repetitive work. The daily chores you face in order to keep your life and your relationships in good order are all at the heart of the call to a truly spiritual life.

After Each Day Comes the Night

When we talk about the role of ordinary labor as part of the spiritual life, it's important to see this in perspective. Work is part of the normal rhythm of being alive, alongside the human need for rest, relaxation, recreation, connection with others, the pursuit of leisure or hobbies—and, of course, time devoted to spiritual endeavors like lectio divina, contemplation, and participation in a faith community. In a similar way, the life of prayer involves a rhythm of those times when God is felt keenly to be present, or close, or even united with us, balanced against those times when God is known to us only in terms of absence, or distance, or simply silence.

Larger rhythms are at work in the Christian spiritual life as well—rhythms that unfold over time. Two of the most powerful metaphors used by mystics over time are the cloud and the dark night. The cloud, as immortalized in *The Cloud of Unknowing*, envelops you with mist and fog and renders all of your attempts to "know" God (in a mental, cognitive sense) ultimately useless. Meanwhile, the dark night, as explained by John of the Cross, can visit you more than once. John distinguishes between a dark night of the senses, in which you are called to surrender inordinate attachments to the things of this world in order to love God more fully, and the far more terrifying dark night of the soul, in which even the pleasure you take in spiritual and religious experience must ultimately be surrendered. For, to love God fully, you must let go of even the "things of God" (religious or spiritual experiences), or you fall into the trap of loving the pleasure you take in God rather than loving God for God alone.

The images of darkness, night, and the cloud can be depressing if not terrifying, and they are easily misunderstood. The cloud of unknowing is not an excuse to retreat into some sort of infantile, anti-intellectual religious sentimentalism or romanticism, where you refuse to wrestle with the challenges of faith "because there's no way I'll ever figure it all out anyway." The commandment to love God with all your mind still stands, even once you enter the cloud of unknowing. The cloud is simply a humbling reminder that the keenest mind will still ultimately fail before the profound silence of the Ultimate Mystery.

Likewise, the dark night of the senses is not a directive to hate the things of this world. Much misery has come out of dualism—a false interpretation of the gospel that suggests that, to be truly spiritual, you must renounce, reject, and even hate your body, your sexuality, and the material pleasures of earthly existence. This kind of dualism is particularly pernicious because it is shot through with sexism. The same logic that deems the human body and sexuality to be evil also regards women as inherently inferior to men, since men are more "spiritual" and women more "carnal."

The purpose of the dark night of the senses is to teach you a light, nonattached relationship to your own "bodiliness" and materiality, to enjoy the good gifts that God has given you without fusing your identity with them or thinking that your happiness is bound up with your material well-being. When you are nonattached from material things, you are in a better position to share your resources with those in need, or to roll with life's punches as you experience the losses that, sooner or later, we all face—financial setbacks, loss of loved ones, loss of health. When God, rather than something material, is your center, you are empowered to suffer life's challenges with grace and at least a degree of serenity. With God at your center, your task is not to reject all other things and relationships, but to love and care for God's creation in a manner consistent with living a God-centered life. If, however, you make the mistake of rejecting all that is "not God," you run the risk of choosing a life of hatred, which, in turn, leads directly to hell.

Finally, the dark night of the soul, which strips away anything that comes between you and God—even religious or spiritual experience—can be a temptation to abandon faith or let go of participation in Christian community. The joy formerly found in the sacraments or in public worship, the pleasure of reading the scripture or other sacred writings, even the joy of contemplation itself is slowly replaced with a profound, wordless, imageless, feeling-transcending trust in God and God alone. In the midst of the dark night, you may be tempted to think that the Christian tradition itself has lost all purpose and meaning, and that the community of faith is no longer important, especially if your community of faith is not particularly sensitive to the wisdom of Christian mysticism. When you begin this descent into the darkness, however, is precisely when you need your grounding in others the most, even if those relationships bring you nothing more than a sense of boredom and ennui.

The experiences of darkness, of the cloud, of unknowing, of radical letting-go may tempt you to abandon the spiritual journey—to retreat into cynicism, into despair, or into ego-driven fantasy. The best safeguard against this derailing of your spiritual journey is continual prayer. Trust in God, even when it feels as if you're barely hanging on, and rely on the love, support, and guidance of others—your spiritual friend(s) and/or director, and your larger community of faith. Dark-night experiences may seem to be episodes of depression, so be careful, when you enter the darkness, to discern whether the sense of profound loss and sadness you are feeling needs psychological care or spiritual support. Sometimes, it may require both.

The journey of a maturing spiritual life has many seasons and nuanced changes. No matter how deeply we fall in love with God, we never stop being embodied human beings with material needs and earthly concerns—not, at least, on this side of death. Each stage of life—childhood, adolescence, young adulthood, midlife, and old age—carries its own set of spiritual issues and life concerns. A young person's need to establish a sense of self differs considerably from a retiree's quest to find grace and humility in facing the limitations of age and the need to provide a legacy to the next generation. Our gender, our experience with addiction or illness, our ethnicity and level of education and socioeconomic status—all these factors contribute to the unique flavor of our own dance with God. As you persevere on the long road to faithful love of God, you will experience both joy and sadness, both breathtaking moments of God's felt presence and the, alas, all more common feelings of God's silence or absence. Times of confident growth and peaceful contentment give way to seasons of loss or unknowing. But through all of life's changes and uncertainties, when you balance the quest for the love of God with a commitment to love your neighbors as yourself, you anchor yourself in the resources and support systems necessary to live the spiritual life well.

CHANGING WATER INTO WINE

I began this chapter with a Zen story. Let's end it with a Christian tale that comes from the second chapter of the Gospel of John:

> On the third day there was a wedding in Cana of Galilee, and the mother of Jesus was there. Jesus and his disciples had also been invited to the wedding. When the wine gave out, the mother of Jesus said to him, "They have no wine." And Jesus said to her, "Woman, what concern is that to you and to me? My hour has not yet come." His mother said to the servants, "Do whatever he tells you." Now standing there were six stone water jars for the Jewish rites of purification, each holding twenty or thirty gallons. Jesus said to them, "Fill the jars with water." And they filled them up to the brim. He said to them, "Now draw some out, and take it to the chief steward." So they took it. When the steward tasted the water that had become wine, and did not know where it came from (though the servants

who had drawn the water knew), the steward called the bridegroom and
said to him, "Everyone serves the good wine first, and then the inferior
wine after the guests have become drunk. But you have kept the good
wine until now." Jesus did this, the first of his signs, in Cana of Galilee,
and revealed his glory; and his disciples believed in him (John 2:1-11).

Even if we ignore the miracle at the center of this story, it relates a marvel-ously human tale. Jesus responds irritably when his mother prods him to help out, and we catch a glimpse of the kind of behind-the-scenes action that takes place at just about any party or social event. Jesus, one of the guests, takes on the role of servant, following his mother's suggestion that he do something to make an ordinary day extraordinary. A miracle occurs, but it slips by when the steward suggests to the groom merely that there's been a mix-up with the wine.

This story can remind us that, whenever we talk about the "nighttime" dimension of mystical spirituality, we ought to keep in mind that, following every night, comes a new dawn. This, then, is the other side of "chop wood, carry water." Living the contemplative life is also all about changing water into wine. While the exercises of the contemplative life cannot guarantee anyone any kind of supernatural or extraordinary encounters with God, for those who are willing to see the possibilities within them, they can help us to see all of life in an entirely new way. And so we arrive at yet another paradox: Become a contemplative, and nothing will change; become a con-templative, and everything changes.

The dark-night experience—whether of the senses or of the soul—transforms you as certainly as Jesus changed the water into wine. The night never lasts forever, and it yields to a new dawn, a new day in which every-thing is changed. When you accept the boredom and confusion, the pain and letting-go that lies at the heart of the dark night, you are, in effect, yielding to the possibility that God is working something wondrous within you. And in accepting the possibility of deep transformation, you choose to embrace the promise of the new dawn.

Like chopping wood and carrying water, however, changing water into wine is not a one-time event. Nothing in the Christian tradition will encourage you to believe that if you, say, spent a year or two in daily prayer and contemplation, then you'll wake up one morning to see everything glowing with an unearthly light because you have been totally and permanently enlightened. What is far more likely to happen after two years of prayer is that you'll wake up one morning with your heart aching for God more than ever before, along with an increasing desire to serve your neighbors, particularly those in the greatest of need.

Contemplation is a gift, but it's by no means a passive one. It is a gift that requires your cooperation and participation in order for the alchemy to work. Every day, you choose to turn the water into wine by choosing to acknowledge that everything you have is a gift. And you choose to keep your eyes and ears open for glimpses and whispers of the giver. In making that choice, you create the space for the Spirit to make a difference in your life—which, in turn, changes everything.

ALL YOU NEED IS LOVE

A Christian rock singer named Larry Norman once made fun of the Beatles for singing "All you need is love," and then breaking up shortly thereafter. There's a cautionary tale here: Even if you know that all you need is love, you have to remind yourself of this continually, for, if you don't, it's far too easy to slip into less-than-loving choices and actions.

There's good news, however. Yes, it's true: all you need *is* love. And every time you choose love, every time you lay down your resistance to God's love, you turn water into wine. Accepting love, and choosing love, and making choices both large and small that, to the best of your knowledge, are in alignment with the love of God and the love of your neighbors, is the heart of the heavenly life. Orienting yourself to love will not magically solve your problems or instantly set you free from your addictions or your imprisonment (real or metaphorical). However, choosing love will, sooner or later, inspire you and impel you to begin changing the water of your ordinary, messy life to the wine of a life radiant with the fruit of the Spirit.

Love is like that. Even while it demands that you take responsibility for your actions, it also creates space in your life—space where light can shine, where hope can emerge, and where a sense of God's joyous and peaceful and playful presence can be felt—if you pay attention. And every time you choose love, that spaciousness within you grows a little bigger. Little by little, the mystery of divine love will transform your life, even while you are busy chopping wood and carrying water and turning water into wine—this is the promise of the contemplative life.

CHAPTER 17

The Heart of the Mystery

Take delight in the LORD, and he will give you the desires of your heart.

Psalm 37:4

*To comprehend and understand God as he is in himself, above and beyond
all likenesses, is to be God with God...Contemplative persons will go out in accordance with the mode of their contemplation, above and beyond reason
and distinction and their own created being. Through an eternal act of gazing
accomplished by means of the inborn light, they are transformed
and become one with that same light with which they see and which they see...
the contemplative life is a heavenly life.*

John Ruusbroec[44]

Christian mysticism is a path without a destination, for the point behind the journey is not to reach a goal, but rather to be reached—by God.

The only reason to embrace the mystical life is to foster intimacy with God, the Ultimate Mystery. Mysticism does not dangle benchmarks or objectives in front of you, like celestial carrots for which you must continually strive. The purpose of contemplation is only to be available for God and to open yourself up to his elusive presence. So the contemplative life is not about becoming someone different from who you are, but rather about being who you *really* are to begin with.

Within contemplative spirituality exists a tension between being and becoming. In a very real sense, mysticism has no incremental objectives or measurable goals, nothing to strive for, since God is always present and already loves you regardless of what you do or don't do to cultivate or accept that love. And yet, you can only experience contemplation in the context of your human life, played out in a universe that is continually changing, evolving, expanding, and mutating. There is, therefore, an aspect of change—and hopefully, growth and development—to the ongoing process of the mystical life. The Triune God may be, in the words of *The Book of Common Prayer*, an "eternal changelessness," and yet it seems that, built into the very structure of the Ultimate Mystery, is the ever-renewing, always-blossoming flower of continual dynamic activity—in other words, at the heart of eternal being is ever-evolving becoming.

Creation, it seems, is the key. The Holy Trinity may be changeless, but is hardly static. The Source of love may have at its center an immovable serenity, yet love is hardly unmoving or unyielding. In the Hebrew Scriptures, God first appears in the act of creation, separating wind from water and giving form to chaos, working in a mythic six-day timeline to bring all of the world and the cosmos as we know it into being. And anyone familiar with scientific theories like evolution, mutation, and the continual expansion of the universe can see that God has been at it ever since.

The contemplative life opens up the door to two simultaneous, and yet clearly paradoxical, possibilities: a state of being, and a state of becoming. In the state of *being*, you are always, already, one with God, immersed in his presence. You do not earn this, you do not create it, you do not make it more real by dint of effort or stretch of mind. It simply is; it always has been, and always will be. But the words we use to describe this state are words that imply a process of change (in other words, *becoming*)—sanctification, deification, divinization, *theosis*. As these process-words imply, you are called to a state of continual change, growth, and development through creativity, expression, and the work of love made visible. Yet, this state of becoming can be described in a way that returns us to the eternality of being: it is the state of "*being* creative."

Like everything about the contemplative life, the best approach for reconciling the being-becoming paradox is simply to try to live it, without necessarily figuring it out in a rational or logical way. Becoming united with God, and being eternally in God's presence, becoming more creative, and yet relaxing into our always-already deified being, this process-state is the summit to which holiness, meditation, contemplation, and simply living out the Christian life as best you can, leads.

The Artistry of Mysticism

Evelyn Underhill asserted that artists are those who, among all people, come closest to being natural mystics. And, indeed, many mystics throughout history were great artists. For example, Augustine, Aquinas, and Simone Weil were world-class philosophers, while George Herbert, John Donne, and John of the Cross were great poets. And many of the world's creative geniuses who achieved renown for their artistic work were almost certainly mystics as well. Consider musicians like Johann Sebastian Bach and Ralph Vaughan Williams; artists like Botticelli and Raphael; writers and poets like Dante, T. S. Eliot, and C. S. Lewis; and the enigmatic artist/poet William Blake. If the luminous, spiritual beauty of the music, art, and literature these figures gave us is any indication, I, for one, would include them in the community of great mystics. Moreover, the splendor and beauty of the

Christian mysteries have, over the ages, inspired countless lesser-known artists and contemplatives who combined elements of mysticism and creativity in their lives, without achieving lasting fame or renown.

The implication of this connection between art and spirituality is fairly clear: creativity supports contemplation—and vice versa. If you have any yearning to live a contemplative life, sooner or later you may find God seeking to manifest in you through some form of creative expression. To the extent that contemplation opens us up to participation in the divine nature, one way to support this realization of the divine mystery is to develop your own capacity to create. Exploring some form of authentic, soulful creativity can be an important part of your overall commitment to ever-deepening intimacy with God.

I'm not suggesting that in order to be a mystic you have to become an artist, writer, or musician. Granted, creative expression will often involve the performing arts like music, dance, or theater; or the visual arts like drawing, painting, sculpture, or computer-generated imagery; or literary arts such as poetry, fiction, and blogging. But your unique call may be to develop some other form of talent: in domestic arts like cooking, interior design, or scrapbooking; in crafts like carpentry or wood turning; or in mechanical or technical skills. Your creativity might find expression through business, or a healing profession, or in landscaping. The key to the spirituality of creation lies not so much in artistry-as-livelihood, but in the pure pursuit of creativity for its own sake. When you open yourself up to the delight that comes from creating for the sake of creating and no other purpose, you more readily participate in God's own delight.

In fostering your creative expression, you need not push yourself to be the very best; this is not about making sure you are as good as Michelangelo or Mozart. Nor it is necessarily about making a profit out of your creativity. Indeed, for contemplation and creativity to enhance one another, I recommend that you maintain a spirit of playful disregard for the normal demands of ambition. If you make your living doing one type of creative work, consider taking on an entirely different creative activity, with no goal other than having fun and enjoying the process. Offer up your creative efforts—no matter how good or amateurish they may be—to the love and delight of God.

Your creative play does not have to be "religious" or "spiritual" in nature. A poem or painting or some other work need not be concerned with the Crucifixion in order for its artistry to be anchored in contemplation. If you keep your work honest and grounded, it will not contradict the hope and love that comes from the heart of God—even if these themes are not explicit in your work.

The first book of the Bible, Genesis, not only reveals that creativity is essential to God, it also describes the fundamental link between creativity and contemplation. In the initial creation story, God manifests everything—the entire cosmos, the solar system, the earth, the ecosystems within the biosphere, eventually even the plants and animals and humankind itself—over the course of six "days." On the seventh day, God rested. In his rest, he contemplated the fruits of his own creativity. Thus, creative effort and contemplative rest naturally complement one another. In fact, they complete each other. A work of art is not complete until the artist stands back from it, gazes upon it, and hopefully smiles in approval—just as God "saw that it was good."

Likewise, contemplation is not "completed" until you rise from your repose, and, nourished and refreshed by the silence and the resting in God's presence, are capable of responding to the universal call to bring new creativity—and healing, hope, and love—to the world. Any contemplative who feels that to endlessly gaze on the beauty of God is the ultimate end of the mystical life is simply unfamiliar with the wisdom of the Bible and of the Christian mystical tradition. Even those who retreated into desert solitude or monastic community found that a life shaped and seasoned by contemplation is a life meant to be given away—through love, service, creativity, and care for family, friends, fellow members of a faith community, and the larger human family in all its need, hunger, and longing for God. Sharing your talents with others is, like resting in contemplative silence, a part of the overall process.

The spiritual path thus incorporates creativity, community, and contemplation in an integral life practice that includes seeking after, experiencing, and letting go of the presence of God, who is the object of your contemplation, the inspiration of your creativity, and the love that binds your community together. And in this mysterious relationship between contemplation and creativity, we come finally to the threshold of the deepest mystery of mysticism: the mystery of *theosis*.

In Chapter 6, I mentioned a monk who doesn't like the idea of the Beatific Vision, because it makes union with God seem to be a spectator sport; instead, he sees the mystery of human destiny in God as the Beatifying Communion, in which we join in the very heart of the loving relationships within the Trinity. I think this holds true not just for eternity, but equally for the contemplative life here and now. We are called not only *to* contemplation, but even *beyond* contemplation. We are called to the deifying life precisely so that we can share the presence of God with others. We receive the gifts of God's love and presence so that we can pass those same gifts on to our neighbors—those we love as ourselves.

Guigo II described lectio divina as involving four steps: reading, meditation, prayer, and contemplation. But his is not the final word on the spiritual exercise. In his book *Conversing with God in Scripture*. Stephen J. Binz suggests that contemplatio leads beyond itself to additional practices, such as *operatio* ("faithful witness in daily life") and *collatio* (forming community). When we offer to God our capacity to create, we are given the opportunity to witness to God's love through our prayerful activity, which includes the opportunity to help establish truly loving community here on earth. In a very real way, then, the spiritual life brings us full circle: we begin by finding nurture in community and in the wisdom of those who have gone before us, and in that wisdom we discern the call to enter ever more deeply into the loving mystery of God through prayer and contemplation, only to find that our highest destiny as contemplatives is to give back to our community, by the operation of our creative skill—arising out of God's transforming and healing love.

THE EVER-EXPANDING JOURNEY INTO GOD

In her pioneering book on mysticism, Evelyn Underhill exhibits a wise reticence when describing what she calls "the unitive life." She knew that her critics would pounce if she tried to recount her own experience of the summit of Christian mysticism, so she prudently played the role of a journalist reporting what others had said (or done) as evidence of what the end of the mystical road looks like.

> *The language of "deification" and of "spiritual marriage," then, is temperamental language: and is related to subjective experience rather than to objective fact. It describes on the one hand the mystic's astonished recognition of a profound change effected in his own personality—the transmutation of his salt, sulphur, and mercury into Spiritual Gold—and on the other, the rapturous consummation of his love. Hence, by a comparison of these symbolic reconstructions, and by the discovery and isolation of the common factor latent in each, we may perhaps learn something of the fundamental fact that each is trying to portray.*[45]

Likewise, Robert Hughes, in his wonderful study of spiritual theology *Beloved Dust*, accompanies his description of "Waves of Glory" with a disclaimer acknowledging that it is a topic of which little can be said. "The witness of all those who have tasted it, however, is that it cannot really be spoken but only alluded to by analogies and art."[46]

Underhill and Hughes agree that deification, or *theosis*, is characterized primarily by humility, which in this context can be defined as "self-forgetfulness." In other words, the truly divinized mystic is perhaps the least likely person to waste a lot of time recounting his or her experience.

It's not that mystics think their experience is unimportant. It's just that mysticism is, in the final analysis, an intimate, precious, and delicate matter. There is a personal, and even a private, dimension to the mystical life, as Jesus himself acknowledged when he said: "Whenever you pray, go into your room and shut the door and pray to your Father who is in secret; and your Father who sees in secret will reward you" (Matthew 6:6). What begins as a closet where prayer is offered in secret becomes, entirely by the grace of God, the most beautiful and intimate marriage chamber, where you give yourself fully, completely, entirely to God.

The spiritual marriage that gleams at the center of mystical experience is far more than just a comfortable intimacy between you and God. By the very nature of the Christian understanding of God, the mystical marriage urges you to join in a joyful circle of love and generativity with God-as-relationship: the Father, the Son, and the Holy Spirit. And the mystery of the Christian understanding of the Body of Christ or the Communion of Saints means that this profound relationship is open to every human being who says "yes" in response to that call. Mysticism may begin in the privacy of intimate contemplation, but it blossoms into the joyful ecstasy of a communion that lasts forever—with God in Three Persons beginning, sustaining, and completing the dance.

THE DANCE BELONGS TO ALL OF US

In a fully blossomed mystical life, the ecstasies and pleasures of knowing God intimately and fully are, as best I can tell, just a small fraction of the entire experience. The beauty and splendor of mystical intimacy in some ways must forever remain hidden, to be shared privately between a contemplative and God. But this beauty will also, in some ways, spill endlessly over to others. Through the splendor of intimacy with God, the contemplative will find wisdom to share with others. Through this beauty, he or she will serve those in need and care for those who suffer. And the glory of the Christian mysteries will find expression in the contemplative's creative work, in whatever form that might take. Out of the silence which is the natural habitat of the contemplative, God leads all who love him to carry that love to others, even as they return again and again to the silence, for their own rest and renewal.

Carmelite priest William McNamara, who has authored several idiosyncratic and visionary books about spirituality in the postmodern age, insists that "the mystic is not a special kind of person; each person is a special kind of mystic." I read this to mean that *every Christian is, to a greater or lesser extent, already a participant in the unitive life.* Consider the paradox: mysticism is a gift that can be given to anyone, even those who have never bothered to seek a holy life, who have never made a disciplined effort to pray or meditate, or who have not shown any particular interest in pursuing any kind of relationship with God. If God can give amazing mystical experiences to anyone, who are we to say that God cannot give some sort of mystical life to everyone?

I believe that William McNamara's vision of mysticism as defining all people is as true as Karl Rahner's assertion that in the future all Christians will be mystics. With these ideas in mind, we need to let go of the idea that some Christians are mystics while others are not; that the natural contemplatives get to enjoy union with God while others do not; that the worthy ones become deified while others do not. Both the teachings of Christianity and the wisdom of the mystics point to a spiritual reality beyond such dualistic thinking. All of Christ's lovers are, to some extent and on some level, "partakers of the divine nature." Most assuredly, some may enjoy the awareness of union with God, or the conscious presence of God, more fully or abundantly than others. But this is a difference of degree, not of kind. Perhaps those who never have any kind of spiritual "experience" at all are simply not mindful of the powerful, but hidden, action of the Spirit in their lives.

We certainly know enough about the reality of the unconscious and subconscious dimensions of the human mind to recognize that God, in his limitless sovereignty, can easily pour divine love and gifts into us on a less-than-conscious level. Perhaps if we want to learn about the mystery of *theosis*—the mystery of the unitive life or, for that matter, any aspect of the Ultimate Mystery—we need to inquire within.

As contemplatives, we can turn to the great mystics of history for guidance: Julian of Norwich, Meister Eckhart, *The Cloud of Unknowing*, John Ruusbroec, Thomas Merton, Teresa of Avila, John of the Cross, and many others. And whether or not we can ever be as brilliant as these giants of the spiritual life, we can take advantage of the store of wisdom they have handed to us. Through lectio divina, silence, meditation, and prayer, we can allow that wisdom to shape us, form us, and nurture our temperament for the ultimate contemplative task: falling, and staying, in love with God. It lets us open our hearts to receive the vast and limitless love he has for us—love that he is eager to pour into us, love that will fill us up and overflow from us to a world that so desperately needs it, and love that will rearrange our values, our ethics, and our sense of right and wrong so that we reorient our entire lives to the expression of grace and joy in ways both large and small.

A FINAL THOUGHT

There is a point in the Catholic Mass when the priest pours water into the wine that will be consecrated as the Blood of Christ. As he pours that water, he is instructed to inaudibly speak this blessing: "By the mystery of this water and wine may we come to share in the divinity of Christ, who humbled himself to share in our humanity."[47] Because these words are inaudible, they are *hidden* from the average person participating in the Mass. But in these hidden words lie the heart of the Christian mystery. Christ, who is one with God, comes to us and shares his divinity with us.

Psalm 82 contains this rather explosive verse: "You are gods, children of the Most High, all of you." We live in an age where plenty of people are willing to say "I am one with God," but these statements are tossed off in such a glib and cavalier way that it has become difficult to recognize just how awe-inspiring these statements really are.

Christianity, as an institutionalized religion, insists on the truth of the transcendence of God. But in doing so, the religion has too often sent out another, less helpful message: God is God, and we are not. Christian mystics, by contrast, merrily aim to deconstruct the walls that separate the immanence of God from the divine transcendence. Of all the paradoxes that mysticism helps to bring together, this may be the most important of all. God is greater than the universe, and God is present, right here and right now, in you and me. We are partakers of the divine nature, and God will always remain as different from us as the ocean is different from a single drop of water.

How do you sort this out and make it relevant to your daily spiritual practice? The answer is encoded in Psalm 82, where we are called "the *children* of the Most High." And Jesus said it even better: "Unless you change

and become like children, you will never enter the kingdom of heaven" (Matthew 18:3).

If, in fact, the mystical life can be likened to a sacred, spiritual marriage between your soul and God, it is fitting that a child be born out of that union of love. This heavenly love child is born inside of you and is, in fact, a part of you—the part who knows that you are a "god" and a child of the Most High, a child who, by knowing this, resides already in the unspeakable glories of heaven, right here, right now.

Mysticism is, ultimately, simply the art of going to heaven before you die—or, perhaps better said, the art of letting heaven emerge within you now. This doesn't take away your sins, or your pain and suffering, or your woundedness. Nor does it take away the brokenness of the world in which you live, and will continue to live on this side of eternity. But it does transform all these things. It empowers you to make God-infused choices and responses to all that life throws your way—and to do it all with the lack of self-consciousness that characterizes every reasonably well-adjusted child. To be fully aware that you partake of the divine nature and to accept that simply and naturally is, perhaps, what you can hope to find at the end of your contemplative journey.

And of course, the end will unfold into ever-new beginnings.

Yes, of course you'll get back to Narnia again some day. Once a King in Narnia, always a King in Narnia. But don't go trying to use the same route twice. Indeed, don't try to get there at all. It'll happen when you're not looking for it. And don't talk too much about it even among yourselves. And don't mention it to anyone else unless you find that they've had adventures of the same sort themselves. What's that? How will you know? Oh, you'll know all right. Odd things, they say—even their looks—will let the secret out. Keep your eyes open.

C. S. Lewis [48]

APPENDIX A

The Communion of Mystics

One of the Christian teachings I love the most is the concept of the "communion of saints," which holds that Christians have a mystical bond in Christ that transcends time and space. In other words, those who have already died in Christ remain just as much a part of the Body of Christ as those who are now alive and striving to live a faithful life. One way they continue to speak to us is through written words they have left behind. The following is a list of what I call "the communion of mystics." These are the great contemplatives, visionaries, and mystics who continue to inspire us today.

The list is by no means comprehensive, as it includes only those mystics who left behind writings. How many great mystics have been lost in the mists of time, simply because they never chose to commit their wisdom and their experiences to words on a page, we will never know. Some of the figures included here are controversial. Indeed, some, like Origen, Meister Eckhart, and Madame Guyon, have been denounced as heretics. And at least one person on my list—C. S. Lewis—specifically denied being a mystic.

The list is chronological by each mystic's date of death. Anonymous works are listed by the approximate date the work was composed. The list ends with individuals from the twentieth century, including a few who are still alive as of this writing. Including these contemporary figures in a list of great Christian mystics may seem somewhat presumptuous. We have no way of knowing if writers like Rufus Jones or George F. Macleod will still be remembered 200 years from now, let alone regarded as key mystics. On the other hand, Simone Weil, Pierre Teilhard de Chardin, and Thomas Merton are already renowned as truly great mystics, and I am confident that their reputations will only grow in the future.

I include these more recent figures because I think it's important to remember that mysticism is not just something that happened "way back then." For many people today, the work of living writers like Cynthia Bourgeault or Richard Rohr will be far more accessible and relevant than the arcane musings of Nicholas of Cusa or Jakob Böhme. I've tried to emphasize a wide and diverse selection of figures from our time and the recent past who are worthy exemplars of the contemplative life.

The Apostle Paul (?–ca. 66)

Author of much of the New Testament, including *The Second Letter to the Corinthians* (in which he recounts an ecstatic experience of being "caught up to the third heaven") and *The Letter to the Philippians*. Two of the most mystical of the New Testament writings, *The Letter to the Ephesians* and *The Letter to the Colossians*, may have been written by Paul, but may also have been written by one of his followers.

John the Evangelist (?–ca. 100)

Traditionally seen as the author of *The Gospel of John* and the three *Letters of John*.

Titus Flavius Clemens (ca. 150–215)

Known as Clement of Alexandria; author of *An Exhortation to the Greeks* and the *Stromata* ("Miscellanies").

Origen Adamantius (ca. 185–253)

Author of numerous works, including the *Commentary of the Song of Songs* and *Homily XXVII on Numbers*.

**The Desert Fathers and Mothers
(third and fourth centuries)**

Rejected the urbane life of the Roman Empire for the austerity of a solitary life in the desert or the wilderness—a life given over to prayer, fasting, and continual seeking after the heart of God. Their wisdom can be found in collections of their stories, including *The Sayings of the Desert Fathers,* and *The Lives of the Desert Fathers*.

Athanasius of Alexandria (ca. 296–373)

Author of *On the Incarnation* and the *Life of St. Antony*.

Ephrem the Syrian (ca. 306–373)

Author of the *Hymns on Paradise*.

Macarius of Egypt (ca. 300–390)

One of the Desert Fathers, traditionally seen as the author of *Fifty Spiritual Homilies*.

Gregory of Nyssa (ca. 330–395)

Author of the *Life of Moses*.

Evagrius Ponticus (345–399)

Also a Desert Father; author of *The Praktikos* and *Chapters on Prayer*.

Augustine of Hippo (ca. 354–430)

Author of many philosophical and theological works, but his mysticism is seen most clearly in his *Confessions*.

John Cassian (ca. 360–435)

Wrote the *Institutes* and the *Conferences*, particularly Conferences 9 and 10 on prayer.

**Pseudo-Dionysius the Areopagite
(late fifth to early sixth centuries)**

Probably a Syrian monk; his work represents the culmination
of the integration of Greek philosophy and Christian spirituality. Works include *The Divine Names* and *The Mystical Theology*.

Benedict of Nursia (480–547)

Author of *The Rule of St. Benedict*.

Gregory the Great (ca. 540–604)

Author of *Dialogues*, which include a biography of Benedict.

John Climacus (ca. 525–606)

Author of *The Ladder of Divine Ascent*.

Maximus the Confessor (ca. 580–662)

Author of *The 400 Chapters on Love* and *The Church's Mystagogy*.

Isaac Cyrus (died ca. 700)

Also known as Isaac the Syrian or Isaac of Nineveh; author of
the *Ascetical Homilies*.

Johannes Scotus Eriugena (ca. 815–877)

Author of the *Periphyseon* and the *Homily on the Prologue to the
Gospel of John*.

Symeon the New Theologian (949–1022)

Also known as Symeon of Studion; author of the *Practical and
Theological Chapters* and the *Discourses*.

William of St. Thierry (ca. 1085–1148)

Author of *The Golden Epistle* and *On Contemplating God*.

Bernard of Clairvaux (1090–1153)

Author of *On Loving God* and the *Sermons on the Song of Songs*.

Elizabeth of Schönau (1129–1164)
Author of the *Three Books of Visions*.

Aelred of Rievaulx (1110–1167)
Author of *Spiritual Friendship* and *The Mirror of Charity*.

Richard of St. Victor (d. 1173)
Author of *On the Trinity* and *The Mystical Ark*.

Hildegard of Bingen (1098–1179)
Author of *Scivias* and *The Book of Divine Works*.

Guigo II (died 1188)
Author of *The Ladder of Monks: A Letter on the Contemplative Life*.

Hadewijch of Antwerp (ca. 1150–1200)
Poet and visionary whose writings have been published in English as the *Collected Works*.

Giovanni Francesco Bernardone (ca. 1181–1226)
Better known as Francis of Assisi; author of several short writings anthologized in *Francis and Clare: The Complete Works*.

Clare of Assisi (1194–1253)
Author of several short writings anthologized in *Francis and Clare: The Complete Works*.

Beatrice of Nazareth (d. 1268)
Author of *The Seven Ways of Holy Love*.

Thomas Aquinas (ca. 1225–1274)
Author of numerous works, most famously the *Summa Theologica*. The year before he died, he had a mystical vision after which he dismissed all of his brilliant theological writing as only so much straw.

Bonaventure of Bagnoregio (1221–1274)
Author of *The Soul's Journey to God*.

Albertus Magnus (1200–1280)
Author of numerous works including the *Commentary on Diony-sius' Mystical Theology*.

Mechthild of Magdeburg (ca. 1210–1285)
Author of *The Flowing Light of the Godhead*.

Mechtilde of Hackeborn (1241–1299)
Author of *The Book of Special Grace*.

Gertrude of Helfta (1256–1302)
Known as Gertrude the Great; author of *The Herald of God's Loving Kindness*.

Jacopone da Todi (ca. 1230–1306)
Author of the *Lauds*.

Angela of Foligno (1248–1309)
Author of *The Book of Angela of Foligno*.

Marguerite Porete (d. 1310)
Author of *The Mirror of Simple Souls*.

Ramon Lull (ca. 1232–1315)
Author of *The Book of the Lover and the Beloved*.

Johannes Eckhart von Hochheim (1260–1328)
Known as Meister Eckhart; author of numerous works, includ-ing sermons in both German and Latin and treatises such as *The Book of Divine Consolation*.

Richard Rolle (ca. 1300–1349)
Author of *The Fire of Love* and *The Mending of Life*.

Theologia Germanica **(mid fourteenth century)**
> Author unknown.

Margaret Ebner (1291–1351)
> Author of *The Revelations of Margaret Ebner*.

Christina Ebner (1277–1355)
> Author of *The Diary of Christina Ebner*. No relation to Margaret Ebner.

Gregory Palamas (ca. 1296–1359)
> Author of *The Triads*.

Johannes Tauler (ca. 1300–1361)
> Known for his *Sermons*.

Henry Suso (ca. 1296–1366)
> Author of *The Exemplar*.

Birgitta Birgersdotter (1303–1373)
> Also known as Bridget of Sweden; author of *The Revelations of Saint Birgitta*.

Catherine of Siena (1347–1380)
> Author of *The Dialogue*.

John Ruusbroec (1293–1381)
> Also known as Jan Ruusbroec or John Ruysbroeck; author of *Spiritual Espousals* and *The Kingdom of the Lovers of God*.

Rulman Merswin (ca. 1307–1382)
> Author of *The Book of the Nine Rocks*.

Geert Groote (1340–1384)
> Author of numerous works, some of which are anthologized in *Devotio Moderna: Basic Writings* (Ed. by J. van Engen).

Walter Hilton (d. 1396)
Author of *The Scale of Perfection*.

The Cloud of Unknowing (late fourteenth century)
Author unknown.

Gerlac Peterson (1378–1411)
Author of the *Divine Soliloquies*.

Julian of Norwich (1342–ca. 1416)
Author of *Revelation of Love*.

Jean le Charlier de Gerson (1363–1429)
Author of *The Mountain of Contemplation*.

Margery Kempe (ca. 1373–1438)
Author of *The Book of Margery Kempe*.

Nicholas of Cusa (1401–1464)
Author of numerous works, including *The Vision of God*.

Thomas à Kempis (1380–1471)
Author of *The Imitation of Christ*.

Denys of Rykel (1402–1471)
Also known as Denis the Carthusian; author of *The Fountain Of Light And The Paths Of Life* and *Contemplation*.

Nikolai Maikov (ca. 1433–1508)
Also known as Nil Sorsky; author of several short works published in English as his *Complete Writings*.

Catherine of Genoa (1447–1510)
Author of *Purgation and Purgatory* and *The Spiritual Dialogue*.

Francisco de Osuna (d. ca. 1540)
Author of *The Third Spiritual Alphabet*.

Ignatius of Loyola (1491–1556)
Author of *The Spiritual Exercises*.

Teresa of Ávila (1515–1582)
Also known as Teresa of Jesus; author of numerous works, including *The Life of Teresa of Jesus*, *The Way of Perfection*, and *Interior Castle*.

Luis de León (1528–1591)
Author of *The Names of Christ*.

John of the Cross (1542–1591)
Author of *The Dark Night of the Soul*, *The Ascent of Mount Carmel*, *Spiritual Canticle*, and *Living Flame of Love*, as well as works of mystical poetry.

Philip Neri (1515–1595)
Author of the *Maxims* and *Sayings*.

Maria Maddalena de' Pazzi (1566–1607)
Author of *Revelations and Knowledge*.

Lorenzo Scupoli (ca. 1530–1610)
Author of *Spiritual Combat*.

François de Sales (1567–1622)
Author of *An Introduction to the Devout Life*.

Jakob Böhme (1575–1624)
or Jacob Boehme; author of *The Way to Christ*.

George Herbert (1593–1633)
Author of *The Temple*; renowned for his mystical poetry.

Gertrude More (1606–1633)
Author of *The Inner Life*.

Augustine Baker (1575–1641)
Author of *Holy Wisdom*.

Blaise Pascal (1623–1662)
Author of *Pensees*.

Jeremy Taylor (1613–1667)
Author of *The Rule and Exercises of Holy Living*.

Marie Guyart Martin (1599–1672)
Also known as Marie of the Incarnation; author of the *Relation* (autobiography).

Thomas Traherne (ca. 1636–1674)
Visionary poet and the author of *Centuries*.

Johann Scheffler (1624–1677)
Also known as Angelus Silesius; author of *The Cherubinic Wanderer*.

Benjamin Whichcote (1609–1683)
Author of *Our Conversation is in Heaven*.

Henry More (1614–1687)
Author of *An Explanation of the Divine Mystery of Godliness*.

George Fox (1624–1691)
Author of *The Journal of George Fox*.

Brother Lawrence of the Resurrection (ca. 1610–1691)
Author of *The Practice of the Presence of God*.

Henry Vaughan (1622–1695)
Visionary poet whose *Collected Poems* are available in several editions.

François Fénelon (1651–1715)
Author of *Christian Perfection*.

Jeanne Marie Bouvier de la Motte Guyon (1648–1717)
Also known as Madame Guyon; author of *Experiencing the Depths of Jesus Christ*.

Jean Pierre de Caussade (1675–1751)
Author of *Abandonment to Divine Providence*.

Jonathan Edwards (1703–1758)
Remembered chiefly for his controversial sermon "Sinners in the Hands of an Angry God," but his masterpiece, *A Treatise Concerning Religious Affections*, suggests that he was a true mystic.

William Law (1686–1761)
Author of *A Serious Call to a Devout and Holy Life*.

John Woolman (1720–1772)
Remembered for *The Journal of John Woolman*.

John Wesley (1703–1791)
Author of *A Plain Account of Christian Perfection*.

Nicholas Kallivourtzis (ca. 1749–1809)
Also known as Nicodemus of the Holy Mountain or Nicodemus the Hagiorite; compiler of *The Philokalia*.

William Blake (1757–1827)
Visionary poet and author of *The Marriage of Heaven and Hell*.

William Wordsworth (1770–1850)
Visionary poet whose works included "Intimations of Immortality" and "Lines Composed a Few Miles Above Tintern Abbey."

Phoebe Palmer (1807–1874)
Author of *The Way of Holiness* and *Entire Devotion to God*.

Matthias Joseph Scheeben (1835–1888)
Author of *The Mysteries of Christianity*.

The Way of a Pilgrim (mid nineteenth century)
Author unknown.

Coventry Patmore (1823–1896)
Author of *The Rod, The Root and the Flower*.

Thérèse de Lisieux (1873–1897)
Author of *The Story of a Soul*.

Maria Gemma Umberta Pia Galgani (1878–1903)
Whose autobiographical writings have been published in English as *The Voices of Gemma Galgani*.

Charles Eugene de Foucauld (1858–1916)
Author of *The Spiritual Autobiography of Charles de Foucauld*.

Maria Faustina Kowalska (1905–1938)
Author of *Divine Mercy in My Soul: The Diary of Saint Faustina*.

Thomas R. Kelly (1893–1941)
Author of *A Testament of Devotion*.

Evelyn Underhill (1875–1941)
Author of numerous works, including *Mysticism: A Study in the Nature and Development of Spiritual Consciousness* and *Practical Mysticism*.

Theresa-Benedicta of the Cross (1891–1942)
Also known as Edith Stein; author of *The Science of the Cross*.

Simone Weil (1909–1943)
Author of *Waiting for God*.

Rufus Jones (1863–1948)
Author of *The Flowering of Mysticism*.

William Ralph Inge (1860–1954)

Author of *Christian Mysticism*.

Caryll Houselander (1901–1954)

Author of *The Reed of God*.

Pierre Teilhard de Chardin (1881–1955)

Author of *Hymn of the Universe* (which includes his luminous essay "The Mass on the World") and *The Divine Milieu*.

John Baillie (1886–1960)

Author of *A Diary of Private Prayer* and *The Sense of the Presence of God*.

Dag Hammarskjöld (1905–1961)

Author of *Markings*.

A. W. Tozer (1897–1963)

Author of *The Pursuit of God* and *The Knowledge of the Holy*.

C. S. Lewis (1898–1963)

Refused to call himself a mystic but wrote luminous mystical fiction, such as *The Voyage of the Dawn Treader* and *Till We Have Faces*.

Reginald Garrigou-Lagrange (1877–1964)

Author of *Christian Perfection and Contemplation*.

Adrienne von Speyr (1902–1967)

Author of *Light and Images: Elements of Contemplation*.

Thomas Merton (1915–1968)

Author of many works, including *New Seeds of Contemplation* and *The Inner Experience: Notes on Contemplation*.

Ní Tuòsheng (1903–1972)

Also known as Watchman Nee; author of *The Normal Christian Life*.

Henri Le Saux (1910–1973)
Also known as Swami Abhishiktananda; author of *Prayer*.

Karl Rahner (1904–1984)
Author of many works, including *Encounters with Silence*.

Anthony de Mello (1931–1987)
Author of *Sadhana: A Way to God*.

George F. MacLeod (1895–1991)
Author of *The Whole Earth Shall Cry Glory*.

Bede Griffiths (1906–1993)
Author of *Return to the Center* and *A New Vision of Reality*.

Matta El-Meskeen (1919–2006)
Also known as Matthew the Poor; author of *The Communion of Love*.

Raimon Panikkar (b. 1918)
Author of *The Experience of God: Icons of the Mystery* and *Christophany: The Fullness of Man*.

Thomas Keating (b. 1923)
Author of *Intimacy with God*.

Jean Borella (b. 1930)
Author of *The Sense of the Supernatural*.

Richard Rohr (b. 1943)
Author of *Everything Belongs: The Gift of Contemplative Prayer* and *The Naked Now: Learning to See as the Mystics See*.

Cynthia Bourgeault (b. 1947)
Author of *Centering Prayer and Inner Awakening*.

APPENDIX B

A Contemplative Reading List

You don't have to read a lot of books to explore the mysteries. But it sure helps if you do. The Christian tradition has been blessed with numerous contemplatives and mystics who have written about their experiences and their life stories, and left advice and direction for those of us who follow in their footsteps.

The following list is meant only to get you started on your own journey of contemplative reading. I've tried to balance this list to include both the writings of the great mystics and more contemporary books of spiritual guidance and instruction. I make no apologies for how subjective the list is; it features authors and works that I myself have found useful or inspiring.

The books are presented in the reading order I think you may find most useful, but of course, if you are drawn to a particular book at the bottom of the list, by all means follow your intuition and read that one first. Meanwhile, for further ideas on books that may be of help to you as you continue your exploration of Christian mysticism, please consult my bibliography.

As you read these books, remember to approach them in the spirit of lectio divina. Read them slowly and with an open heart, not only savoring the wisdom they contain, but also taking time to ponder the often challenging or paradoxical insights they give into the nature of God and the dynamics of the spiritual life. There is more to being a contemplative than learning how to read meditatively. But as you embrace the prayerful rhythm of lectio divina, your journey into the world of mystical wisdom will be so much the richer for it.

This list is hardly exhaustive, and probably anyone with more than a passing knowledge of Christian mysticism and spirituality will howl with indignation over the many worthy books I did not include. My purpose is simply to whet your appetite. There are enough interesting and provocative writings by the great mystics—and about their wisdom—to fill a lifetime of study. Even in my relatively short list, you will find many different styles of writing and approaches to mysticism. Some are academic; some are informal; some emphasize the experiential side of mysticism; some focus on the values and teachings that undergird such experience. Only by exploring the literature for yourself can you discern which authors and writings speak most richly to you. Take the time to explore. But remember: as good as it is to read about prayer, it is even better to set aside the book and give God your undivided attention.

The Holy Bible. Not only is the Bible the text *par excellence* for lectio divina, it is also the single most important document for Christian mysticism. Reading the Bible can be challenging in our time, particularly because of its images of God as angry or vengeful, or the passages on gender relations that come across as sexist or demeaning to women. But for those who are willing to wrestle with the text, the Bible contains luminous passages of mystical insight. Start with the Gospel of John, then move on to Ephesians, Colossians, Philippians, the first Letter of John, the Psalms, and the Song of Songs. And don't stop there; shimmering glimpses of mystical insight can be found throughout this essential book. I strongly suggest that you avoid historical translations like the King James and the Douay-Rheims versions; newer translations are easier to read and generally more accurate. The New Jerusalem Bible and the New Revised Standard Version are both excellent, respected translations, worthy for both Bible study and for use in lectio.

C. S. Lewis, *The Voyage of the Dawn Treader.* Jesus told us to become like little children. With that in mind, here is a superb introduction to the mystical life under the charming guise of a children's book. Not only is this installment from C. S. Lewis's beloved Narnia books a delight to read, it is also a masterful integration of an ancient Celtic myth (the *immram*, or the wondrous sea voyage that leads to paradise) with the key elements of the Christian mystical journey. All the important dimensions of the contemplative life are here: conversion, repentance and growth in holiness, the embrace of silence, the encounter with darkness, and finally, the glorious union with God in light.

Bernard McGinn, *The Essential Writings of Christian Mysticism.* Numerous anthologies of writings by the great mystics have been published over the years, but this one towers over them all. It includes lengthy selections from the writings of the mystics arranged topically, as well as insightful introductions and commentaries on the various selections.

Harvey Egan, *An Anthology of Christian Mysticism.* An excellent complement to McGinn's *Essential Writings*, this anthology presents the writings of the greatest mystics in chronological, rather than topical, order, allowing you to get a feel for how mystical literature has evolved over the past 2,000 years.

Cynthia Bourgeault, *Centering Prayer and Inner Awakening.* The centering prayer movement began in a Trappist monastery, so its earliest proponents (Basil Pennington, Thomas Keating, and William Meninger) were all Trappists. But centering prayer soon spread widely, crossing denominational lines as people from all walks of life embraced this simple approach to silent prayer. As a leading "second-generation" teacher of centering prayer, Anglican priest Cynthia Bourgeault brings to this book a keen insight, not only of centering prayer itself, but also of the dynamics of inner growth and healing that can occur as part of a sustained contemplative practice.

Richard Rohr, *Everything Belongs: The Gift of Contemplative Prayer.* This is a general introduction to the beauty of contemplative spirituality, in which Rohr poetically explores how contemplation fosters new ways of seeing and thinking and understanding. His message, that contemplation transforms us from ordinary consciousness (which is dualistic, competitive, and oppositional) to unitive consciousness (a holistic recognition of God's grace and presence in all things), falls squarely in the heart of mystical wisdom.

Julian of Norwich, *Revelation of Love.* In my opinion, this is the single most important written record of Christian mystical experience (at least so far). On the surface, it is the tale of a devout woman who experienced visions while suffering from illness; but as Julian shares the details of her visions, a powerful theology of divine love and transforming grace emerges that supports her central conviction that, in Christ, "all shall be well."

Thomas Merton, *The Inner Experience: Notes on Contemplation.* In the 1940s, Merton wrote a short book called *What is Contemplation?* which he revised and expanded in the 1950s. That manuscript was revised yet again shortly before he died in 1968. Now published as *The Inner Experience*, it offers an in-depth look at Merton's understanding of contemplation, and how average men and women (i.e., those who are not called to monastic life) can embrace the path of contemplation in our day.

Evelyn Underhill, *Practical Mysticism.* Many of Underhill's books on mysticism and Christian spirituality are scholarly in tone, but this short book presents her understanding of how Christian mysticism can be applied to ordinary life in the modern world. A century after its publication, it feels a bit dated, but nevertheless contains keen insight on how mysticism can transform the spirituality of anyone, no matter how "practical" he may be.

Anonymous, *The Cloud of Unknowing* and *The Book of Privy Counseling*. These two manuals on contemplative spirituality were originally written in the fourteenth century. *The Cloud of Unknowing* affirms the primacy of love over mental ability in the mystical life, and served as a direct inspiration for the centering prayer movement that emerged in the late twentieth century. *The Book of Privy Counseling* offers additional instruction for the serious student of silent prayer.

Mary Margaret Funk, *Thoughts Matter: The Practice of the Spiritual Life*. A Benedictine nun explores the wisdom of the Desert Fathers and Mothers, particularly the teachings of Evagrius and John Cassian, to reveal how their insights about meditation and managing the unruly nature of the mind remain relevant even today.

Anonymous, *The Way of a Pilgrim* and *The Pilgrim Continues His Way*. These nineteenth-century Russian novels provide an accessible explanation of the spirituality of the Prayer of the Heart—the Eastern Orthodox practice of repeating the Jesus Prayer continually, thereby cultivating an ongoing awareness of Christ's presence.

Brother Lawrence, *The Practice of the Presence of God*. This is a slender volume of collected papers by and about a seventeenth-century Carmelite friar which captures his simple spirituality of intentionally and continually choosing awareness of God's presence moment by moment throughout the day.

John Ruusbroec, *The Spiritual Espousals and Other Works*. Evelyn Underhill considered Ruusbroec her favorite mystic, and it's easy to see why. His spirituality is deeply Trinitarian, and his understanding of the mystical summit of union with God that nevertheless does not erase the distinction between creator and creature makes him one of the most articulate

Christian mystics. *The Spiritual Espousals* is generally regarded as his masterpiece. Three minor works are included in the Classics of Western Spirituality edition.[49]

Teresa of Avila, *Collected Works, Volumes 1 and 2*. The first two volumes of Teresa's collected works include three mystical classics: her autobiography, one of the finest statements of personal spiritual experience; *The Way of Perfection*, her commentary on prayer and particularly on the Lord's Prayer; and *The Interior Castle*, a survey of the mystical life built around the metaphor of the soul as a castle fashioned out of a glittering diamond, in whose center God reigns. As we travel through the rooms or "mansions" of the castle, we are called to grow in virtue and holiness.

Benedicta Ward (translator), *The Sayings of the Desert Fathers: Sayings of the Early Christian Monks*. Most of the early Christian hermits and monks who retreated into the deserts of Egypt and Syria to surrender their lives to prayer did not write about their experiences, but tales of their teachings were eventually collected and anthologized. Today, the sayings of the desert read like parables and sometimes even riddles, offering insight into lives where everything was held secondary to the quest for God.

Meister Eckhart, *Selected Writings*. One of the most celebrated, but also most controversial, of Christian mystics, Eckhart, a thirteenth-century Dominican theologian, wrote scholarly works but also preached in both Latin and his native German about the experience of union with God that is available to the ardent contemplative. The Penguin Books anthology of his writings includes three treatises, along with a selection of sermons.

Pseudo-Dionysius, *The Complete Works*. The Classics of Western Spirituality has published a one-volume edition of all the known writings by the elusive and mysterious sixth-century theologian who calls himself Dionysius the Areopagite, a minor figure in the New Testament. Evidence in his writings shows that he isn't really Dionysius, but an anonymous figure who lived and wrote sometime around the year 500 CE. What this author has to say is just as mysterious (and controversial) as his identity. He expresses his understanding of God, the angels, and even the church using language and concepts that are clearly influenced by pagan Greek philosophy. Pseudo-Dionysius has had an enormous impact on the mystical tradition as a whole, influencing figures as diverse as Thomas Aquinas, the author of *The Cloud of Unknowing*, and lesser-known mystics like John Scotus Eriugena. This anthology includes his four major works: *The Celestial Hierarchy*, his enormously influential treatise on the nature of heaven; *The Ecclesiastical Hierarchy*, in which he explores the mystical nature of church organization; *The Divine Names;* and *The Mystical Theology*, profound, seminal works of apophatic (imageless) theology.

Thérèse of Lisieux, *The Story of a Soul.* Immensely popular when published, this autobiography of a nineteenth-century French nun who died of tuberculosis while still in her twenties has become a modern classic. Thérèse promotes what she calls "the little way" of serving God in humble and ordinary ways, acknowledging that the spiritual life is not just for martyrs or others who are heroic in their stature, but also for even the most down-to-earth people in the lowliest of circumstances who nevertheless have much to offer to God and their neighbors.

John of the Cross, *Collected Works.* One of the greatest of Christian mystics, John of the Cross was a world-class Spanish poet and a gifted writer with a keen understanding of the psychology of the inner life. His collected works include his four major mystical treatises: *The Ascent of Mount Carmel, The Dark Night of the Soul, Living Flame of Love,* and the *Spiritual Canticle.*

Anthony Bloom, *Beginning to Pray*. Most of the books on this list are concerned primarily with contemplation, but this book takes us back to the basics of prayer in its most down-to-earth form (even including recited or memorized prayer). Written by an orthodox archbishop, this introductory work offers gentle encouragement and insight into practical questions (and common obstacles) for anyone wishing to foster a greater sense of intimacy and connection with God.

Hildegard of Bingen, *Selected Writings*. A twelth-century nun who has become celebrated in our time because of her beautiful music, Hildegard was also a visionary who wrote of her mystical experiences and corresponded with some of the leading figures of her day, including Bernard of Clairvaux.

Jean-Pierre de Caussade, *Abandonment to Divine Providence*. This short eighteenth-century mystical text, originally written as letters of spiritual direction for a convent of nuns, promotes the freedom that arises from living in the present moment and joyfully offering all our concerns to the loving care of God.

Nikodimos of the Holy Mountain and Makarios of Corinth (compilers), *The Philokalia*. This multi-volume anthology of writings from the fathers of the Eastern Orthodox churches provides detailed instructions on asceticism and the life of prayer, particularly the "Prayer of the Heart." Among the great mystics whose writings are included in *The Philokalia* are John Cassian, Evagrius Ponticus, Maximus the Confessor, and Gregory Palamas.

Douglas V. Steere (editor), *Quaker Spirituality*. This installment in the Classics of Western Spirituality series presents key writings from the Religious Society of Friends, including works by George Fox, Isaac Penington, John Woolman, Rufus M. Jones, and Thomas R. Kelly, all of whom celebrate the rich Quaker tradition, whose profound attentiveness to silence and to God's presence within has resulted in a strong heritage of social justice.

Michael Casey, *Fully Human, Fully Divine.* The mystery of deification is explored and, as much as possible, explained in this meditative commentary on the Gospel of Mark—and how Mark's story of Christ can, in turn, illuminate our own experience as members of Christ's Body, here and now.

Walter Hilton, *The Scale of Perfection.* A contemporary of both Julian of Norwich and *The Cloud of Unknowing*, Hilton is not as well known now, but, during their lives, his work was the most widely circulated of the three. This may be because *The Scale of Perfection* is an astute study of the psychology of spiritual development that explains the dynamics of the inner life in a down-to-earth, practical style.

Ignatius of Loyola, *The Spiritual Exercises.* Ignatius's spiritual exercises are designed to assist in the process of discernment. But they also stand on their own as a powerful method for using imagination and visualization to embrace Christ as encountered through scripture, and for using meditation and prayer to draw closer to God.

Simone Weil, *Waiting for God.* One of the twentieth century's most enigmatic figures, Weil was a Jewish philosopher who had mystical experiences of Christ and who explored the teachings of the Christian faith. She was never baptized, however, preferring to remain an "outsider" to the institutional church. Her masterpiece, *Waiting for God*, collects a number of her essays and letters, including a powerful reflection on the various forms of the implicit (not readily visible) love of God.

Evagrius Ponticus, *The Praktikos & Chapters on Prayer.* Perhaps the most important of the Desert Fathers, Evagrius influenced later monks like John Cassian and Benedict, thereby influencing monasticism as a whole. This book gathers his pithy, concise writings about the struggle to overcome sin, become holy, and enter into the serene state where true contemplation may occur.

Gerald May, *Will and Spirit: A Contemplative Psychology.* Combining the scientific thinking of a psychiatrist with the deep interior knowingness of a mature contemplative, May explores how the prayerful process of surrendering to God in a spirit of "willingness" can transform us both psychologically and spiritually.

Ruth Burrows, *Guidelines for Mystical Prayer.* Drawing on the rich wisdom of Carmelite spirituality, Burrows describes what contemplative prayer is, and why it is ultimately a spirituality that involves surrendering to Christ and trusting in his initiative—trusting Christ to draw us into union with God.

Martin Laird, *Into the Silent Land: A Guide to the Christian Practice of Contemplation.* Ideal for both beginners and proficients in the spiritual life, this book examines the landscape of interior prayer, drawing on both the eastern and western traditions of Christian wisdom. The book offers practical advice on such topics as attentiveness to the breath as an aid to contemplation, dealing with distractions, and learning how to pray through suffering.

APPENDIX C

Online Resources

www.anamchara.com
My blog and website, with information about Christian spiritual formation and the writings of the great Christian mystics.

www.benedictine-oblates.org
Benedictine oblates "donate their own being to God… infusing the values of the Holy Rule of Benedict into their paths of faith."

www.cistercianfamily.org
Website for an international association of Catholic and ecumenical contemplative communities associated with Cistercian monasteries.

www.contemplativeoutreach.org
Dedicated to the practice and promotion of centering prayer and the teachings of Thomas Keating.

www.laycarmelites.com
Catholic organization of laypersons dedicated to the spiritual tradition of Teresa of Avila, John of the Cross, and Thérèse of Lisieux.

www.nafra-sfo.org
Secular (Third Order) Franciscans date back to Francis of Assisi himself, and follow Franciscan spirituality while living "in the world." This site is for Catholic Franciscans; other websites serve Anglicans (*www.tssf.org*) and ecumenical Franciscans (*www.franciscans.com*).

www.sdiworld.org
Interfaith organization dedicated to promoting the ministry of spiritual direction. The site includes a directory of spiritual directors.

www.shalem.org
Programs and resources for those who want to open themselves more fully to God in their daily lives and work.

www.universalis.com
Website that provides the text of the Catholic Daily Office each day. The text can be downloaded to your computer or iPhone.

www.wccm.org
Center for Christian meditation, following the teaching of Benedictine monk John Main.

Endnotes

1. Karl Rahner, *Concern for the Church* (New York: Crossroad, 1981), p. 149.

2. Evelyn Underhill, *Mystics of the Church* (Cambridge, UK: James Clarke & Co. Ltd., 1925), p. 10.

3. Maximus the Confessor, *On the Cosmic Mystery of Jesus Christ* (Crestwood, NY: St. Vladimir's Seminary Press, 2003), p. 126.

4. Augustine, *Confessions*, XI, 14 (London: Penguin Books, 1961), p. 264.

5. *The American Heritage Dictionary.*

6. Evelyn Underhill, *The Mystics of the Church* (Cambridge, UK: James Clarke & Co., Ltd., 1925), p. 9–10.

7. Margaret Smith, "The Nature and Meaning of Mysticism," from *Understanding Mysticism,* Ed. Richard Woods, OP (Garden City, NY: Image Books, 1980), p. 19.

8. Harvey D. Egan, SJ, *An Anthology of Christian Mysticism* (Collegeville, MN: The Liturgical Press, 1996), p. xvi.

9. Timothy Freke & Peter Gandy, *The Complete Guide to World Mysticism* (London: Piatkus, 1997), p. 9.

10. Swami Abhayananda, *History of Mysticism: The Unchanging Testament* (Olympia, WA: Atma Books, 1996), p. 1.

11. F. C. Happold, *Mysticism: A Study and an Anthology* (London: Penguin Books, 1990), p. 16.

12. Andrew Harvey, *The Essential Mystics: The Soul's Journey to Truth* (New York: HarperCollins, 1996), p. x.

13. Thomas Keating et al., *Spirituality, Contemplation & Transformation: Writings on Centering Prayer* (New York: Lantern Books, 2008), p. xii.

14. Louis Bouyer, in *Understanding Mysticism,* Ed. Richard Woods, OP (Garden City, NY: Image Books, 1980), p. 43.

15. George Maloney's *The Mystery of Christ in You* (New York: Alba House, 1998) explains much of the meaning behind the concept of "mystery" in the New Testament, particularly in the writings of St. Paul.

16. Quoted in Antoine Thomas, *Praying in the Presence of Our Lord for Children* (Huntington, IN: Our Sunday Visitor, 2003), p. 28.

17. Patrick Henry and David Steindl-Rast, *Benedict's Dharma* (New York: Riverhead Books, 2001), p. 128.

18. *http://tinyurl.com/ylsjfll*

19. S. Abhayananda, *History of Mysticism: The Unchanging Testament* (Olympia, WA: Atma Books, 1996), p. 232.

20. Quoted in *The Soul Afire: Revelations of the Mystics.* Ed. by H. A. Reinhold (Garden City, NY: Image Books, 1973), p. 420.

21. Quoted by Richard Rohr in *The Naked Now* (New York: Crossroad, 2009), p. 113.

22. Jean-Yves Leloup, *Being Still: Reflections on an Ancient Mystical Tradition* (New York: Paulist Press, 2003), p. 59.

23. Thomas Dubay, *Deep Conversion Deep Prayer* (San Francisco: Ignatius Press, 2006), p. 64.

24. C. S. Lewis, *The Great Divorce* (San Francisco: Harper One, 2009), p. 75.

25. Gerald May, *Will and Spirit* (San Francisco: Harper & Row, 1982), p. 46.

26. Quoted in *Sermons in a Sentence: A Treasury of Quotations on the Spiritual Life Volume 4: St. Teresa of Avila.* Selected and arranged by John P. McClernon (San Francisco: Ignatius Press, 2005), p. 107.

27. *The Cloud of Unknowing* and *The Book of Privy Counseling*, Tr. by William Johnston (New York: Image Books, 1973), p. 146.

28. Thomas Merton, *The Inner Experience* (New York: HarperCollins, 2003), p. 22.

29. Meister Eckhart, *Selected Writings* (London: Penguin Books, 1994), p. 179.

30. These include John Wesley, founder of Methodism; George Fox, founder of the Religious Society of Friends, commonly known as the Quakers; Jonathan Edwards, leader of the "Great Awakening" religious revival; Phoebe Palmer, a Methodist woman renowned for her advocacy of living a holy life; and A. W. Tozer, a minister with the evangelical Christian Missionary Alliance.

31. To learn more, visit *www.shalem.org* or *www.sdiworld.org*—two websites devoted to the ministry of spiritual guidance.

32. *De Incarnatione*, 54, quoted in A.M. Allchin, *Participation in God: A Forgotten Strand in Anglican Tradition* (London: Darton, Longman & Todd, 1988), p. 1.

33. Julian of Norwich, *Revelations of Divine Love*, Chapter 4, Tr. by Clifton Wolters (New York: Penguin Books Ltd., 1966), p. 66.

34. Quoted in *The Soul Afire: Revelations of the Mystics,* edited by H. A. Reinhold (Garden City, NY: Image Books, 1973), p. 129.

35. Quoted in Paul Verdeyen, *Ruusbroec and His Mysticism* (Collegeville, MN: The Liturgical Press, 1994), p. 72.

36. Brian Haggerty, *Out of the House of Slavery: On the Meaning of the Ten Commandments* (New York: Paulist Press, 1978), p. 135–136.

37. Quoted in Jonathan Wilson-Hartgrove, *New Monasticism* (Grand Rapids, MI: Brazos Press, 2008), p. 147.

38. Guigo II, *Ladder of Monks and Twelve Meditations* (Kalamazoo, MI; Cistercian Publications, 1979), p. 90–91.

39. Bonaventure, *The Soul's Journey to God and Other Works* (New York: Paulist Press, 1978), p. 63.

40. Quoted in *Sermons in a Sentence: A Treasury of Quotations on the Spiritual Life Volume 2: St. Francis de Sales* (San Francisco: Ignatius Press, 2003), p. 138.

41. Fr. John-Julian, OJN, *The Complete Julian of Norwich* (Brewster, MA: Paraclete Press, 2009), p. 171.

42. Quoted in *The Soul Afire: Revelations of the Mystics.* Ed. by H. A. Reinhold (Garden City, NY: Image Books, 1973), p. 112.

43. Richard Rohr, *The Naked Now: Learning to See as the Mystics See* (New York: Crossroad, 2009), p. 159.

44. John Ruusbroec, *The Spiritual Espousals and Other Works* (New York: Paulist Press, 1985), pp. 146, 150.

45. Evelyn Underhill, *Mysticism* (London: Methuen & Co. Ltd., 1930), p. 415.

46. Robert Davis Hughes, *Beloved Dust* (New York: Continuum, 2008), p. 373.

47. Tony Castle, ed., *The Catholic Prayer Book* (Ann Arbor, MI: Servant Books, 1986), p. 74.

48. C. S. Lewis, *The Lion, the Witch and the Wardrobe* (New York: Collier Books, 1970), pp. 185–186.

49. Paulist Press' Classics of Western Spirituality series of great mystical books is an excellent resource for students of Christian mysticism, as well as Jewish, Muslim, and even Native American spirituality.

Selected Bibliography

WRITINGS BY THE GREAT CHRISTIAN MYSTICS

Abhishiktananda. *Prayer*. Delhi: ISPCK, 1989.

Aelred of Rievaulx. *Spiritual Friendship*. Kalamazoo, MI: Cistercian Publications, 1977.

Anonymous. *The Cloud of Unknowing* and *The Book of Privy Counseling*. Newly edited with an introduction by William Johnston. New York: Image Books, 1973.

Anonymous. *The Way of a Pilgrim* and *The Pilgrim Continues His Way*. Blanco, TX: New Sarov Press, 1993.

Augustine of Hippo. *Selected Writings*. New York: Paulist Press, 1984.

Baker, Augustine. *Holy Wisdom*. Wheathampstead, UK: Anthony Clarke Books, 1972.

Bernard of Clairvaux. *Selected Works*. New York: Paulist Press, 1987.

Birgitta of Sweden. *Life and Selected Works*. New York: Paulist Press, 1990.

Bonaventure. *The Soul's Journey Into God and Other Works*. New York: Paulist Press, 1978.

Brother Lawrence. *The Practice of the Presence of God*. Washington, DC: ICS Publications, 1994.

Catherine of Genoa. *Purgation and Purgatory: The Spiritual Dialogue*. New York: Paulist Press, 1979.

Catherine of Siena. *The Dialogue*. New York: Paulist Press, 1980.

Climacus, John. *The Ladder of Divine Ascent*. New York: Paulist Press, 1982.

de Caussade, Jean-Pierre. *Abandonment to Divine Providence*. Tr. by John Beevers. New York: Image Books, 1975.

Du Boulay, Shirley, ed. *Swami Abhishiktananda: Essential Writings*. Maryknoll, NY: Orbis Books, 2006.

Egan, Harvey D., ed. *An Anthology of Christian Mysticism*. Second edition. Collegeville, MN: The Liturgical Press, 1996.

Ephrem the Syrian. *Hymns*. New York: Paulist Press, 1989.

Evagrius Ponticus. *The Praktikos & Chapters on Prayer*. Kalamazoo, MI: Cistercian Publications, 1980.

Fox, George. *The Journal*. London: Penguin Books, 1998.

Francis and Clare. *The Complete Works*. New York: Paulist Press, 1982.

Fremantle, Anne, ed. *The Protestant Mystics: An Anthology of Spiritual Experience from Martin Luther to T. S. Eliot*. Introduction by W. H. Auden. Boston: Little, Brown and Company, 1964.

Fry, Timothy, OSB, ed. *RB 1980: The Rule of St. Benedict in Latin and English with Notes*. Collegeville, MN: The Liturgical Press, 1981.

Gregory of Nyssa. *The Life of Moses*. Tr. by Everett Ferguson and Abraham J. Malherbe. New York: Paulist Press, 1978.

Gregory Palamas. *The Triads*. New York: Paulist Press, 1983.

Guigo II. *Ladder of Monks and Twelve Meditations*. Kalamazoo, MI: Cistercian Publications, 1979.

Herbert, George. *The Country Parson* and *The Temple*. New York: Paulist Press, 1981.

Hildegard of Bingen, *Selected Writings*. London: Penguin Books, 2001.

Hilton, Walter. *The Stairway of Perfection*. Tr. by M. L. Del Mastro. Garden City, NY: Image Books, 1979.

Houselander, Caryll. *Essential Writings*. Selected with commentary by Wendy M. Wright. Maryknoll, NY: Orbis Books, 2005.

_____. *The Reed of God*. New York: Sheed and Ward, 1944.

Ignatius of Loyola. *The Spiritual Exercises*. Garden City, NY: Image Books, 1964.

John Cassian. *Conferences*. New York: Paulist Press, 1985.

John of the Cross. *Collected Works*. Washington, DC: ICS Publications, 1991.

Julian of Norwich. *Revelation of Love*. Ed. and tr. by John Skinner. New York: Image Books, 1996.

Kempe, Margery. *The Book of Margery Kempe*. London: Penguin Books, 1985.

Lewis, C. S. *Letters to Malcolm: Chiefly on Prayer*. San Diego: Harcourt, Inc., 1964.

_____. *The Lion, the Witch and the Wardrobe*. New York: Macmillan Books, 1950.

_____. *The Voyage of the Dawn Treader*. New York: Macmillan Books, 1952.

Macleod, George F. *The Whole Earth Shall Cry Glory*. Glasgow, Scotland: Wild Goose Publications, 1985.

_____. *Daily Readings with George Macleod*. Ed. by Ron Ferguson. London: HarperCollins, 1991.

Maximus the Confessor. *On the Cosmic Mystery of Jesus Christ*. Crestwood, NY: St. Vladimir's Seminary Press, 2003.

McClernon, John P., ed. *Sermons in a Sentence: A Treasury of Quotations on the Spiritual Life Volume 4: St. Teresa of Avila*. San Francisco: Ignatius Press, 2005.

Meister Eckhart. *Selected Writings*. London: Penguin Books, 1994.

_____. *The Complete Mystical Works*. New York: Crossroad, 2010.

Merton, Thomas. *Contemplative Prayer*. New York: Image Books, 1971.

_____. *New Seeds of Contemplation*. New York: New Directions, 1961.

_____. *The Inner Experience: Notes on Contemplation*. Ed. by William H. Shannon. San Francisco: HarperSanFrancisco, 2003.

_____. *An Introduction to Christian Mysticism: Initiation into the Monastic Tradition 3*. Ed. by Patrick F. O'Connell. Kalamazoo, MI: Cistercian Publications, 2008.

_____. *Thomas Merton, Spiritual Master: The Essential Writings*. Ed. by Lawrence S. Cunningham. New York: Paulist Press, 1992.

_____. *The Seven Storey Mountain*. Garden City, NY: Image Books, 1970.

McGinn, Bernard, ed. *The Essential Writings of Christian Mysticism*. New York: The Modern Library, 2006.

Mechthild of Magdeburg. *The Flowing Light of the Godhead*. New York: Paulist Press, 1998.

Nicholas of Cusa. *Selected Spiritual Writings*. New York: Paulist Press, 1997.

Nikodimos of the Holy Mountain and Makarios of Corinth (compilers). *The Philokalia: The Complete Text* (Volumes 1–4). London: Faber and Faber, 1979, 1981, 1984, 1995.

Origen. *An Exhortation to Martyrdom, Prayer, and Selected Works*. Tr. by Rowan A. Greer. New York: Paulist Press, 1979.

Pascal, Blaise. *Pensées*. London: Penguin Books, 1966.

Palmer, Phoebe. *The Way of Holiness*. Charleston, SC: Bibliolife, 2009.

Patmore, Coventry. *The Rod, the Root and the Flower*. Freeport, NY: Books for Libraries Press, 1950.

Ponticus, Evagrius. *The Praktikos & Chapters on Prayer*. Kalamazoo, MI: Cistercian Publications, 1972.

Pseudo-Dionysius. *The Complete Works*. New York: Paulist Press, 1987.

Pseudo-Macarius. *The Fifty Spiritual Homilies and the Great Letter*. New York: Paulist Press, 1992.

Rahner, Karl. *Spiritual Writings*. Maryknoll, NY: Orbis Books, 2004.

Reinhold, H. A., ed. *The Soul Afire: Revelations of the Mystics*. Garden City, NY: Image Books, 1973.

Richard of St. Victor. *The Twelve Patriarchs and Other Works*. New York: Paulist Press, 1979.

Rolle, Richard. *The Fire of Love and the Mending of Life*. Tr. with an introduction by M. L. del Mastro. Garden City, NY: Image Books, 1981.

Ruusbroec, John. *Spiritual Espousals*. New York: Paulist Press, 1985.

Steere, Douglas V., ed. *Quaker Spirituality: Selected Writings*. New York: Paulist Press, 1984.

Symeon the New Theologian. *The Practical and Theological Chapters & The Three Theological Discourses*. Kalamazoo, MI: Cistercian Publications, 1982.

Teilhard de Chardin, Pierre. *The Divine Milieu*. New York: Harper & Row, 1965.

_____. *Hymn of the Universe*. New York: Harper & Row, 1965.

Teresa of Avila. *Collected Works* (Volumes 1–3). Washington, DC: ICS Publications, 1976, 1980, 1985.

Thérèse of Lisieux. *Story of a Soul: The Autobiography*. Washington, DC: ICS Publications, 1996.

Tozer, A.W. *The Pursuit of God*. Camp Hill, PA: Wing Spread Publishers, 2006.

Underhill, Evelyn. *Mysticism: A Study in the Nature and Development of Spiritual Consciousness*. Twelfth edition, revised. London: Methuen & Co. Ltd., 1930.

_____. *Practical Mysticism*. New York: E. P. Dutton & Co., 1915.

_____. *The Evelyn Underhill Reader*. Compiled by Thomas S. Kepler. New York: Abingdon Press, 1962.

_____. *The Letters of Evelyn Underhill*. Ed. with an introduction by Charles Williams. London: Longmans, Green and Co. Ltd., 1943.

_____. *The Mystics of the Church*. Cambridge, UK: James Clarke & Co., Ltd., 1925.

Ward, Benedicta, tr. *The Desert Fathers: Sayings of the Early Christian Monks*. London: Penguin, 2003.

Weil, Simone. *Gravity and Grace*. London: Routledge, 1952.

_____. *Waiting for God*. New York: Harper & Row, 1973.

Wesley, John. *A Plain Account of Christian Perfection*. Annotated edition by Mark K. Olson. Fenwick, MI: Alethea in Heart, 2005.

William of St. Thierry. *On Contemplating God, Prayer, Meditations*. Kalamazoo, MI: Cistercian Publications, 1977.

Recent and Contemporary Christian Contemplatives

A Monk of the West. *Christianity and the Doctrine of Non-Dualism*. Hillsdale, NY: Sophia Perennis, 2004.

Baillie, John. *The Sense of the Presence of God*. New York: Charles Scribner's Sons, 1962.

Behrens, James Stephen, OCSO. *Portraits of Grace: Images and Words from the Monastery of the Holy Spirit*. Skokie, IL: Acta Publications, 2007.

Benson, Robert. *In Constant Prayer*. Nashville, TN: Thomas Nelson, 2008.

Bloom, Anthony. *Beginning to Pray*. New York: Paulist Press, 1982.

Bourgeault, Cynthia. *Centering Prayer and Inner Awakening*. Cambridge, MA: Cowley Publications, 2004.

_____. *Mystical Hope: Trusting in the Mercy of God*. Cambridge, MA: Cowley Publications, 2001.

_____. *The Wisdom Way of Knowing: Reclaiming an Ancient Tradition to Awaken the Heart*. San Francisco: Jossey-Bass, 2003.

Burrows, Ruth. *Guidelines for Mystical Prayer*. Denville, NJ: Dimension Books, 1976.

Carter, Sydney. *Dance in the Dark*. New York: Crossroad, 1982.

Casey, Michael, OCSO. *Fully Human Fully Divine: An Interactive Christology*. Liguori, MO: Liguori/Triumph, 2004.

_____. *Sacred Reading: The Ancient Art of Lectio Divina*. Liguori, MO: Liguori/Triumph, 1996.

_____. *Strangers to the City: Reflections on the Beliefs and Values of the Rule of Saint Benedict*. Brewster, MA: Paraclete Press, 2005.

_____. *Toward God: The Ancient Wisdom of Western Prayer*. Liguori, MO: Liguori/Triumph, 1996.

_____. *The Undivided Heart: The Western Monastic Approach to Contemplation*. Petersham, MA: St. Bede's Publications, 1994.

Chu-Cong, Joseph, OCSO. *The Contemplative Experience: Erotic Love and Spiritual Union*. New York: Crossroad, 1999.

Delisi, Anthony, OCSO. *Praying in the Cellar: A Guide to Facing Your Fears and Finding God*. Brewster, MA: Paraclete Press, 2005.

Doherty, Catherine De Hueck. *Molchanie: The Silence of God*. New York: Crossroad Publishing Company, 1982.

Dubay, Thomas. *Deep Conversion, Deep Prayer*. San Francisco: Ignatius Press, 2006.

Edwards, Tilden. *Living Simply Through the Day: Spiritual Survival in a Complex Age*. New York: Paulist Press, 1977.

Foster, David, OSB. *Deep Calls to Deep: Going Further in Prayer*. London: Continuum, 2007.

Funk, Margaret. *Thoughts Matter*. New York: Continuum, 1998.

Grant, Sara, RSCJ. *Toward an Alternative Theology: Confessions of a Non-Dualist Christian*. Notre Dame, IN: University of Notre Dame Press, 2002.

Huggett, Joyce. *The Joy of Listening to God*. Downers Grove, IL: Intervarsity Press, 1986.

Jones, Rufus. *Essential Writings*. Maryknoll, NY: Orbis Books, 2001.

Keating, Thomas OCSO, et al. *Spirituality, Contemplation & Transformation: Writings on Centering Prayer*. New York: Lantern Books, 2008.

Kelsey, Morton. *The Other Side of Silence: A Guide to Christian Meditation*. New York: Paulist Press, 1976.

Laird, Martin. *Into the Silent Land: A Guide to the Christian Practice of Contemplation*. Oxford: Oxford University Press, 2006.

Leech, Kenneth. *Soul Friend: The Practice of Christian Spirituality*. San Francisco: Harper & Row, 1977.

_____. *Experiencing God: Theology as Spirituality*. San Francisco: Harper & Row, 1985.

_____. *The Eye of the Storm: Living Spiritually in the Real World*. San Francisco: HarperCollins, 1992.

_____. *Subversive Orthodoxy: Traditional Faith & Radical Commitment*. Toronto: Anglican Book Centre, 1992.

_____. *True Prayer: An Invitation to Christian Spirituality*. San Francisco: Harper & Row, 1980.

Marechal, Paul. *Dancing Madly Backwards: A Journey Into God*. New York: Crossroad, 1982.

May, Gerald G. *Will & Spirit: A Contemplative Psychology*. San Francisco: Harper & Row, 1982.

McNamara, William. *Earthy Mysticism: Contemplation and the Life of Passionate Presence*. New York: Crossroad, 1987.

O'Donohue, John. *Anam Cara: A Book of Celtic Wisdom*. San Francisco: HarperCollins, 1997.

Panikkar, Raimon. *Christophany: The Fullness of Man*. Maryknoll, NY: Orbis Books, 2004.

_____. *The Experience of God: Icons of the Mystery*. Minneapolis: Fortress Press, 2006.

Rohr, Richard. *Everything Belongs: The Gift of Contemplative Prayer*. New York: Crossroad, 2003.

_____. *Things Hidden: Scripture as Spirituality*. Cincinnati: St. Anthony Messenger Press, 2008.

_____. *The Naked Now: Learning to See as the Mystics See*. New York: Crossroad, 2009.

Pennington, M. Basil, O.C.S.O. *Centering Prayer: Renewing an Ancient Christian Prayer Form.* New York: Image Books, 1980.

Rolheiser, Ronald. *The Holy Longing: The Search for a Christian Spirituality.* New York: Doubleday, 1999.

Rollins, Peter. *How (Not) to Speak of God.* Brewster, MA: Paraclete Press, 2006.

_____. *The Fidelity of Betrayal: Towards a Church Beyond Belief.* Brewster, MA: Paraclete Press, 2008.

Ross, Maggie. *Pillars of Flame: Power, Priesthood, and Spiritual Maturity.* San Francisco: Harper & Row, 1988.

Slade, Herbert. *Exploration into Contemplative Prayer.* London: Darton, Longman and Todd, 1975.

Resources on Christian Mysticism

Ahlgren, Gillian T. W. *Entering Teresa of Avila's Interior Castle: A Reader's Companion*. New York: Paulist Press, 2005.

Allchin, A. M. *Participation in God: A Forgotten Strand in Anglican Tradition*. London: Darton, Longman & Todd, 1988.

Armstrong, Christopher. *Evelyn Underhill: An Introduction to Her Life and Writings*. Oxford, UK: A. R. Mowbray & Co. Ltd., 1975.

Arseniev, Nicholas. *Mysticism & the Eastern Church*. Crestwood, NY: St. Vladimir's Seminary Press, 1979.

Bailey, Raymond. *Thomas Merton on Mysticism*. Garden City, NY: Image Books, 1976.

Barry, William A. and William J. Connolly. *The Practice of Spiritual Direction*. San Francisco: HarperCollins, 1986.

Bondi, Roberta. *To Pray and to Love: Conversations on Prayer with the Early Church*. Minneapolis: Fortress Press, 1991.

Borys, Peter N., Jr. *Transforming Heart and Mind: Learning from the Mystics.* New York: Paulist Press, 2006.

Bouyer, Louis. *A History of Christian Spirituality, Volume I: The Spirituality of the New Testament and the Fathers.* Minneapolis: Winston Press, 1963.

Bouyer, Louis, Jean Leclarcq, and Francois Vandenbroucke. *A History of Christian Spirituality, Volume II: The Spirituality of the Middle Ages.* Minneapolis: Winston Press, 1968.

Bouyer, Louis. *A History of Christian Spirituality, Volume III: Orthodox Spirituality and Protestant and Anglican Spirituality.* Minneapolis: Winston Press, 1969.

_____. *The Christian Mystery: From Pagan Myth to Christian Mysticism.* Edinburgh, Scotland: T & T Clark, 1991.

Bradley, Ritamary. *Julian's Way: A Practical Commentary on Julian of Norwich.* London: HarperCollins, 1992.

Chesterton, G. K. *Saint Thomas Aquinas: The Dumb Ox.* Garden City, NY: Image Books, 1956.

Clément, Olivier. *The Roots of Christian Mysticism.* London: New City, 1993.

Cross, F. L. and E. A. Livingstone, eds. *The Oxford Dictionary of the Christian Church.* Oxford, UK: Oxford University Press, 1983.

Cupitt, Don. *Mysticism After Modernity.* Oxford, UK: Blackwell Publishers Inc., 1998.

Davies, Oliver. *God Within: The Mystical Tradition of Northern Europe.* Hyde Park, NY: New City Press, 1988.

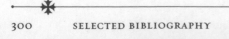

de Dreuille, Mayeul, OSB. *The Rule of Saint Benedict: A Commentary in Light of World Ascetic Traditions*. New York: The Newman Press, 2,000.

Downey, Michael, ed. *The New Dictionary of Catholic Spirituality*. Collegeville, MN: The Liturgical Press, 1993.

Dupré, Louis. *The Common Life: The Origins of Trinitarian Mysticism and its Development by Jan Ruusbroec*. New York: Crossroad, 1984.

Egan, Harvey D., S.J. *What Are They Saying About Mysticism?* New York: Paulist Press, 1982.

Fanning, Steven. *Mystics of the Christian Tradition*. London: Routledge, 2001.

Finlan, Stephen, and Vladimir Kharlamov, eds. *Theosis: Deification in Christian Theology*. Eugene, OR: Pickwick Publications, 2006.

Frost, Bede. *The Christian Mysteries*. London: A. R. Mowbray & Co. Limited, 1950.

Fry, Timothy, OSB, ed. *RB 1980: The Rule of St. Benedict in Latin and English with Notes*. Collegeville, MN: The Liturgical Press, 1981.

Gatta, Julia. *Three Spiritual Directors for Our Time: Julian of Norwich, The Cloud of Unknowing, Walter Hilton*. Cambridge, MA: Cowley, 1986.

Hardy, Richard P. *John of the Cross: Man and Mystic*. Boston: Pauline Books & Media, 2004.

Harton, F. P. *The Elements of the Spiritual Life: A Study in Ascetical Theology*. London: SPCK, 1957.

Heath, Elaine A. *The Mystic Way of Evangelism: A Contemplative Vision for Christian Outreach*. Grand Rapids, MI: Baker Academic, 2008.

Henry, Patrick, ed. *Benedict's Dharma: Buddhists Reflect on the Rule of Saint Benedict*. New York: Riverhead Books, 2001.

Holdaway, Gervase, OSB, ed. *The Oblate Life*. Collegeville, MN: Liturgical Press, 2008.

Holmes, Urban T. *A History of Christian Spirituality: An Analytical Introduction*. New York: The Seabury Press, 1980.

Hughes, Robert Davis, III. *Beloved Dust: Tides of the Spirit in the Christian Life*. New York: Continuum, 2008.

Huxley, Aldous. *The Perennial Philosophy*. New York: Harper and Brothers, 1945.

Jantzen, Grace M. *Julian of Norwich: Mystic and Theologian*. New York: Paulist Press, 2,000.

Johnson, Luke Timothy. *Mystical Tradition: Judaism, Christianity, and Islam*. Chantilly, VA: The Learning Company, 2008.

Jones, Cheslyn, Geoffrey Wainwright, and Edward Yarnold S.J., eds. *The Study of Spirituality*. New York: Oxford University Press, 1986.

Keating, Daniel A. *Deification and Grace*. Naples, FL: Sapientia Press, 2007.

King, Ursula. *Christian Mystics: Their Lives and Legacies Throughout the Ages*. Mahwah, NJ: HiddenSpring, 2001.

Leloup, Jean-Yves. *Being Still: Reflections on an Ancient Mystical Tradition*. Tr. by M. S. Laird, OSA. Leominster, UK: Gracewing, 2003.

Llewellyn, Robert. *With Pity Not With Blame: The Spirituality of Julian of Norwich and the Cloud of Unknowing for Today*. London: Darton, Longman and Todd, 1982.

Louth, Andrew. *The Origins of the Christian Mystical Tradition from Plato to Denys*. Oxford, UK: Clarendon Press, 1981.

MacQuarrie, John. *Two Worlds Are Ours: An Introduction to Christian Mysticism*. Minneapolis: Fortress Press, 2004.

Maloney, George A., S.J. *Abiding in the Indwelling Trinity*. New York: Paulist Press, 2004.

_____. *The Mystic of Fire and Light: St. Symeon, the New Theologian*. Denville, NJ: Dimension Books, 1975.

_____. *The Mystery of Christ in You: The Mystical Vision of Saint Paul*. New York: Alba House, 1998.

_____. *Invaded by God: Mysticism and the Indwelling Trinity*. Denville, NJ: Dimension Books, 1979.

McGinn, Bernard, and Patricia Ferris McGinn. *Early Christian Mystics: The Divine Vision of the Spiritual Masters*. New York: Crossroad, 2003.

McGinn, Bernard. *The Mystical Thought of Meister Eckhart: The Man From Whom God Hid Nothing*. New York: Crossroad, 2001.

_____. *The Foundations of Mysticism*. New York: Crossroad, 1992.

_____. *The Growth of Mysticism*. New York: Crossroad, 1994.

_____. *The Flowering of Mysticism*. New York: Crossroad, 1998.

_____. *The Harvest of Mysticism in Medieval Germany*. New York: Crossroad, 2005.

Miller, Gordon L. *The Way of the English Mystics: An Anthology and Guide for Pilgrims*. Ridgefield, CT: Morehouse Publishing, 1996.

Moorcroft, Jennifer. *He is My Heaven: The Life of Elizabeth of the Trinity*. Washington, DC: ICS Publications, 2002.

O'Connor, Patricia. *In Search of Thérèse*. Wilmington, DE: Michael Glazier, 1987.

Olivera, Bernardo, OCSO. "Solus Deus Vacare Deo: Towards a Renewed Christian Mysticism," *Cistercian Studies Quarterly* Vol. 43.3, pp. 253–270.

Papanikolaou, Aristotle. *Being With God: Trinity, Apophaticism, and Divine-Human Communion*. Notre Dame, IN: University of Notre Dame Press, 2006.

Perl, Eric D. *Theophany: The Neoplatonic Philosophy of Dionysius the Areopagite*. Albany, NY: State University of New York Press, 2007.

Roden, Frederick S., AOJN, and John-Julian, OJN. *Love's Trinity: A Companion to Julian of Norwich*. Collegeville, MN: Liturgical Press, 2009.

Russell, Norman. *The Doctrine of Deification in the Greek Patristic Tradition*. Oxford, UK: Oxford University Press, 2004.

Sells, Michael A. *Mystical Languages of Unsaying*. Chicago: University of Chicago Press, 1994.

Spidlík, Tomas. *Drinking from the Hidden Fountain: A Patristic Breviary*. Kalamazoo, MI: Cistercian Publications, 1994.

_____. *The Spirituality of the Christian East*. Kalamazoo, MI: Cistercian Publications, 1986.

_____. *Prayer: The Spirituality of the Christian East, Vol. 2*. Kalamazoo, MI: Cistercian Publications, 2005.

Stavropoulos, Archimandrite Christoforos. *Partakers of Divine Nature*. Minneapolis: Light and Life, 1976.

Thornton, Martin. *Christian Proficiency*. London: SPCK, 1959.

_____. *English Spirituality: An Outline of Ascetical Theology According to the English Pastoral Tradition*. London: SPCK, 1963.

Upjohn, Sheila. *In Search of Julian of Norwich*. London: Darton, Longman and Todd, 1989.

Verdeyen, Paul. *Ruusbroec and His Mysticism*. Collegeville, MN: The Liturgical Press, 1994.

Von Hügel, Friedrich. *The Mystical Element of Religion as Studied in Saint Catherine of Genoa and Her Friends*. Second edition. With an introduction by Michael Downey. New York: Crossroad, 1999.

Woods, Richard, OP, ed. *Understanding Mysticism*. Garden City, NY: Image Books, 1980.

Other Worthwhile Sources

Batterson, Mark. *Wild Goose Chase: Reclaim the Adventure of Pursuing God*. Colorado Springs, CO: Multnomah Books, 2008.

Binz, Stephen J. *Conversing with God in Scripture: A Contemporary Approach to Lectio Divina*. Ijamsville, MD: The Word Among Us Press, 2008.

Blake, William. *The Complete Illuminated Books*. Introduction by David Bindman. New York: Thames & Hudson, 2,000.

Boylan, Eugene, OCSO. *The Mystical Body*. Westminster, MD: The Newman Bookshop, 1948.

_____. *Partnership with Christ: A Cistercian Retreat*. Kalamazoo, MI: Cistercian Publications, 2008.

Carmichael, Alexander, ed. *Carmina Gadelica: Hymns & Incantations*. Hudson, NY: Lindisfarne Press, 1992.

Cary, Phillip. *The History of Christian Theology*. Chantilly, VA: The Learning Company, 2008.

Chesterton, G.K. *Orthodoxy*. Garden City, NY: Image Books, 1959.

Chittister, Joan. *Called to Question: A Spiritual Memoir*. Lanham, MD: Sheed & Ward, 2009.

Claiborne, Shane. *The Irresistible Revolution: Living as an Ordinary Radical*. Grand Rapids, MI: Zondervan, 2006.

Claiborne, Shane, and Jonathan Wilson-Hartgrove. *Becoming the Answer to Our Prayers: Prayer for Ordinary Radicals*. Downers Grove, IL: Intervarsity Press, 2008.

Cron, Ian Morgan. *Chasing Francis: A Pilgrim's Tale*. Colorado Springs, CO: NavPress, 2006.

Freke, Timothy, and Peter Gandy. *The Complete Guide to World Mysticism*. London: Piatkus, 1997.

Garrison, Becky. *Rising from the Ashes: Rethinking Church*. New York: Seabury Books, 2007.

Greeley, Andrew M. *The Great Mysteries: Experiencing Catholic Faith from the Inside Out*. Lanham, MD: Sheed & Ward, 2003.

Haggerty, Brian A. *Out of the House of Slavery: On the Meaning of the Ten Commandments*. New York: Paulist Press, 1978.

Johnson, Elizabeth A. *Quest for the Living God: Mapping Frontiers in the Theology of God*. New York: Continuum, 2007.

Lamott, Anne. *Bird by Bird: Some Instructions on Writing and Life*. New York: Pantheon Books, 1994.

Linn, Dennis, Sheila Fabricant Linn, and Matthew Linn. *Good Goats: Healing Our Image of God*. Mahwah, NJ: Paulist Press, 1994.

Louf, André. *The Cistercian Way*. Tr. by Nivard Kinsella. Kalamazoo, MI: Cistercian Publications, 1983.

Manser, Martin H. *The Westminster Collection of Christian Quotations*. Louisville, KY: Westminster/John Knox Press, 2001.

Mathewes-Green, Frederica. *The Lost Gospel of Mary: The Mother of Jesus in Three Ancient Texts*. Brewster, MA: Paraclete Press, 2007.

McHugh, Adam S. *Introverts in the Church: Finding Our Place in an Extroverted Culture*. Downers Grove, IL: IVP Books, 2009.

McLaren, Brian D. *A Generous Orthodoxy*. Grand Rapids, MI: Zondervan, 2004.

_____. *Finding Our Way Again: The Return of the Ancient Practices*. Nashville, TN: Thomas Nelson Publishers, 2008.

Miller, Donald. *Blue Like Jazz: Nonreligious Thoughts on Christian Spirituality*. Nashville, TN: Thomas Nelson Publishers, 2003.

Murray, Seth. *Lord, Open My Lips: The Liturgy of the Hours as Daily Prayer*. El Sobrante, CA: North Bay Books, 2004.

Nolan, Albert. *Jesus Before Christianity*. Maryknoll, NY: Orbis Books, 1976.

Nolan, William Michael. *Growing Up as a Trappist Monk*. New York: Vantage Press, 2003.

Norris, Kathleen. *The Cloister Walk*. New York: Riverhead Books, 1996.

_____. *Acedia & Me: A Marriage, Monks, and a Writer's Life*. New York: Riverhead Books, 2008.

Ramsey, Michael. *Be Still and Know: A Study in the Life of Prayer*. Cambridge, MA: Cowley Publications, 1993.

Rowling, J. K. *Harry Potter and the Chamber of Secrets*. London: Bloomsbury, 1998.

_____. *Harry Potter and the Philosopher's Stone*. London: Bloomsbury, 1997.

Sellner, Edward C. *Finding the Monk Within: Great Monastic Values for Today*. Mahwah, NJ: Hidden Spring/Paulist Press, 2008.

Smith, Martin L., SSJE. *Reconciliation: Preparing for Confession in the Episcopal Church*. Cambridge:, MA: Cowley Publications, 1985.

_____. *The Word is Very Near You: A Guide to Praying with Scripture*. Cambridge, MA: Cowley Publications, 1989.

Sweeney, Jon. *Cloister Talks: Learning from My Friends the Monks*. Grand Rapids, MI: Brazos Press, 2009.

Steere, Douglas V. *Prayer and Worship*. Richmond, IN: Friends United Press, 1978.

Wakefield, Gordon S., ed. *The Westminster Dictionary of Christian Spirituality*. Philadelphia: The Westminster Press, 1983.

Wathen, Ambrose G., OSB. *Silence: The Meaning of Silence in the Rule of St. Benedict*. Washington, DC: Cistercian Publications/Consortium Press, 1973.

Wilber, Ken. *Integral Spirituality: A Startling New Role for Religion in the Modern and Postmodern World*. Boston: Integral Books, 2006.

Young, Wm. Paul. *The Shack*. Newbury Park, CA: Windblown Media, 2007.

AUTHOR BIO

Carl McColman is an author, teacher, and spiritual director. He is the creator of the Website of Unknowing (*www.anamchara.com*), a blog devoted to Celtic and mystical spirituality. He studied Christian meditation and contemplation at the Shalem Institute for Spiritual Formation, and received additional training in the art of spiritual direction from the Institute for Pastoral Studies in Atlanta.

He is the author of twelve books, including *366 Celt: A Year and a Day of Celtic Wisdom and Lore, The Aspiring Mystic: Practical Steps for Spiritual Seekers, Spirituality: A Postmodern and Interfaith Approach to Cultivating a Relationship with God,* and *The Complete Idiot's Guide to Celtic Wisdom.*

Carl is a lay associate of the Trappist Monastery of the Holy Spirit in Conyers, Georgia. He lives near Stone Mountain, Georgia, with his wife and stepdaughter.

HAMPTON ROADS PUBLISHING COMPANY

. . . for the evolving human spirit

Hampton Roads Publishing Company publishes books on a variety of subjects, including spirituality, health, and other related topics.

For a copy of our latest trade catalog, call 978-465-0504, or visit our website at *www.hrpub.com*.

Index

C

Charismatic Renewal, 53
Carthusians, 138
Cassian, John, 154, 210, 228, 258
Catherine of Siena, 181
Catholicism, 62, 145
Catholic Mass, 254
Catholic Sacrament of Reconciliation, 96
centering prayer, 150, 226–227
charismatic prayer, 214–215
Charismatic Renewal, 53
Chesterton, G. K., 115
child consciousness, 109
Christ, 49
Christ, Jesus, 89
Christianity
    defined, 136
    liminal, 151–153
    mystical tradition and, 62–64
    mysticism and, origin of, 37–46
Christian mediation groups, 150
Christian mysticism, 18
    charter of, 41–46
    concept of, 20
    elements of, 62–63
    history of, 16
    love and, 72–74
    New Testament and, 40–41
    practicing, 133–135
Christian mysticism, evolution of, 47–55
    enacting the mysteries, 49–51
    mystery and revelation, 54–55
    narrating the mysteries, 51–52
    rehabilitation of mysticism, 52–54
Christian mysticism and world mysticism, 57–64
    in global village, 58–60
    mystical tradition and, 62–64
    vs. tofu, 60–61
Chrysostom, John, 50

church
    attending, 136–140
    exploring, 142–148
    joining, 148–151
    types of, 144–147
churched, 143
Church of England, 145
Clemens, Titus Flavius, 257
Clement of Alexandria, 48, 63
Climacus, John, 183, 259
Cloud of Unknowing, The (anonymous), 113, 123, 129, 154, 228, 229, 230, 238, 253
Colossians, 106, 165
Coltrane, John, 166
communion of saints, 256
complaint, 214
confession, 212
consciousness, 109–110
consecrated act, 50
conservatives, 93
contemplatio, 194
contemplation, 219–220
    contemplating, 230–231
    defined, 220
    forms of, 224–225
    methods of, 222–224
    objections to, 227–229
    significance of, 220–222
contemplative life, 182–185
conversational prayer, 212–214
Conversing with God in Scripture (Binz), 250
cool spiritual experiences, 17
Crucifixion, 51
cynicism, 68–72
Cyril of Alexandria, 49
Cyrus, Isaac, 259